"LOEX" of the West:
Collaboration and Instructional Design in a Virtual Environment

**FOUNDATIONS IN LIBRARY AND
INFORMATION SCIENCE, VOLUME 43**

Editor: Thomas W. Leonhardt, *Director of Library Technical Services, Bizzell Memorial Library, University of Oklahoma*

Foundations in
Library and Information Science

Edited by **Thomas W. Leonhardt,** *Director of Library Technical Services, Bizzell Memorial Library, University of Oklahoma* and **Murray S. Martin,** *University Librarian and Professor of Library Science Emeritus, Tufts University*

Volume 8.
Management of a Public Library
Harold R. Jenkins, *Kansas City Public Library*

1980, 258 pp. LC 76-13957 $78.50/£49.95
ISBN 0-89232-038-9

Volume 9.
(Omitted from Numbering)

Volume 10.
Collection Development in Libraries: A Treatise
Edited by **Robert D. Stueart,** *Dean, Graduate School of Library and Information Science, Simmons College-Boston* and **George B. Miller, Jr.,** *Assistant Director for Collection Development, University of New Mexico Libraries*

Part A, 1980, 288 pp. LC 79-93165 $78.50/£49.95
ISBN 0-89232-106-7

PART B, 1980, 314 pp. LC 79-93165 $78.50/£49.95
ISBN 0-8232-162-8

Volume 11.
Introduction to Serial Management
Marcia Tuttle, *University of North Carolina, Chapel Hill*

1983, 324 pp. LC 81-81658 $78.50/£49.95
ISBN 0-89232-107-5

Volume 12.
Developing Collections of U.S. Government Publications
Peter Hernon, *Graduate School of Library and Information Science, Simmons College, Boston* and **Gary R. Purcell,** *Graduate School of Library and Information Science, University of Tennessee, Knoxville*

1983, 289 pp. LC 82-81208 $78.50/£49.95
ISBN 0-89232-135-0

Volume 13.
Library Management Without Bias
Ching-Chih Chen, *Graduate School of Library and Information Science, Simmons College, Boston*

1981, 225 pp. LC 80-82482 $78.50/£49.95
ISBN 0-89232-163-6

Volume 14.
Issues in Personnel Management
Murray S. Martin, *Pennsylvania State University Libraries*

1981, 226 pp. LC 81-81649 $78.50/£49.95
ISBN 0-89232-136-9

Volume 15.
Information Needs of the 80s: Libraries and Information Services Role in Bringing Information to People Based on the Deliberations of the White House Conference on Library and Information Services
Edited by **Robert D. Stueart,** *Graduate School of Library and Information Science, Simmons College, Boston*

1982, 192 pp. LC 81-81657 $78.50/£49.95
ISBN 0-89232-164-4

Volume 16.
ALMS: A Budget Based Library Management System
Betty Jo Mitchell, *California State University Library, Northridge*

1983, 235 pp. LC 82-81208 $78.50/£49.95
ISBN 0-89232-246-2

Volume 17.
Options for the 80s: Proceedings of the Second National Conference of the Association of College and Research Libraries, October 1-4, 1981, Minneapolis, Minnesota
Edited by **Michael D. Kathman,** *College of St. Benedict and St. John's University* and **Virgil F. Massman,** *James J. Hill Reference Library*

1982, 687 pp., LC 82-7721 (2 Volume Set)
SET ISBN 0-89232-276-4 $157.00/£99.90

Volume 18.
The Library Services and Construction Act: An Historical Overview from the Viewpoint of Major Participants
Edward G. Holley and **Robert F. Schremser,** *School of Library Science, The University of North Carolina at Chapel Hill*

1983, 165 pp. LC 83-48088 $78.50/£49.95
ISBN 0-89232-410-4

Volume 19.
Fundraising for Nonprofit Institutions
Edited by **Sandy Dolnick,** *Executive Director, Friends of Libraries, U.S.A.*

1987, 268 pp. LC 87-31200 $78.50/£49.95
ISBN 0-89232-387-6

Volume 20.
Changing Technology and Education for Librarianship and Information Science
Edited by **Basil Stuart-Stubbs,** *School of Librarianship, University of British Columbia*

1985, 188 pp. LC 84-21330 $78.50/£49.95
ISBN 0-89232-515-1

Volume 21.
Videotex and Teletext: New Online Resources for Libraries
Michael B. Binder, *Director of Libraries, Fairleigh Dickinson Library*

1985, 160 pp. LC 85-5246 $78.50/£49.95
ISBN 0-89232-612-3

Volume 22.
Research Libraries and Their Implementation of AACR2
Edited by **Judith Hopkins,** *Technical Services Research and Analysis Officer, Central Technical Services, University Libraries, State University of New York at Buffalo* and **John A. Edens,** *Director, Central Technical Services, University Libraries, State University of New York at Buffalo*

1986, 360 pp. LC 85-23825 $78.50/£49.95
ISBN 0-89232-641-7

Volume 23.

An Encyclopedia of Film Festivals

Robert A. Nowlan and **Gwendolyn Wright Nowlan,**
Southern Connecticut State University

1986, 360 pp. LC 85-23825 $78.50/£49.95
ISBN 0-89232-641-7

Volume 24.

**A Guide to the Literature of Electronic Publishing: CD-ROM,
DESKTOP Publishing, and Electronic Mail, Books, & Journals**

Edited by **Michael R. Gabriel,** *Mankato State University Library*

1989, 187 pp. LC 8932430 $78.50/£49.95
ISBN 1-55938-044-6

Volume 25.

Technical Services in Libraries: Systems and Applications

Edited by **Thomas W. Leonhardt,** *Bizzell Memorial Library,
University of Oklahoma*

1991, 279 pp. LC 91-43729 $78.50/£49.95
ISBN 1-55938-214-7

Volume 26.

Collection Management: A New Treatise

Edited by **Charles B. Osburn,** *Amelia Gayle Gorgas Library,
University of Alabama* and **Ross W. Atkinson,** *Cornell University Library*

1991, 474 pp. LC 91-33499   (2 Part Set) $157.00/£99.90
SET ISBN 1-55938-231-7

Volume 27.

**The Role of the American Academic Library
in International Programs**

Edited by **Bruce D. Bonta,** *The University Libraries, Pennsylvania State
University* and **James G. Neal,** *University Libraries, Indiana University*

1992, 283 pp. LC 92-4314 $78.50/£49.95
ISBN 1-55938-383-6

Volume 28.

Academic Library Budgets

Edited by **Murray S. Martin,** *University Librarian and
Professor of Library Science Emeritus, Tufts University*

1993, 270 pp. LC 91-30103 $78.50/£49.95
ISBN 1-55938-597-9

Volume 29.

Academic Libraries and Training

Edited by **Maryruth Phelps Glogowski,** *Associate Director,
E.H. Butler Library, State University College at Buffalo*

1994, 238 pp. LC 94-37215 $78.50/£49.95
ISBN 1-55938-598-7

Volume 37.

The Changing Face of Reference

Edited by **Lynne M. Stuart,** *Penn State University*
and **Dena Hutto,** *Reed College*
1996, 250 pp.   LC 96-45479 $78.50/£49.95
ISBN 0-7623-0217-8

Volume 38.

Genre and Ethnic Collections: Collected Essays

Edited by **Milton T. Wolf,** *Assistant Director for Collection Development,*
University of Nevada, Reno and **Murray S. Martin,** *University Librarian and*
Professor of Library Science Emeritus, Tufts University

1996, 467 pp.   (2 Part Set) $157.00/£99.90
SET ISBN 0-7623-0218-6   LC 96-45501

Volume 39.

Libraries and Other Academic Support Services for Distance Learning

Edited by **Carolyn A. Snyder** and **James W. Fox,**
Library Affairs, Southern Illinois University at Carbondale

1997, 344 pp.   LC 97-9941 $78.50/£49.95
ISBN 0-7623-0229-1

Volume 40.

Starting and Managing Fee-Based
Information Services in Academic Libraries

By **Suzanne M. Ward,** *Technical Information Service, Purdue University*

1997, 224 pp.   LC 97-4997 $78.50/£49.95
ISBN 0-7623-0225-9

Volume 41.

Recognizing Excellence in the Mathematical Sciences:
An International Compilation of Awards, Prizes, and Recipients

Edited by **Janice M. Jaguszewski,** *Science and Engineering Library,*
University of Minnesota

1997, 271 pp.   LC 97-29849 $78.50/£49.95
ISBN 0-7623-0235-6

Volume 42.

Dynamics of the Internet

Carl H. A. Dassbach, *Michigan Technological University,*
Houghton, Michigan

Publishing in 1999 $78.50/£49.95
ISBN 0-7623-0409-X

"LOEX" of the West:
Collaboration and Instructional Design in a Virtual Environment

Edited by KARI ANDERSON,
ELIZABETH BABBITT,
EMILY HULL, THERESA MUDROCK, AND
HELENE WILLIAMS
UNIVERSITY OF WASHINGTON LIBRARIES

 **JAI PRESS INC.**
Stamford, Connecticut

Library of Congress Cataloging-in-Publication Data

"LOEX" of the West : collaboration and instructional design in a
virtual environment / edited by Karl Anderson . . . [et al.].
p.   cm. -- (Foundations in library and information science :
v. 43)
Papers presented at the Second LOEX of the West Conference held in
Seattle, June 1996.
Includes bibliographical references and index.
ISBN 0-7623-0549-5
1. Library orientation for college students--United States-
-Congresses.   2. Electronic Information resources literacy--Study and
teaching (Higher)--United States--Congresses.   I. Anderson, Kari J.
II. LOEX of the West Conference (2nd : 1996 : Seattle. Wash.)
III. Series.
Z711.2.L79   1999
027.6'2--dc21   99-12397
                                                      CIP

ISBN: 0-7623-0549-5

Library of Congress Catalog Number: 99-12397

Manufactured in the United States of America

CONTENTS

FOREWORD

The University of Washington Libraries was pleased to host the second "LOEX" of the West Conference in June 1996, continuing a tradition begun by Oregon librarians in 1994. A major part of the University Libraries' services program has been focused on integrating information literacy into the university curriculum by working in collaboration with campus partners within the UWired program. The opportunity offered by the Conference to reflect on experiences and to hear about innovative initiatives at other institutions was very timely.

The Conference Steering Committee is to be congratulated on such a successful event. Excellent presentations were heard throughout the two days and social occasions were rich with conversations about ideas presented. The sharing of experiences and learning from one another so characteristic of our profession were clearly present.

It was especially satisfying that the University Libraries was able to support the Conference through the Kenneth S. Allen Library Endowment. Ken Allen served many years as a librarian in the University Libraries, including several years as associate director.

Such occasions are a fitting memorial to his work and contributions.

Betty G. Bengtson
Director of University Libraries
University of Washington

INTRODUCTION

Kari Anderson, Elizabeth Babbitt, Emily Hull, Theresa Mudrock, and Helene Williams

---

New ideas, shared experiences, renewed inspiration and good food are the hallmarks of a successful conference. Instruction librarians from the West, the country, and abroad, gathered in Seattle for the second "LOEX" of the West in the summer of 1996.[1] Held at the University of Washington, the conference was co-sponsored by Pierce College, St. Martin's College, Seattle Central Community College, Seattle Pacific University, and the University of Puget Sound. Additional support was provided by Microsoft Library, EBSCO Industries, Inc., and Highsmith, Inc.

Inspired both by the original annual LOEX Clearinghouse for Library Instruction conferences and by the first "LOEX" of the West held at Willamette University in 1994, a group of intrepid librarians set out to plan a conference which would celebrate the innovation and creativity of instruction librarians.[2] The theme, "Collaboration and Instructional Design in a Virtual

Environment," focused on the development and use of collaborative relationships in library instruction—between libraries and computer centers, university libraries and public or school libraries, and between libraries at different academic institutions.

The subjects of the papers presented at the conference[3] divide into three categories:

- Building collaborations—practical ideas and suggestions on developing successful working relationships with other libraries, academic departments and computing centers.
- Instructional design—examples of how successful programs are created and the necessary steps in this process.
- Virtual environment—ways that the World Wide Web is freeing library instruction from the physical walls of the library and campus.

In their keynote address, "Campus Partnerships: Collaborating for the 21st Century," Carla Stoffle, Karen Smith, and Karen Williams touch on each of these issues as they discuss new innovative collaborations at the University of Arizona. Carla Stoffle begins by exploring challenges that face higher education and libraries which are pressuring institutions to become learning-centered rather than teaching-centered. Karen Smith describes the Faculty Development Partnership which is providing support for faculty as they begin to take advantage of innovations in instructional technology. Karen Williams finishes by explaining how this collaborative effort has expanded the traditional roles of librarians in new directions which support the changing instructional goals of the campus.

The theme of collaboration runs through many of the papers. Andrea Bartelstein, Louis Fox, Pamela Stewart, Lizabeth Wilson, and Anne Zald describe the collaborative development of the UWired project which is helping to make information and technology literacy a distinguishing characteristic of University of Washington graduates by creating a learning community of students, faculty, librarians, and technology specialists. Karen Diller and Chuck Harrsch reach across the traditional boundaries between academic libraries and computing centers to create a series of workshops on various technology-related topics for the students, staff, and faculty of Washington State University, Vancouver.

Collaboration between staff in the Corvallis School District, Oregon State University Libraries, and the Corvallis-Benton County Public Library enables these libraries to overcome constraints imposed by property tax limitations and the challenges of school reform and the information explosion. Jan Deardorff, Loretta Rielly, and Kim Thompson describe the web of cooperative relationships between the three institutions which has resulted in improved library service to the community's school children.

In another collaboration success story, Laura Bender and Jennalyn Tellman discuss how a team approach within the University of Arizona Library prepares librarians to forge instructional partnerships with faculty, and increases their comfort level in teaching information literacy skills. Larry Berk and Patricia Carroll-Mathes highlight the challenges and successes involved in implementing an across-the-curriculum information literacy initiative at Ulster County Community College. Carolyn Johnson, Lisa Kammerlocher, and Diane Gruber describe a collaborative effort between the Library, the Center for Writing Across the Curriculum, and the School of Management at Arizona State University West, which integrates research and writing skills into an undergraduate gateway course in global business. Susan Waterman MacLean of the University of Guelph illustrates the process, successes, and pitfalls of developing a collaborative course in computer and information literacy.

Two papers focus on cooperative projects that tailor instruction for special populations. Calvin Williams of Bowling Green State University reminds us that traditional bibliographic instruction methods do not necessarily meet the needs of different cultural groups. He finds that successful instruction for African-American and Hispanic-American students relies heavily on the development of personal ties between instructor and student to facilitate the learning process. Keith Gresham of the University of Colorado at Boulder shows us how a university library faces the challenge of increasing use by high school students. An innovative outreach program opens the resources of the university to high schools, introducing the students to information navigation and evaluation skills.

The theme of instructional design is also evident in nearly all the conference presentations; four sessions concentrate specifically on the design of a single class or an entire program. Kyzyl Fenno-Smith and Deb Gilchrist from Pierce College lay some important groundwork for improving the design of instruction programs and remind participants of the importance of keeping the student in the center of the educational framework. Buhle Mbambo and Ann Roselle, from the University of Botswana, also look at the larger picture of designing an instruction program. Both of their approaches incorporate information literacy into the curriculum; one provides library instruction throughout a student's course of study, while the other relies on intensive library sessions during the first year of classes. Designing a program around one resource, the LEXIS/NEXIS database, is the focus of Mary Strow and Emily Okada's presentation. Time, space, and technology constraints are some of the topics the authors tackle in this discussions of their collaborative efforts between academic units and librarians.

The session by Michael Bertsch, Randy Burke Hensley, and Margit Misangyi Watts of the University of Hawaii centers on taking instructional design to its technological limits, which provides a level of interaction different from the traditional teacher-learner roles assumed by librarians and students. This discussion of the high-tech environment of MOOs, the Web, and library databases shows opportunities for dynamic, learner-centered instruction.

Using the World Wide Web to enhance course development is the focus of four papers. Margaret Zarnosky and John Tombarge contribute information about a collaborative information literacy venture with faculty from the Hospitality and Tourism Management department at Virginia Tech. Nancy Lombardo of the University of Utah and Deleyne Wentz of Utah State University describe an alliance between librarians from the higher education institutions in Utah, providing insight into a multi-institutional approach to Internet training. Anne Scholz-Crane of Purdue University discusses the development, implementation, and evaluation of an interactive tutorial which emphasizes the essential skills of database searching for undergraduates. Fred Roecker of Ohio State University delineates the key elements of the successful OSU library instruction program as it wrestles with changes in technology.

In her paper based on the conference active learning workshop, Sharon Mader of Christian Brothers University provides practical information and exercises for building collaborative relationships with faculty. She illustrates the qualities necessary for library leadership and methods of developing and evaluating our potential leadership skills. We also learn to recognize the mutual misconceptions between faculty and librarians and ways to bridge these differences.

It took the better part of two years to plan the second "LOEX" of the West, and then, in what seemed like the blink of an eye, it was over. For those of us involved in its planning, the end of the conference was something akin to sending a child off to college. In this case, the college in question is Southern Utah University, which will host the third "LOEX" of the West in Cedar City, Utah, June 18-20, 1998. Attendees who expressed a desire to meet in smaller, more intimate surroundings will be pleased with the 1998 venue—a much smaller campus than the University of Washington. The setting will be completely different, but the spirit of sharing and learning together that has become the hallmark of "LOEX" of the West will continue.

NOTES

1.   There is no formal connection yet between the national LOEX Clearinghouse for Library Instruction at Eastern Michigan University and this conference. We have permission from Linda Shirato to use the "LOEX" name and we thank her and are inspired by the example of the original LOEX.

2.   Members of the planning group were Kari Anderson, Elizabeth Babbitt, Esther Daniels, Emily Hull, Linda Lambert, Theresa Mudrock, and Helene Williams.

3.   All the papers presented at the conference are included in the proceedings with the exception of Barry Brown's "Biological Literature Instruction in the Age of Networked Information."

COLLABORATION AND INSTRUCTIONAL DESIGN:
NECESSARY CAMPUS PARTNERSHIPS FOR SUCCESS IN THE TWENTY-FIRST CENTURY

Carla Stoffle, Karen Smith, and Karen Williams

ABSTRACT

To prepare students for success in the global information-based economy of the twenty-first century, institutions
of higher education must restructure their education programs and academic support services to be learning-centered rather than teaching-centered.

For most colleges and universities, this translates to a mandate to provide students with a learning environment that
incorporates state of the art information and telecommuni-
cation technologies into instructional programs. It removes
the educational barriers of time and place which are by their
nature a part of the traditional classroom and information
seeking process.

The Faculty Development Partnership at the University of
Arizona is working to bring about these changes. The Partnership began with a vision and an attitude. The Vision:
supporting faculty with inspiration, information, and infrastructure will lead to innovation in teaching and the gradu-
ation of information and technology literate, lifelong
learners. The Attitude: transforming teaching in order to
realize this vision will require a willingness to collaborate in

order to maximize the combined resources and expertise of faculty and campus support units.

New roles for librarians include training faculty in information literacy, library and Internet resources, and the creation of instructional World Wide Web pages. Librarians also consult with faculty to integrate information literacy skills into courses and assignments. The Library provides facilities and equipment for faculty to develop multimedia and Internet resources, and to support completion of assignments requiring the use of sophisticated personal computing equipment.

COLLABORATION AND INSTRUCTIONAL DESIGN: NECESSARY CAMPUS PARTNERSHIPS FOR SUCCESS IN THE TWENTY-FIRST CENTURY

Carla Stoffle

I really appreciate being invited to participate in what I think will be an important and stimulating conference. When called about participating, I was intrigued and interested because I must admit that, after twenty-five years in academic librarianship, I still believe in the importance of the educational role of the library. I believe even more strongly that education and educational librarians are at the heart of where the profession is going and where the future of academic librarianship lies. However, I feel a great sense of urgency for us. I believe we need to begin to make radical changes in our thinking and our strategies for achieving our educational goals. We cannot be satisfied with having defined information literacy as our special responsibility and with the baby steps we have taken to create programs to achieve this end. We need to move even beyond information literacy to something that may not have a name yet, but includes a role in which we help faculty redesign the teaching/learning process. We need to think more boldly and creatively about what we can do and how we would do it. We have a unique opportunity to move center stage and to help our institutions make the critical adjustments needed for survival in the twenty-first century. If we act, I have great hope and see a tremendously meaningful future for us.

Having shared this perspective, let me now describe how we hope to use this session as a framework for the rest of the conference. We have divided this keynote speech into three parts. I will open with a discussion of the issues facing higher education and libraries. I will focus on why librarians must collaborate, what this collaboration means, and how it is different from our previous efforts. Then I will turn the program over to Karen Smith, who is director of the Faculty Development Partnership at the University of Arizona. Karen has led campus efforts to transform instruction at the university from a "sage on the stage" to a "guide on the side" model that focuses on students and learning outcomes, rather than on faculty and the mechanics of teaching. The new model advocates active student involvement in learning. It requires collaboration between faculty and a variety of campus professionals to support the development and delivery of content, and to structure meaningful experiential learning activities. It also requires collaboration among students to unleash the intelligence and experience that they bring. Karen will describe the components necessary to successful collaboration and discuss how they fit together to enhance the learning program. She will also address the goal of reducing instruction costs over time. Then Karen Williams, Social Sciences team leader at the University of Arizona Library, will describe how collaboration efforts at Arizona have impacted library activities and how librarians interact with the campus. For those of you interested in specifics about how front-line librarians are putting this into practice, there is a separate session from their perspective. Finally, we plan to leave time at the end of this program for questions or reactions from you. In that manner we hope to unleash some of the intelligence and experience in this room to enrich our thinking on this topic.

It is no secret to any of you that higher education is under great pressure to change. We read articles about how the public has grown disillusioned with the ability of higher education to solve societal problems and with the quality of our products. In general, the public believes that higher education is fat and that the faculty are a group of self-absorbed, self-interested individuals with no public accountability. The public sees educational programs as being out of control with rampant duplication, and "add on" programs that continuously cost more money. They do not see what they want: faculty interacting with students, and reengineering efforts, like those in business and government, resulting in reduced costs and fulfillment of new needs. They do not see productivity savings from years of investment in computing technology.

At the same time, students are complaining about their experiences in and out of the classroom. They are tired of large impersonal classes, canned lectures and heavy use of teaching assistants. They are demanding higher quality from instructional programs and support services. They fear that what they are learning has no meaning in the job market, or that the market will change and they will be unprepared to adjust and thrive.

This general dissatisfaction, combined with other pressing demands for public funding (prisons, health care, and a rapidly deteriorating public infrastructure), results in decreased funds to support existing educational programs. Tuition increases will not be a viable solution to funding problems much longer. To make matters worse for research institutions, federal funding programs face drastic cuts and private grant sources are drying up. All of this is happening after a decade of deferred maintenance on our physical plants, coupled with incredible demands for investment in telecommunications infrastructure. Hardware and software needs are escalating and, once purchased, both equipment and software require continual refreshing as well as extensive human support and user training.

To add insult to injury, institutions of higher education are being challenged by the possibility of virtual universities and instructional programs developed by commercial entities (McGraw-Hill, McDonald's) delivered through the emerging telecommunications infrastructure. These programs threaten long-held concepts about what constitutes a degree program (for example, seat time expressed as hours per week in the classroom). They are competitors for the "just-in-time" learning market that is emerging as a result of globalization and the transformation of world economy away from manufacturing-based toward knowledge or information-based. Higher education is in the midst of a paradigm shift, and those institutions which have been most successful in the past are now in the greatest danger.

The situation for libraries is just as dire. The cost of information has finally exceeded the ability, and more importantly, the willingness of our institutions to pay. The traditional collusion between faculty, librarians, and publishers in the scholarly communication process is broken. Change must occur. Technology has created new means of access and the possibility of "just-in-time" delivery of information, but so far change has come at a great price with minimal results.

The cost of new information technologies with their annual maintenance charges and continual need for upgrades is shifting the traditional configuration of library budgets. We cannot afford the status quo, and are not likely to secure sufficient budget increases for maintaining traditional collections and services while introducing new ones.

Our library employees feel used, abused, and victimized. There is not enough staff to do our traditional work, let alone the work our future hinges on. We are not able to learn at the pace necessary to view ourselves as experts on the new information systems.

If the foregoing were not bad enough, we face incredible competition both on and off-campus for what librarians think of as our roles: information selection, organization, and delivery, information education, and the provision of related services. For example, we don't normally think of the campus book store as a competitor. When they viewed themselves as textbook vendors, they were not. Increasingly, they define their business as information dissemination, which opens opportunities for new roles and markets. Professionals in teaching centers, computing centers, media units, and even faculty themselves are taking on new roles that overlap with those of librarians. Publishers and online vendors who used to reach their customers through libraries are bypassing us and going directly to clients.

What is most ironic about the current situation is that we are entering what could be the most exciting time for higher education and libraries since the invention of the printing press. We now have the capability to transform the learning experience. Across the country, varying only by degree, this transformation is already underway in our institutions. Individual faculty are experimenting with collaboration and active learning techniques largely enabled by new technologies.

Librarians face this time and these opportunities with insight and shared values gained from decades of working with faculty in their teaching and research activities. We know a great deal about teaching and learning theory. We have made the transformation from teaching how to use our libraries, to how to use tools, to how to think about information issues and information problems. We have a unique understanding of the existing and emerging information structure and information policy, including copyright issues. This latter understanding will be critical as learning experiences are structured around electronic access to information and the creation of interactive multimedia courseware.

Librarians understand how faculty work, and we know how the revolution stimulated by advances in telecommunications and information technologies is different from the audiovisual movement in the 1960s and 1970s. We know that the new tools impact the very activity of knowledge creation. Helping faculty use those tools to enhance their own scholarly and professional work can lead faculty to introduce the tools in the classroom. We are not interested in technology for technology's sake. We understand that most faculty do not want to create courseware, nor do they want to learn skills that they will use only for teaching. We know that our new partnerships and collaborations must bring them support and at the same time free them from dependence they don't want.

Librarians are non-threatening partners to the faculty and we generally have good relations with other academic support professionals in the institution. We are used to working in groups and cooperating for success, and our organizations are set up to focus resources on the roles of individual disciplines.

So what will be required of us in the immediate future that is so different from the past? Why is collaboration more critical and what will these partnerships look like?

First, we cannot afford duplication or the time it would take for us or our potential partners to learn individually all the skills we would need. We have to recognize that none of us can do it alone—not even the faculty. We must leverage our resources and gain the advantage that goes beyond merely the sum of the individual contributions. Our collaboration and partnerships must be true give-and-take relationships with each unit or person recognizing and valuing the skills and resources that others bring. We have to do what is right for the institution and share the credit. We also must trust that others in the collaboration/partnership will do their share.

Then we have to admit that we have only collaborated in the past where it did not infringe upon our turf. We defined the limits of the relationships in terms of what was good for us and our goals. When faculty called, we taught their students how to use our libraries and our bibliographic tools, or even how to think about information. We occasionally tried to help faculty rethink the learning experience, but that was not our primary purpose or role. With other academic professionals, we collaborated to use their skills and resources to achieve our purposes and ends. We must now move beyond turf and beyond doing things that only advantage us. We must take the lead in reaching out, offering support, and trusting.

In the new environment, we must see our role as helping to improve learning and the way learning experiences are structured and delivered. We must accept that we have a responsibility for instructional redesign. We have to be good change agents that can bring together the necessary configuration of resources to change the learning result. We must carry information to faculty about resources that go beyond traditional library information. We need to become the front line for the change effort. We must go beyond our focus on information literacy and information seeking skills, although these are critical skills that all college graduates will need to compete effectively in the future. We must be open to new partnerships and see potential productive relationships where none existed in the past. We must be learners.

While the foregoing will not be easy and our achievements will come slowly, the end result will truly be rewarding both in the relationships experienced and the results gained. Clearly, my colleagues from Arizona feel this and now will describe our faculty development process and its results.

PROVIDING SUPPORT FOR CHANGE:
THE FACULTY DEVELOPMENT PARTNERSHIP

Karen Smith

The transformation into a learner-centered environment cannot happen without a change in the roles teachers play in the learning process. Nor can it occur without easy and convenient access to appropriate technologies as well as to support personnel. Access, technology, and support are all critical elements in the process of developing new learning environments. In addition, teachers must be inspired to change by understanding how new instructional approaches will further their goals and aid their students in attaining desired outcomes. Teachers must be trained to select and use appropriate technologies. Finally, they must be given the opportunity to become independent users of expert tools for the purpose of creating new learning environments. Developing teachers requires a complex training program that nurtures emerging as well as advanced courseware developers.

As a first step toward transforming itself into a learner-centered research university, the University of Arizona has shifted its focus to enhancing the learning process rather than continuing to concentrate on modifying traditional teaching or presentation methods. Students and faculty are encouraged to become life-long learners, using technology in the learning environment to facilitate information access and organization, data collection and analysis, and communication between learners. Students find new opportunities to pursue their individual learning interests and to enhance their experiences by using technology that is associated with their own career goals as a means of accessing information, solving problems, and communicating with peers and experts. Faculty efforts are supported by a campus-wide faculty development initiative that meets changing instructional requirements as instructors shift their attention from curriculum-driven goals to learner needs.

To supply support for a number of individual projects, the administration encouraged faculty and support personnel from a variety of units to establish the Faculty Development Partnership. This Partnership provides a flexible technological and pedagogical infrastructure for instructional research and curriculum development. The Faculty Development infrastructure is an extensive network of partners and referral units that provide faculty with access to technology, funding, and personnel support. Through this infrastructure, faculty become familiar with new learning theories, innovative teaching methods, curriculum design techniques, and technology use. Participating units in the Partnership include:

- The Center for Computers and Information Technology provides telecommunications and campus network support as well as general consulting through the HELP desk, advanced computing and consulting through its Multimedia and Visualization Lab, and access to current software library through the Faculty Resources for Instruction. CCIT Research Support assists in the design and analysis of instructional research projects. Open access labs spread across campus provide delivery environments for courseware and serve as part-time electronic classrooms.
- The University Library serves as a gateway to electronic information sources worldwide. Librarians develop and support information literacy among faculty and students, emphasizing lifelong learning in a technology-based, global information society.
- The University Teaching Center offers the New Technologies Training Program for faculty who are new to high technology teaching tools. In addition, all faculty can obtain the most current information on learning theories and teaching methods through the Center's library and seminars.
- The Peter Treistman Fine Arts Center for New Media specializes in animation, video and audio editing, and graphics design. Faculty use high technology artistic tools to refine their instructional materials for clear, effective visual communications.
- VideoServices supports the University of Arizona faculty through production and transmission of local and distributed learning environments. Satellite, microwave, digital video, cable, and wireless cable technologies are used to distribute educational material. VideoServices is an

educational broadcast resource of the University of Arizona and member of the KUAT Communication Group.

- The Partnership Coordination Office coordinates all research and workshop projects. It oversees the activities of the Partnership and its interaction with other organizations for curricular change. These organizations include the Instructional Resources Coordination Council, the Faculty Development Team, the University Composition Board, and the Faculty Fellows. It also spearheads efforts to create alliances with corporations and community groups to expand external support networks for faculty projects.

The uniqueness of the Faculty Development support infrastructure lies in its comprehensive programs and creative use of resources. Established programs include symposia and workshops for awareness building, training programs for new users, grants to initiate and expand curriculum change projects, and expert support for faculty seeking to bridge the chasm from emerging user to independent courseware creator. The five independent units mentioned above moved beyond traditional roles in order to provide easy access to a comprehensive, integrated support infrastructure for faculty and curriculum development projects. The units have worked to identify common goals and individual strengths so that the Partnership can support projects without duplicating effort or ignoring any need. The result has been a system that attracts novice as well as intermediate and advanced users and provides customized support packaged to meet most individual needs. In essence, the Faculty Development Support Center for Innovative Teaching and Learning already exists in the distributed form of the Partnership.

Novice users enter the system by seeking services from a variety of entry points. Typically, a group will learn about Faculty Development initiatives through a symposium or workshop, or through a department or college-wide meeting with the Partnership Coordinator. Basic training opportunities include e-mail/Internet and computer conferencing training through the University Library and CCIT, and a global approach to technology use through UTC's New Technologies Training Program. This program combines the talents and resources of all Partners. Faculty receive hands-on training in the selection and use of appropriate technologies including basic computer use, teaching methods, presentation software, decision lab strategies, and Internet strategies. Graduating groups receive development equipment (computer, printer, and scanner) as a shared incentive to apply their new skills immediately.

Intermediate users receive support in multimedia production through CCIT, the Library, and the Treistman Center. These units collaborate to provide design support for faculty who are prepared to progress to more complex programming and package design. At this level, faculty focus on creating interactive packages that promote learner independence. UTC staff and volunteer faculty help developers at this level design products that are pedagogically sound instructional packages. Advanced users collaborate with experts in animation and visual design from CCIT and the Treistman Center to refine instructional modules. With help from CCIT and VideoServices, faculty create delivery mechanisms based on network and cable/satellite technologies that maintain personal contact while transcending the limits of time and distance. The collaborations yield learner-centered courseware and worldware that in turn generate new training standards and procedures for faculty who follow.

Overcoming Obstacles

Moving from a traditional education system to a learner-centered one requires profound change in a number of areas. Students become learning process partners who develop information management, critical thinking, and critical analysis skills and enrich the course content as a result. Teachers learn to select and employ technologies that will free learners to use their own strategies and styles. Institutions adopt a position of support. Thus they create opportunities to guide and help faculty as they strive to reach expert levels of control of learning theories, methods, curriculum design techniques, information search, retrieval, and organization procedures, and courseware design. Ultimately, rewards systems must change to recognize and honor innovative teaching and course development efforts.

No single unit can provide such a comprehensive support system; thus it is vital that units combine efforts to create a comprehensive infrastructure. An integrated approach based on partnerships, mentoring, and resource sharing dramatically reduces duplication of effort and surrounds faculty with the resources they require to create innovative learning environments that meet learner needs. Members of the Faculty Development Partnership at the University of Arizona suggest that faculty development efforts:

- find a leader in the central administration to carry the message to higher levels;
- integrate all aspects of technological and instructional support into a single support system;
- focus on faculty volunteers who are willing to take risks;
- enable creative development initiatives;
- provide easy and adequate access to appropriate technologies;
- focus on goals rather than on territories;
- emphasize faculty-to-faculty mentoring opportunities to expand the support system across disciplines;
- encourage and design changes in the institution's rewards system;
- cultivate external alliances with corporations and community;
- move through three recursive stages of development:

    1. basic training in theories, methods, curriculum design, and technology use;
    2. development of the means to apply the new skills and knowledge in novel environments;
    3. achievement of independent use of expert tools.

THE FACULTY DEVELOPMENT PARTNERSHIP AND THE TEACHING LIBRARY: THE UNIVERSITY OF ARIZONA EXPERIENCE

Karen Williams

Background

Most academic libraries are not currently structured in a way that will allow them to accommodate the changes Carla and Karen outlined. At the University of Arizona we undertook an eighteen-month restructuring process that rebuilt the organization from the ground up. One of the basic principles behind this process was to get more librarians working directly with the clientele. As a result, the majority of librarians now have a public service role. They spend less time in technical processes and at reference desks waiting for the clientele to come to us. More time is spent proactively engaged in education, needs assessment, and other outreach activities. More effort is also spent in planning and designing flexible systems and services that take advantage of technological advances and can be adapted to reflect changing needs. Many academic libraries are experimenting with rethinking reference desk services. At our library, staff from technical services have been trained to provide on-demand reference services along with librarians.

The University of Arizona Library has five strategic objectives, one of which addresses education. This objective states that we will work to improve student achievement through a focus on learning, and by capitalizing on new and emerging technologies to enhance teaching effectiveness. The projects designed to fulfill these objectives define priority work for librarians and library staff. We allocate our resources, both fiscal and human, to completing the strategic projects.

The Faculty Development Partnership

All campus colleagues must realize that we will not be successful educators in the future working alone. So why the emphasis on faculty development? The ultimate goal is to improve the quality of education for students—all students. This cannot be achieved systemically if we focus on those students who find their way into the library or other campus support units. Librarians must learn how to use our skills and resources in tandem with faculty and other support personnel if we are to transform education, instead of merely tweaking it. With this outlook as our frame of reference, we were able to recognize the advantage to be gained by working with four other units on campus to create the Faculty Development Partnership. This is a very important point. An evolution is underway in librarianship. A few years ago we would have been most likely to view the Partnership as something outside of librarianship, rather than an opportunity to create and fulfill new roles. We were in a position to recognize the opportunity and had created a climate that supports risk taking.

Karen Smith described the goals of the Faculty Development Partnership. With campus support, our proposal to form this Partnership went forward to the state legislature and was funded at $940,000. Once the euphoria over receiving the funding faded, we realized that we needed to be in a position to accommodate the demand we were hoping to create. A project of this nature must begin with a vision, and we certainly had that. It is one thing, however, to write a mission statement and quite another to figure out how to turn that statement into action. We needed to figure out how all the partners would fit together to create a seamless whole. What roles and activities would librarians have in this new environment?

The Teaching Library

Carla suggested that we may not yet have a name for what we will call our activities in the future. I think this is true, but the fact that we know we can no longer call what we do "bibliographic instruction" is a recognition of the changes we are facing; the ACRL Bibliographic Instruction Section changed its name to Instruction Section in 1995. I did not invent the term "teaching library," but I am comfortable with it as a descriptor of the directions we are taking. Is being a teaching library different from offering traditional bibliographic instruction? Yes, it is much broader. Being a teaching library includes educating the campus on a variety of information issues and being an integral part of the educational process. Thinking of ourselves as a teaching library helped to define the following initial roles and activities for us as Partnership members:

- Provide basic Internet training for faculty and for their classes
- Introduce faculty to the World Wide Web as an instructional tool
- Support faculty creation of World Wide Web pages for instructional purposes
- Team teach walk-in Internet related courses with the Computing Center
- Model effective use of new learning technologies and appropriate teaching techniques in our instructional sessions
- Be proactive with faculty
- Provide equipment, collaborative work spaces, and support for faculty to use in teaching, and for students carrying out assignments
- Become familiar with Partnership resources in order to make referrals
- Serve as a resource for faculty on issues of copyright, especially relating to new technologies
- Serve as a resource for faculty on electronic access to resources.

I describe this as an initial list in acknowledgment of the fact that our roles will change as the environment changes. Two years ago I could not have included the creation of instructional pages, as the Web was an unfamiliar entity to most faculty. A few years from now, the Web may be overshadowed by an application that does not exist today. Does this mean that our investment in the Web will have been wasted? Not if we are doing the right things with that investment. More than a dozen partnerships were created between faculty and librarians at the University of Arizona last year, many of which made use of the Web. These partnerships involve true collaboration with each individual bringing expertise, and this collaboration is the lasting element. The specific technologies, information issues, and teaching techniques may change, but collaborative efforts that lead to enhanced learning experiences will be remembered and cultivated in the future.

Let me add that we still do a tremendous number of instructional sessions that require less investment than a partnership (688 sessions reached 16,000 students last fiscal year). Although very few sessions could be described as the traditional fifty-minute stand, a partnership goes beyond simply responding to stated requests. How do our partnerships come about? Many of them are a result of librarians being proactive. When difficult assignments turn up at the desk, we contact faculty. When faculty call us requesting "the usual" instructional session we begin a conversation on how we might enhance that session—if the faculty member is receptive and the course objectives would be furthered. But as our expertise becomes recognized on campus we are also receiving referrals in new ways. The Office of Undergraduate Education offered faculty who are piloting new core curriculum courses a menu of support services and about seventy-five percent of them requested librarian assistance with Web page development. The University Teaching Center offers an eight-week New Learning Technologies course to groups of faculty. Not only do we help teach those sessions, but faculty who want more personalized assistance with Internet options are referred to librarians. The campus offers significant instructional computing grants every year for which faculty compete. Awardees who request Internet-related assistance are referred to librarians.

As with any new venture, we must be willing to take risks. I have heard suggestions that what we are experiencing now is just another wave in the ocean of educational reform. I know colleagues who express anxiety about change because the path is not clear. I have learned that there is always an excuse for inaction. We have a chance now to help chart the path rather than waiting to have it revealed to us, and this does require a leap of faith. Not everything that looks like an opportunity will turn out to be one. We will use our best judgment and information to make decisions about where to invest our time and resources, but we will make some mistakes. Karen Smith told us that faculty development efforts at the institutional level must have administrative support in order to be successful. The same is true within libraries. We must create library environments that encourage exploration, support risk taking, and provide training and resources. We undertook a significant training effort which several of my colleagues will describe in a session later at this conference.

Partnership Funding

The Faculty Development Partnership funding supported a number of initiatives, the single largest of which was a series of curriculum transformation grants for faculty. Each Partnership unit also got some funding to put support mechanisms in place. We used our first round of funding for three different purposes in the library.

The electronic classroom in the Main Library was upgraded to provide full network capabilities, powerful workstations, a scanner, one low-end video production station, and software to support Web authoring, presentations, creation of personal bibliographic databases, graphics support, word processing, and spreadsheets. This classroom is used heavily by librarians doing instruction. It is also available to faculty two evenings per week for their own use, and it serves as a walk-in lab on Saturdays.

A prototype Information Commons was created in the reference room of the Main Library. This Commons area provides six workstations that mirror what is available in the electronic classroom. Commons stations are large enough for students to work together on assignments. Why a prototype? Plans are underway to construct a building on campus called the Integrated Instructional Facility (IIF). This facility is designed to accommodate the new Core Curriculum which provides a foundational experience that will give students the flexibility to succeed in a world in which many people have multiple career changes. The IIF will have an Information Commons housed in an area that connects this building to the library. The future Information Commons will house not only library personnel, but also staff from the Computing Center, the Learning Center and Faculty Fellows. We will work cooperatively to meet the needs of students using this facility.

The remainder of our funding was used to hire a computer support staff person, which will be an ongoing position, and students. This configuration of equipment and support staff will provide faculty with a classroom they can use for teaching and two places that students can carry out assignments. Faculty who do not have state-of-the-art equipment in their offices can also use our stations to create course materials. There are open access computer labs available on campus, but our facilities offer software not available elsewhere, greater hours of access than many of the labs, and easy access to many library materials that support the creation of new learning packages. It goes without saying that we still do not have enough computer stations on campus to support demand. The classroom and prototype Information Commons also provide us with working laboratories to help us understand how faculty and students will seek, evaluate, and use information in the future.

Our budget request to the Partnership for next year includes a request for another staff support person and a copyright librarian. There is tremendous evidence of need for the latter on our campus and librarians are in the right position to fulfill that need.

For The Future

Librarians as a group have tended to be somewhat insular. We can no longer afford to do this. We must see ourselves as part of the higher education picture. We must participate in higher education organizations and conferences such as CAUSE, EduCom, and AAHE. The excitement here is palpable. We need to know what leaders in this area are saying about the future. It is also important to know what our campus leaders are saying about teaching, where faculty are in their thinking, and how students are responding to new ways of teaching. I have spent a significant amount of time this past year working on several campus faculty development groups. Some of my activities are directly related to the library, and some are more directly related to furthering the goals of the University as we strive to become a learner-centered, student-friendly institution.

Bibliography

University of Arizona Resources

Educational Technology at the University of Arizona [Online]. Available: http://www.u.arizona.edu/ic/edtech/ (June 6, 1996). This page was developed to encourage faculty to experiment with new technologies and teaching methods. It includes examples of how some faculty are using technology in courses.

Faculty Development Partnership [Online]. Available: http://www.library.arizona.edu/users/kwilliam/partners.htm (March 28, 1997).

Interim Report to Faculty Development Partnership [Online]. Available: http://www.library.arizona.edu/users/kwilliam/intrpt.htm (June 6, 1996).

Sample Faculty/Librarian Partnerships

Dickstein, Ruth. *Women's Studies on the Internet* [Online]. Available: http://www.library.arizona.edu/users/dickstei/homepg.htm (August 30, 1997). Ruth Dickstein (Library) and Susan Craddock (Women's Studies) incorporated six sessions on library and Internet research into Women's Studies 584—Feminist Research Methodologies.

Pfander, Jeanne. *BIOL 181L Library Research* Page [Online]. Available: http://www.library.arizona.edu/users/jpfander/biol181.html (September 11, 1996). Jeanne Pfander, Laura Bender, and Pat Morris (Library) and John Aronson (Molecular and Cellular Biology) developed an assignment that would work for the 1500 students enrolled in Biology 181.

Other Resources

Dolence, Michael G. and Donald M. Norris. *Transforming Higher Education: A Vision for Learning in the 21st Century*. Ann Arbor, MI: Society for College and University Planning, 1995.

Shapiro, Jeremy J. and Shelley K. Hughes. "Information Literacy as a Liberal Art: Enlightenment Proposals for a New Curriculum." *Educom Review 31*, no. 2 (1996): 31-5. Also available at: http://www.educom.edu/web/pubs/review/reviewArticles/31231.html.

Smith, Karen L. "The Student, the Learner, and the Obsolescent Professor: Changing Roles Through Technology." Presented at CCUMC, April 13, 1996; and "The Shift to a Learner Centered University: New Roles for Faculty, Students, and Technology." Presented at ASCUE, June 10, 1996.

Stoffle, Carla J. and Karen Williams. "The Instructional Program and Responsibilities of the Teaching Library." In *Information Technology and the Remaking of the University Library*, ed. Beverly P. Lynch. New Directions for Higher Education, no. 90. San Francisco: Jossey-Bass, 1995.

APPENDIX

Transformation in Higher Education

American Association for Higher Education's TLTR

"The AAHE Teaching, Learning, and Technology Roundtable (TLTR) seeks to improve the quality and accessibility of higher education through the selective use of information technology and information resources in teaching and learning—while controlling costs."
http://www.aahe.org/technology/tltr.index.htm

Coalition for Networked Information's New Learning Communities

"CNI's New Learning Communities Program seeks to promote cross-fertilization of professionals in higher education institutions across the country who use networks such as the Internet and networked information resources to enrich their curriculum and broaden their students' learning experiences. The program brings together institutional or inter-institutional teams of faculty, librarians, information technologists, instructional technologists, and students, to share perspectives, critique each other's programs, and develop a set of "best practices" for the benefit of the larger educational community."
http://www.cni.org/projects/nlc/

EDUCOM's National Learning Infrastructure Initiative

"There is widespread recognition that American higher education needs restructuring in order to contain or reduce rising costs, to increase access, and to promote significant improvements in the quality of student learning. To achieve these restructuring goals, reform efforts must include the creation of new kinds of learning environments that harness the power of information technology."
http://www.educom.edu/program/nlii/nliiHome.html

Annenberg Foundation/Corporation for Public
Broadcasting Flashlight Project

"In order to deal with [today's] challenges, one must focus on programmatic teaching-learning practices and organizational structures because nothing less can change programmatic learning outcomes, accessibility and costs. Improvements in single assignments or even in single courses almost never have an impact on the average graduate. Such isolated improvements may affect a few students a lot, or many students a tiny bit, but rarely do changes in a single assignment (thanks to new software) or course meaningfully affect ultimate learning outcomes, access chances, or costs—the Triple Challenge."

"The Flashlight Project is developing, testing and disseminating evaluation procedures that a postsecondary institution or department could use to periodically assess its evolving educational strategies, in particular those educational strategies supported by its uses of computing, video and telecommunications."

http://www.learner.org/edtech/rscheval/

UWIRED:
ENHANCING TEACHING, LEARNING, AND TECHNOLOGY THROUGH COLLABORATION

Andrea Bartelstein, Louis Fox, Pamela Stewart, Lizabeth Wilson, and Anne Zald

ABSTRACT

In response to the challenges of bringing technology into the service of teaching and learning, the new information literacy, and the creation of community at a large university, the University of Washington developed a holistic, campus-wide approach called UWired. The primary goal of UWired is to create an electronic community in which communication, collaboration, and information technologies become integral to teaching and learning. UWired addresses faculty development, active student learning, and facilities redesign. UWired brings together diverse expertise and support to enhance campus-wide learning and teaching. UWired seeks to go beyond technology—offering sustained discipline-specific instruction, useful educational applications of technology, faculty and librarian development, and requisite facilities and infrastructure.

INTRODUCTION

New technologies have the potential to change profoundly the ways students learn and faculty teach. Colleges and universities across the nation are struggling to discern which instructional applications will provide pedagogical advantages and cost-benefits in student learning. Until UWired, the University of Washington's adaptation to technology in the classroom had been piecemeal, fitful, and slow. Some faculty had used educational technology to produce dramatic and powerful results. Conversely, there were instances when technology resulted in expensive and pointless uses of time and resources. Most faculty confessed that they were "stumbling along, backing into" the use of technology in teaching and learning.

Technology has driven equally significant changes in libraries and scholarly communication. As research and teaching increasingly rely on global networks for the creation, storage, and dissemination of knowledge, a new information literacy has emerged. Excess of, not access to, information is the new challenge. Students often lack the skills necessary to succeed in this evolving environment. Librarians and faculty have worked together in promoting information literacy; however, these initiatives have tended to be spotty and not part of the curriculum.

The quality of the student experience is both heightened and harmed by the size and complexity of a large research university such as the University of Washington (UW). While students have a great breadth of opportunities for learning, they often feel isolated from both the faculty and one another. A documented benefit of the UW's Freshman Interest Group (FIG) program has been cohesive learning communities within this larger environment. However, not all freshmen and a very small proportion of faculty have the opportunity to participate in a FIG. A challenge for the large, non-residential research university is how to foster educational conditions in which undergraduates can be engaged with faculty and become full participants in the academic community.

UWIRED: AN INNOVATIVE CONCEPT

In response to the three-pronged challenge of bringing technology into the service of teaching and learning, the new information literacy, and the creation of community at a large research university, the UW developed a holistic, campus-wide approach called UWired.[1] The primary goal of UWired is to create an electronic community in which communication, collaboration, and information technologies become ongoing, integral parts of teaching and learning. UWired is a collaboration of faculty, librarians, computing staff, administrators, and students from a number of units, including Undergraduate Education, Computing & Communications, University Libraries, and University Extension. UWired addresses faculty development, active and engaged student learning, and facilities management and redesign. Few efforts have brought to bear the diverse expertise and support needed to enhance campus-wide learning and teaching. Although initiatives on other campuses have provided computers to faculty or students, UWired seeks to go beyond technology—offering sustained discipline-specific instruction, useful applications of technology in the classroom, faculty development, and requisite facilities and infrastructure.

BUILDING ON THE UW MISSION AND STRENGTHS

UWired reflects the UW's mission to provide an undergraduate education which emphasizes the mastery of methods of inquiry and fosters those qualities of mind that encourage mature and independent judgment. UWired is predicated on the distinguishing strengths of a research university—the faculty's scholarly and creative achievements. UWired allows faculty to directly engage students in learning through the use of electronic communication. UWired capitalizes on a campus information infrastructure that has been called one of the best in the world. Students, faculty, administrators, and librarians have benefited immeasurably from greater access to information, enhanced communication, and connections to otherwise unreachable resources. Over 54,000 active electronic mail accounts are evidence that UW's information network is enjoyed throughout the campus.

THE EVOLUTION OF UWIRED

UWired started in 1994 when former UW Provost Wayne Clough, now president of the Georgia Institute of Technology, put together a team to seek ways to integrate information technology and electronic learning communities into the undergraduate experience. UWired has grown from a small pilot project reaching 65 students and 12 faculty and teaching assistants to a program enjoyed by over 2,000 students and more than 1,000 faculty. Funding for UWired has been pieced together creatively from a variety of sources including Apple Computer, the

W 94	Sp 94	Su 94	A 94	W 95	Sp 95	Su 95	A 95	W 96	Sp 96	SU 96	A 96	W 97
Provost's Initiative												
			UWired FIGS (3 of 60)				UWired FIGs EXPANDED to 8 (of 60) FIGS Librarian/Peer Teams Intercollegiate Athletics				UWired FIGs EXPANDED to all 60 FIGs	
		Laptop Collab Built										
			Lectures Demos									
				Coordinator Hired Innovative Courses Program Begun								
					Workshops ~ 18 Topics per quarter							
					Pentium Collab Built							
						Telecourse Project						
							Drop-in Collab Built & Opens					
								Center for Teaching, Learning & Technology Opens				
									Community College Symposia			
										K-12 In-service		
											Linked Courses	

Figure 1.

Kenneth Allen Library Endowment, the Provost's Office, capital projects, and each of the participating units.

A timeline of the development of UWired is provided in Figure 1. This timeline provides an overview of the many projects under the UWired umbrella which share the broad goal of integrating information technology into the curriculum and across the disciplinary spectrum.

Freshman Interest Groups

The Freshman Interest Group (FIG) program began on the UW campus in 1987. FIGs are a highly successful effort to assist students in adjusting to life and work at a large urban university. Twenty to twenty-five students enroll in a suite of thematically linked courses during their first quarter. In addition they take a one-credit course taught by a peer advisor who is a UW junior or senior. The peer advisor covers topics such as registering for classes, campus resources, time management, and choosing a major. The peer advisor also facilitates informal student contact with a senior faculty member, a discussion on a social issue (which is often relevant to campus life), and an outing to a cultural event.

During the UWired pilot year (1994-1995), the sixty-five freshmen enrolled in three of these FIGs (anthropology, fisheries, and architecture) and twelve faculty and teaching assistants were targeted for intensive technology and information literacy instruction; each was loaned a laptop computer for the year. Librarians taught a year-long two-credit Information and Technology Seminar focused on hardware and software skills, sophisticated and responsible use of the Internet and the Web, and critical use and evaluation of information. UWired's electronic learning communities required a new type of classroom. A collaboratory (a learning space that blends the best features of classrooms and computer labs) was built in the undergraduate library. The collaboratory departed radically from other electronic classrooms that mirror traditional lecture halls, where rows of computer tables face the instructor who is stationed at the front of the room poised near an LCD projection panel. Instead, the collaboratory is organized in four-person pods and oriented around a center utility pole that provides power and Ethernet connections. Not only are work spaces configured to facilitate collaboration, but the network connections also allow students and faculty to share work and ideas.

In 1995-1996, eight of the sixty FIGs were UWired, but the peer seminar and the information technology seminar merged and the resulting quarter-long two-credit course was team taught by a librarian, peer advisor, and UWired Lead (i.e., computer student assistant). The natural synergy of the topics of the two courses combined with the team teaching experiment yielded many useful lessons. Two additional collaboratories were built adjacent to the first to accommodate the expanded scope of UWired.

Based on the first two years of experience, the program has now been expanded to all sixty FIGs. The first two years of UWired demonstrated the effectiveness of integrating information technology into instruction. Although there were significant differences between the 1994-1995 and the 1995-1996 programs, both were successful in getting students plugged into the electronic information and communication environment. For 1996-1997, the number of instructional sessions will be reduced from the weekly ones offered in pilot UWired FIGs to three sessions spread over ten weeks. The sessions will focus on core competencies: electronic communication, Internet and the World Wide Web, and library resources.

Information Link Courses

To address the demonstrated need for more intensive information and technology instruction later in the first year or in the second year of undergraduate studies, UWired will offer an information technology seminar linked to a specific course during winter quarter 1997. FIG graduates interested in learning more about technology in a discipline-specific context may enroll in one of the information link courses. Sociology of Deviance, Introduction to Anthropology, Introduction to Fisheries, and Introduction to Psychology will pilot the use of technology and information seeking in a way relevant to the discipline. The information link course will be team taught by a librarian and a peer advisor in collaboration with the discipline-based faculty member.

Intercollegiate Athletics

Another initiative of the 1995-1996 year was the involvement of Intercollegiate Athletics. The men's and women's basketball teams were loaned laptop computers for the year and enrolled in an information technology seminar taught by a team of two librarians. The laptops provided these student athletes with an innovative means of receiving extended academic support during their travel time. Student athletes were able to continue working on course work while on the road, communicate with instructors, and turn in assignments.

Upper Division Innovative Courses

An RFP was issued in 1995 to elicit faculty proposals for integrating information resources and technology into teaching and learning. Over thirteen courses in a wide variety of disciplines have been transformed to incorporate technology and networked information into course delivery and content. Courses have included Czech literature, environmental statistics, economic geography, journalism, and radiology. Faculty selected through the RFP process enjoyed use of a collaboratory for class meetings, high-level technical support, funding for specialized software, and a librarian teaching partner.

Faculty Development

UWired provides an institutional structure for accessible, meaningful, and sustained faculty development. UWired faculty, peer advisors, technologists, and librarians attend a week-long series of workshops not only to learn technical skills, but more importantly, to also have an opportunity to work in collaborative teams. Over 1,000 faculty and librarians have participated in a campus-wide series of seminars on teaching and technology. This series has provided an opportunity for faculty to showcase their work, and has promoted a healthy dialogue concerning the advantages and pitfalls of technology. An ongoing curriculum for faculty and librarians provides a variety of specially designed workshops ranging from electronic mail for class communication, to putting a syllabus in HTML, to copyright in cyberspace.

The UWired Center for Teaching, Learning, and Technology (CTLT) opened adjacent to the third collaboratory in May 1996. The Center provides support to faculty, librarians, and teaching assistants in the use of technology and information resources in teaching and learning by offering:

- Consultation services on instructional development, instructional technology, and information resources
- Access to computer hardware and software for the purpose of developing a curriculum, producing course materials such as World Wide Web pages, or learning to use computer technology
- Workshops on pedagogical as well as technical aspects of teaching, learning, and technology
- Resources, such as books, conference announcements, journals, manuals, and model course materials
- Space for instructors to meet for the purpose of collaborating or sharing ideas and tips on using technology and information resources in teaching and learning.

In keeping with the collaborative spirit of UWired, the CTLT staff includes a faculty member, a librarian, a computing professional, and several student consultants. The staff works with instructors in various team configurations based on the nature of the project, bringing in other librarians, faculty, and computing staff as appropriate. Faculty and teaching assistants currently using the CTLT come from diverse fields, including law, medicine, sociology, English, geography, statistics, writing, business, nursing, chemistry, drama, communications, and music. Some faculty are learning how to put their course materials on the World Wide Web or are looking for digital images to incorporate into classroom presentations. Others are consulting with CTLT staff as they develop new courses or redesign existing ones with a substantial emphasis on electronic communication or networked information resources.

Outreach and Partnerships

Recognizing that the University does not operate in an educational vacuum, UWired has extended its focus to include connections with the state's community colleges and K-12 teachers. Teams from the thirty-two community colleges in Washington State participated in a week-long UWired symposium on teaching and technology during summer 1996. The symposium included sessions, demonstrations, and discussions on the use of technology in teaching and learning, training and facilities issues, strategies for collaboration, and planning for inter-institutional cooperation. In October 1996, UWired is hosted an in-service day for 700 Seattle Public School teachers entitled "Educating the Citizen for the 21st Century: Information Literacy and Service Learning." UWired and its partners outside the academy provide structure for a seamless educational experience for the state's students with technology and information literacy at its core.

COSTS, FACILITIES, AND INFRASTRUCTURE

UWired is a project that, up until recently, was funded around the edges with contributions from vendors, endowment funds, capital projects, the Provost, and the collaborating units. First-year start-up costs for UWired were just over $600,000, the bulk of which (about 84%) were devoted to the purchase of equipment, furniture and construction of the first collaboratory. The remaining operating component was a mix of contributions, including in-kind, from Undergraduate Education, University Libraries, and Computing & Communications, and some Libraries endowment monies. Included in the equipment amount was Apple Computer's donation of half of the pool of laptops. It should be noted that the University did not consider UWired a particular risk in this first year. The bulk of the resources was spent on equipment and the collaboratory, all of which could continue to be used regardless of the outcome of the UWired pilot.

Second-year costs approached $1 million, again with the majority of funds spent to construct and equip two more collaboratories and the CTLT. Operating costs (about 30% of the budget) came primarily from resources contributed by Undergraduate Education, non-budgeted staff time from the various units involved, and a large infusion from the Provost. The Libraries by this point had also reallocated close to 10,000 square feet to accommodate the program. Another large infusion from the Provost will enable the third-year program to get off the ground, with the budget now under half a million dollars since no additional capital construction or major equipment purchases are required. Unless additional collaboratories are constructed, future equipment funds will be for maintenance and replacement only.

Funding for UWired has stabilized, and the program is being viewed more now as a department, requesting funds and competing for resources in the normal budget process. UWired planners estimate future annual budgets at approximately this half a million dollar level. Within the operating cost component, approximately 65 percent is devoted to personnel costs. For the purposes of planning for lab construction and outfitting, the UW spent approximately $6,300 per seat—$3,800 of that amount for the workstation, software, and a pro-rata printer share, and $2,500 for capital construction (or $60/square foot). Anyone contemplating starting a program such as UWired should:

- be creative about harnessing in-kind contributions of all kinds, including staff time, from participating units
- expect temporary, and in some cases, permanent reallocations of staff, space, and other resources to occur
- seek out resources to the extent possible from outside the institution.

LESSONS LEARNED

What has been the impact of UWired on students, faculty, librarians, computing professionals, and the institution? What lessons have been learned from UWired that will guide the UW in the future?

Impact on Students

The first two years of UWired have demonstrated the effectiveness of integrating information technology instruction into teaching and learning at the freshman level.[2] UWired was introduced in autumn quarter 1994 with a goal of using information technology to build upon the community and collaborative aspects of the FIG program and also as an integral part of instruction. UWired recognized that computers and information technology had made substantial changes in the ways people communicate with each other and utilize information resources. Areas such as e-mail, library catalogs and databases, Internet and World Wide Web resources, and application software (e.g., word-processing and presentation programs) have all become part of the learning and communication processes. If UWired can help students learn how to collect, evaluate, and synthesize information technologies and resources for their academic careers, it will also equip them to compete effectively in the working world when they leave the University.

Evaluations were done in both 1994 and 1995 and included a general survey given to all FIGs, pre- and post-surveys on technology and library skills administered to UWired FIGs and comparison FIGs, and a focused debriefing for students. Since the second year of UWired differed substantially from the first year in duration (just autumn quarter) and equipment (laptops were not loaned to most students), the results below pertain primarily to the 1995-1996 program. The results have been impressive. UWired has provided a "jump-start" for entering freshmen by enabling them to develop information and technology skills during their first quarter which they can then apply to other academic work.

UWired students were much more likely to know about and use campus computing resources than students in other FIGs. The collaboratories have been crucial in providing access to computing resources and assistance when needed. UWired students used e-mail to a much more significant degree than non-UWired students and they used it for more academic-related activities. E-mail was used on a regular basis to communicate with instructors and other students on class-related work. E-mail contact also helped reinforce the sense of community and collaboration among students. The figures below compare e-mail use among UWired and non-UWired FIGs:

	UWired	Other
Ask instructor questions	85%	71%
Schedule a meeting	66%	22%
Turn in assignments	83%	21%
Discuss with classmates	69%	30%

Not only did UWired students use e-mail more often to communicate with their instructors, they were also more comfortable doing so. On a scale of 1 (very uncomfortable) to 5 (very comfortable), UWired students averaged 4.62 while those in comparison FIGs averaged 3.91. UWired students also used other campus computing resources more often than those in other FIGs. For example, they used the campus-wide information system (UWIN) to find information 45% more often than non-UWired students and also felt more comfortable in using UWIN.

UWired students were introduced to the World Wide Web and taught how to "surf" the Web knowledgeably and evaluate information. When compared to students in other FIGs, those in UWired:

- were five times more likely to know how to evaluate Web information
- used the Web twice as frequently
- were better able to describe specific ways in which this information would help them
- felt far more comfortable using the Web to find information.

Fred Johnson, professor in Fisheries and UWired faculty, compares the UWired freshmen to "... rocket ships: once they left the earth, they kept going faster and faster. In one quarter, these students had gone past what juniors and seniors in our department had mastered in terms of transferable skills. Teaching is never going to be the same again. It brings in a whole new suite of possibilities and allows me to think about teaching more broadly."[3]

Impact on Student Athletes

The UWired student athletes became adept at a broad spectrum of information literacy and technology skills. Students were comfortable communicating through e-mail with professors, coaches, and classmates, searching the World Wide Web, retrieving information from online databases and indexes, creating written documents and slide presentations, transferring files from one computer to another, and connecting to the campus network while on the road. Students improved their skills in evaluating online sources, using source material properly, citing electronic and printed sources, and becoming more familiar with alternate sources of information. The students wonder how they were ever able to get along before without the use of a laptop on their trips. The laptop has become an integral part of their traveling baggage and a boost to efficient use of preparation time while away from campus. The laptops have expanded their academic day and helped address the severe time constraints under which student athletes operate. For the first time ever, the women's basketball team had a cumulative GPA of over 3.0; the coaches credit UWired.

Student-athlete Patrick Femerling used his computer skills while on a road trip to Arizona to send his portion of a geography project back to classmates in Seattle. And while doing a search for his English paper, Patrick joked, "I go to all the best parties and I go to all the best databases."[4]

Impact on Faculty

Modes of teaching in higher education have remained relatively static for nearly a century. The linear presentation of material in the lecture mode that allows students to be isolated and passive in their learning has been changed through the creation of electronic learning communities. UWired has opened new possibilities, including: distributed learning over time and place; more interaction with students; student-directed learning; and enhancement of traditional modalities. Along with the possibilities come new challenges. What is the best way to manage the e-mail workload? How can faculty ensure that the technology does not become a distraction or a barrier? How can faculty assess and evaluate these new forms of learning and teaching? Questions of student access to computing on and off campus have taken on critical importance. A faculty interest group meets regularly in the CTLT and is working collectively to find answers to these challenges.

Impact on the Evolving Role of Librarians

Through UWired, librarians have become active partners in the educational process. They have further honed their technical and instructional talents into highly sophisticated and marketable skills. Librarians have piloted models for integrating information literacy into the curriculum. As the models become increasingly curriculum-based rather than course-based, the librarians are moving away from the traditional stand-alone, one-shot library session. The new model requires more collaboration and, consequently, time. In the instructional teams, librarians are able to use their experience in collaboration to organize efforts and keep initiatives and groups moving forward.

Impact on the Evolving Role of Computing Professionals

Prior to UWired, the role of campus computing professionals was that of technology and applications consultants, trainers, and, of course, cynics and naysayers. Through UWired, computing professionals have become full partners in the planning process and formal instructors in the program. They have collaborated on instructional teams with faculty, librarians, and peer advisors. Computing staff are now closer to their users, particularly faculty, and more aware of the usability of applications. They are placing less emphasis on the technology and more on transparency. Their consulting roles have become more intimate and focused and they have expanded and enhanced their participation in training. UWired has affected overall physical planning for computer laboratories and has provided a filter for prioritizing projects. Student computer assistants have taken on new teaching and advising roles. Computing staff have become believers in the value of collaboration.

Impact on the Institution

UWired has provided an institutional structure for prototyping and testing technology and teaching. Strong educational collaborations, funding partnerships, and a test bed environment have allowed the UW to move from what was once a piecemeal approach to one that is comprehensive, innovative, and sustainable. UWired has allowed for coordinated and wise use of scarce resources. UWired has provided a successful model for budgeting and resource allocation for institutional collaborations. UWired has supported facilities redesign and construction to support technology in teaching and learning and is serving as a prototype for Mary Gates Hall, a technology-intense undergraduate education building set to open in 2000. UWired has enhanced the sense of community at a large research university while providing a test environment for innovation and transformation. Ultimately, UWired is facilitating the institutional goal of making information and technology literacy distinguishing characteristics of a UW graduate.

NIL FACILE

The lessons learned from UWired during its first two years now guide teaching, learning, and technology at the UW. UWired reaffirmed that students must be at the center of the University's efforts; that students are invaluable in the development and implementation of educational efforts; and that, with technology, students can become teachers and ultimately masters of content. In the area of collaboration, we found that much more can be accomplished collectively than individually; that diverse expertise is needed from throughout campus; that no one unit or department can go this alone; and that collaboration takes place on many different levels (among students, between faculty and students; among UWired instructional teams; and among administrative units). A loose and fluid organizational structure is necessary for innovation; flexibility and agility are required; and the best administrative commitment is manifested as a trusting hands-off approach. UWired participants learned to pilot and test, discard and readjust, and that most change is incremental. Appropriate technology used effectively enables more than it constrains, appropriate technology used efficiently disappears more than it interferes; and appropriate technology used effectively and efficiently is neither cheap nor easy.[5] Perhaps the most important lesson learned is *nil facile*: nothing is simple.

NOTES AND REFERENCES

1. Interested readers can find detailed information about all facets of UWired at the project's World Wide Web site at http://www.washington.edu/uwired/.

2. Much of the section on the impact of UWired on students is taken from an internal UW report by Steve Hiller, "UWired FIG Program Concludes Two Year Pilot," (March 1996).

3. Fred Johnson, "Plugging into UWired," *Paideia: Undergraduate Education at the University of Washington* 3, no. 2 (1995), pp. 1-3.

4. Jill McKinstry, "Husky Athletes: Taking Care of Business; ICA UWired Participants in 24 Hours in Cyberspace" [Online]. Available: http://weber.u.washington.edu/~icawired/24hours.html/ (February 8, 1996).

5. Credit for this pithy comment goes to Mark McNair, Consultant and Software Engineering, Computing & Communications, and member of UWired Planning Group.

HARD DRIVES AND HARDBACKS:
PARTNERSHIPS BETWEEN COMPUTER CENTERS AND LIBRARIES

Karen Diller and Chuck Harrsch

ABSTRACT

Recently, the Information Technology Department and the Library at Washington State University Vancouver were combined into one department called Vancouver Information Services (VIS). The two authors, each a member of a sub-department of VIS, worked collaboratively to design an instructional program for the campus. In this paper the authors describe the process of creating an instructional program administered and taught by members of the Library and the Information Technology Department. The original needs assessment and the resulting program implemented in the Spring of 1996 are described. Insights gained from the instructors' experiences and the participants' evaluations are offered.

INTRODUCTION

Since the early 1980s, there have been articles in the professional literature detailing the collaboration of librarians and information technology professionals. The earliest articles showed how these two groups worked together on technical problems surrounding early automation projects.[1] Later articles discussed the merging of computer centers and libraries. Many of these either listed the perils of one department being overrun by members of the other or promised benefits through a tighter integration between the departments. In addition, they also discussed organizational and administrative issues relating to integrating the two departments.[2]

In the early 1990s the focus of the literature changed. Although a number of articles discussing the organization and administration of joint library-computer center departments still appeared, articles focusing on successful joint ventures involving computer center staff and librarians began to emerge.[3] Despite this trend, very few articles focused on these two groups working together on instructional programs. Many articles detailing the advantages of the computer center and library working together did not even mention advantages in the area of instruction.

Only with the growth of the Internet, and the need to have a working knowledge of the Internet and related technology, do we see evidence of computer centers and libraries working together in a teaching mode. In early 1994, articles started appearing which detailed successful collaboration between the staff of the two departments in order to provide Internet instruction.[4] What has not appeared in the literature to this point is a discussion of a jointly organized and administered program designed to meet the instructional needs of an entire campus in an electronic learning environment.

Perhaps one reason for this dearth of information regarding such a complete integration is that each department usually has a long history of its own and has not generally collaborated with the other department except in specific instances. Washington State University Vancouver, as a relatively new branch campus, did not have such long-standing departmental histories and was in the unique position of being able to create a model of integration which included a combined approach to technology instruction. This was made easier by the fact that the two departments were small, with a total staff of six.

Although Washington State University Vancouver started in much the same state as nearly every other school, with the library and computer center as separate departments, around July of 1995 Vancouver Information Services (VIS) was created by combining the Library, Information Technology Department, and the educational television system (WHETS). The Campus Librarian was in charge of the new VIS department. By late 1995 two independent factors coalesced to create a clear mandate for action by this new entity.

First, it became clear to the Head of VIS that the three parts of this new unit needed to work together more closely so that the unit could begin operating as a single entity.[5] Second, during the same period, the campus' need for technology training was becoming more evident. With the explosion of information technology, faculty, staff, and students needed instruction in order to more successfully navigate the campus' electronic environments. However, neither the library nor the computer center had the staff or facilities to provide this instruction on their own. Cooperating to provide technology instruction to the campus appeared to be the perfect project for VIS to work on collaboratively.

WSUV students, staff, and faculty posed a unique set of circumstances which made this collaboration both necessary and proper. The WSUV student body profile was (and continues to be) indicative of part of the need. Of the 983 students at WSUV, the average age is 32 and 70 percent of the students are female. Many of WSUV's students returned to an academic setting after being away from it for a long time. Some needed training to bring them up-to-date while others were looking for the chance to improve their skills to become more competitive in the workplace. The staff and faculty of 88 people also needed additional training. The staff needed training because, as the campus grew, they were looking for ways to further automate their procedures. The faculty requested additional technology training as they became interested in incorporating technology into the classroom. In addition, the Dean, in his commitment to creating a virtual university component at WSUV, had started to move the campus to the forefront of incorporating technology into education.

Clearly, the campus needed an organized program for technology training and the staff of the newly-created VIS were anxious to answer this need. However, some significant problems needed to be overcome or at least acknowledged. As with most programs, technology instruction had a past. The computer center had offered some classes on Word, Excel, e-mail and the Internet, but these were never well attended. Part of the problem was that until recently, technology instruction was not a priority for faculty and staff and the students were not very aware of their need for technology instruction.

An inadequate staffing level was another significant problem. As of November 1995, VIS had two librarians and two systems coordinators in addition to two support staff. It was clear that the brunt of the organization and instruction would have to be carried by two people with a little help from guest instructors. In addition, it was clear that the VIS workshop series should be up and running within two months, that is, by January of 1996.

The biggest obstacle was facilities. At the time there was only one small room on the campus that was equipped with computers. This lab functioned as the students' computer lab, the instruction lab, and office space for the information technology staff. In addition, the workstations in this lab were of variable age and operating systems. There were seven Macintosh computers and twelve PCs ranging from the most recent models to old models incapable of running up-to-date software. It was impossible to project an image so that all could see. Attendees either had their backs to the image or were so close that they could not see the image without significant neck strain. Since this area was also the work area for staff, there were constant interruptions and traffic. In addition, because this room was also the campus computer lab, the times that it could be used for instruction were severely restricted. As a result, many of the classes were scheduled during the early morning hours when the lab was normally closed.

Despite these problems, we did put together a successful series of workshops. It was not perfect. We made mistakes along the way and had to scale back some of our more elaborate plans, but overall it was successful.

How did we plan, organize and conduct workshops with so little planning time? We recognized from the beginning that we would not be able to meet everyone's needs and thus, in December, we conducted a campus needs assessment. As good academics, the first person we consulted was our Dean and what we heard from him was Web, Web, and more Web. In addition, since both of us work on the front lines, we had a good idea of campus needs based on the questions that we were most frequently asked.

Using a more formal approach, we also designed and distributed a survey to all faculty and staff and to as many students as we could reach. Thirty-five percent of all faculty and staff and twelve and one-half percent of the students returned surveys.

Based on the results of our needs assessment, we created a list of workshops that we should offer. We then edited this list based on the reality of the available staff time and resources. Once we had a manageable list, workshops were scheduled based on lab availability and staff time. We were the main instructors, teaching as a team and individually. In addition, we had a few other instructors teaching several workshops.

The problem that took the most time to work through was that of the dual operating systems (Macintosh and PC). We knew that we had users of both and yet did not have the resources to double our workshop load by separately offering every workshop for each operating system. After a long discussion, we decided on several methods to solve this dilemma. We did teach some of the basic computer programs individually, one PC and one Mac, on the assumption that those who were most unfamiliar with common programs would be the most uncomfortable in a dual operating system workshop. Secondly, we asked student lab monitors to help out in some sessions that used both operating systems in order to have more staff available to give individual assistance during the workshop. Finally, we decided that for the HTML sessions we would project both PC and Mac screens on the wall and give instruction on both systems.

Once we had the workshop schedule, we blanketed the campus with announcements and advertisements. We e-mailed, posted, and mailed flyers across campus describing the workshops. In addition, we asked a handful of faculty to distribute the flyers in their classes. During this time, we also designed our evaluation form. Optimistically, we decided to have two levels of evaluations. The goal was to have workshop participants fill out one evaluation directly after class, thereby giving us immediate feedback on our instruction and the content of the class. We then planned a secondary evaluation to be sent to class participants three to four weeks after the workshop. This evaluation would see how useful the workshop content was to the participants' real-life needs. Unfortunately, because of time constraints, this second level evaluation was never completed.

By April the workshops were completed and we were pleased with the results. Attendance at the workshops was very good, especially among faculty and staff, 40 percent of whom attended at least one workshop. Unfortunately, only 7 percent of the students at WSUV attended a workshop, although those who did usually attended more than one. There are several reasons which account for this pattern. First, there were no campus mailboxes for individual students and a high percentage of students were only on campus for one or two classes so their exposure to campus was limited. As a result, it was difficult to notify the students of the workshops. Another potential reason for this low attendance was the workshop schedule. With so little flexibility in the scheduling, we could not use a wider variety of time slots which would have accommodated a greater number of students.

The VIS workshops were highly rated by those faculty, staff, and students who attended. Although we would like to claim that the very favorable evaluations were entirely due to the quality of teaching, we must admit that the evaluations may have been slightly skewed because of the nature of WSUV and the people who make up WSUV. In short, it is a small campus with a relatively small number of people. Frequently, everyone in the room was on a first-name basis with everyone else, including the instructors.

Although the majority of the evaluations were quite good, two areas generally scored lower than the others. As can be seen in Figure 1, the two areas that were given the lowest scores were "organization" and "content level." This was not a surprise. The "organization" rating was lowest at the beginning of the semester when the instructors were unfamiliar with each other's styles. These scores steadily improved as the semester progressed and we operated more as a team. We also had problems in the beginning with conducting the dual operating system sessions but we learned with each class and made adjustments over time.

In talking with the participants it became clear that they had certain expectations as to the content level of the class. When these expectations were not met, the "content level" scores suffered. Because the workshops were not described in the flyers,

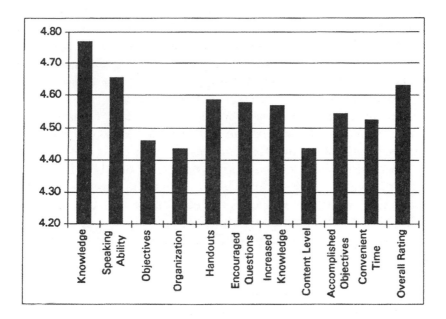

Evaluation Results

Figure 1.

participants had widely varying expectations regarding the complexity and depth of topics to be covered in any one workshop.
Therefore, there sometimes was a great discrepancy between a
participant's expectations and our goals for the class.

Overall, however, the workshops were very successful in the
eyes of the attendees. Ninety-four percent of all participants said
that they would recommend the workshop to a friend or
coworker. These results, we hope, will encourage others who are
short-staffed and have poorly-equipped facilities, to start
technology training programs.

As instructors, we noted several unexpected benefits beyond
imparting knowledge to the attendees. VIS, as a new department,
was able to build a reputation as a department able to provide quality instruction. In addition, Chuck, the "computer techie"
improved his image from that of the computer support person to
that of a skilled instructor. This, in turn, gave him more confidence

as an instructor. As a new faculty member, the workshops introduced me to the campus and its needs. I learned more about the campus and the campus became acquainted with me. Finally, team teaching proved to be an advantage. Our teaching and technology skills expanded because we learned from each other and were able to provide each other with constructive criticism.

One consistent problem, however, was the lack of basic computer skills on the part of the participants. Workshop attendees frequently were not familiar with how to use a mouse, how to open and close files, and other basics. In our HTML classes we also found a lack of knowledge about the Internet in general. As a result, we will offer several classes on the basics of using the Windows and Macintosh operating systems. In addition, we will be including an introduction to the Internet in future HTML classes.

We also underestimated the need for paper. Although help documentation was available on the campus web site, and, for the HTML classes, disks containing help information were distributed, participants clearly preferred paper handouts.

One problem that was anticipated, especially due to the age of our equipment, was the ubiquitous "technical glitch." These glitches, added to the technical inexperience of our participants, could quickly escalate the classroom atmosphere to near panic. It was essential to have a computer-literate assistant in larger classes to provide individual assistance to those having problems.

Finally, both of us learned that in a hands-on setting, personalities are even more likely to dictate the ebb and flow of the class than in a more traditional classroom setting. This was especially true since we had faculty, staff, and students in the same workshops. The expectations for individual attention varied significantly, with students generally expecting less individualized attention.

Despite these problems, WSUV will continue to offer the VIS Workshop Series. Our present plans are to survey the faculty to ask them what technology expectations they have for their students, which is information that we did not get in our original needs assessment. Additionally, we plan to coordinate our efforts with the new student orientations so that we provide incoming students with some basic information (e-mail, introduction to the online catalog and Netscape) and then encourage them to attend VIS workshops to further their knowledge.

Due to the initial success of the VIS program, WSUV intends to expand the program to include a greater variety of workshops. In addition, once the faculty became aware of the potential for this program we began receiving offers of assistance in developing and teaching future workshops. Fortunately, since the presentation of this paper in June 1996, WSUV has moved to an entirely new facility that is capable of accommodating the increased activity that VIS has planned. Recognizing, however, that there are practical limits to what can be done with classes and workshops, WSUV has begun creating "Web Workshops" in which mini-workshops are presented via World Wide Web pages so that many people can access the workshops at their convenience.

As a result of our experience with the program we offer the following advice to those contemplating starting their own programs.

1. Look before you leap. Discover the needs of your campus before starting your project.
   a. We found that it was important to know what plans the faculty had for the technology that was available and how they intended to use it. Thus, we could tailor the workshops to meet the needs of the students and faculty. In addition, it was important to know what training the staff needed so that they could use the technology most effectively.
   b. We also found that it was very important to understand the level of computer literacy on campus. Ascertain as much information as possible about the level of technology literacy on your campus and match the level of your workshops to that level of literacy.
2. To thine own self be true. Begin by teaching those areas that you know you can teach well. Do not be overly ambitious in the early stages. Start small and the program will grow as other people come to you with their resources and ideas because they will recognize the quality program that you are building.
3. Take a page from Madison Avenue. Make sure that you are reaching your target audience with your flyers and work-

shop descriptions. If they do not know what you are offering, you cannot expect them to attend. In addition, most campuses already have established methods of distributing information. Know them and use them to your advantage.

4. Pair your "hard drives" with your "hardbacks." We noticed that workshop content and instruction improved because we had the technology expert and the instruction expert working together. This created a synergy that expanded our skills as both instructors and technologists.

5. Expanding the (teaching) pie. Your resources, whether they be time, personnel, or money, are limited. Maximize your current resources and your future teaching pool by using and training computer lab and library assistants in the initial sessions and then utilizing them as additional instructors in subsequent semesters. Train them by having them assist in the initial sessions so that they become familiar with the material and you benefit by having a skilled assistant.

6. Paper, paper, paper. We have not reached a point where people are completely comfortable obtaining their information entirely online. Although you may (and should) provide very good supplemental training materials on the Web or by other electronic means, people are still firmly wedded to paper and are rarely happy unless they leave with paper in their hands.

7. Don't stick your head in the sand. Once you have started your program and established it as a credible asset, you can begin to collaborate with other campus departments. These new collaborative frontiers can offer you a wealth of opportunities and assets that will help you improve and expand technology training.

In conclusion, as a collaborative effort, that is, "...an act of shared creation and/or shared discovery,"[6] this project was perfect. Not only were we creating a new program entitled the "VIS Workshop Series" but the two principal organizers discovered a lot about each other's roles, prior functions, and professional philosophies as we debated, discussed, argued, and finally created and taught the VIS workshops. If we had not pooled our resources and started it, no organized technology training would currently exist on the WSUV campus. We were able to build a strong foundation of trust and respect that will be communicated to others on campus. This will make it easier to expand the program and gain support for staff and equipment in the future.

ACKNOWLEDGMENTS

The authors would like to thank Doug Stephens, Phil Garcia, Michelle Eccles, and Dena Keller for their help with advertising, web page creation and number-crunching. We would also like to thank David Carlson for his editorial assistance.

NOTES AND REFERENCES

1. For a general discussion, see Pat Moholt, "On Converging Paths: The Computing Center and the Library," *Journal of Academic Librarianship* 11, no. 6 (1985), pp. 284-288.

2. Excellent examples are Richard Dougherty, "Libraries and Computing Centers: A Blueprint for Collaboration," *College & Research Libraries* 48, no. 4 (1987), pp. 289-296 and Marilyn J. Martin, "Academic Libraries and Computing Centers: Opportunities for Leadership," *Library Administration and Management* 6, no. 2 (1992), pp. 77-81.

3. See Anita K. Lowry, "The Information Arcade at the University of Iowa," *Cause/Effect* 17, no. 3 (1994), pp. 38-44 and Gayle S. Baker, "The Knoxville Library/Computer Center Partnership," in *Building Partnerships Computing and Library Professionals*, ed. Anne G. Lipow and Sheila D. Creth (Berkeley: Library Solutions Press, 1995), pp. 51-53.

4. Nancy Schiller, "Internet Training and Support: Academic Libraries and Computer Centers: Who's Doing What?," *Internet Research* 4, no. 2 (1994), pp. 35-47.

5. For an extended discussion, see Sheila Creth, "Creating a Virtual Information Organization: Collaborative Relationships Between Libraries and Computing Centers," *Journal of Library Administration* 19, nos. 3-4 (1993), pp. 111-132.

6. Michael Schrage, *Shared Minds: The New Technologies of Collaboration.* (New York: Random House, 1990), p. 6.

BUILDING BRIDGES THROUGH COLLABORATION:
ONE CITY'S SUCCESS STORY

Jan Deardorff, Loretta Rielly, and Kim Thompson

ABSTRACT

Adversity often creates new partnerships and creative solutions. That is the case in Corvallis, Oregon, where, despite severe cutbacks in funding and reductions in staff, the school, public, and academic libraries are working together to provide library services to the students in their community.

INTRODUCTION

Two summers ago, a friend from Illinois visited us in Corvallis. On the night he arrived, we took him to an outdoor jazz concert. After an hour of listening to the music mingled with the sounds of the river flowing by, and watching kids playing and friends visiting over picnic dinners and bottles of wine, he turned to us and said, "You live in the twilight zone."

To some extent, Rick is correct. Located on the Willamette River and in the foothills of the coastal range, Corvallis is picturesque, mild of climate, and benign in temperament. The largest employers are Oregon State University and Hewlett-Packard, both of which attract other clean industries and a skilled workforce. The University's farms and forest land form a pastoral and wooded greenbelt around the city. The population is educated:

according the 1990 census, 41 percent of the county's population are college graduates, the highest in the state. It's a primarily white collar community with activist citizens who support the arts, the environment, and education. And it does not rain as much as it does in the rest of Oregon! Honest!

CHALLENGES AND OPPORTUNITIES

We recognized early on that three major external factors affected the collaboration between the Corvallis School District, the Oregon State University Libraries, and the Corvallis-Benton County Public Library: Measure 5 property tax limitation, twenty-first century school reform, and the technology and information explosion.

Measure 5

In November of 1990, Oregonians passed a property tax limitation bill. This measure limited local non-school taxes, and gradually limited taxes for public schools from $15.00 per thousand of assessed value to $5.00 per thousand. This meant that in 1989, Corvallis schools received $19.69 per thousand and now receive $5.00. This measure also prohibited school districts from proposing a bond measure for operating funds, and local control and support were lost. Measure 5 meant disaster to many of the programs that Corvallis schools once offered. Gone are the school nurses, 28 percent of the art teachers, 17 percent of the PE teachers, 7 percent of the music teachers, and 74 percent of the specialists and counselors. The library program receives 18 percent less money.

Because of the requirement to replace a portion of the lost revenue for schools, lawmakers used $2.9 billion from the general fund over the six-year time period of 1990-1996. This loss of money from the general fund impacted other state spending for such necessities as higher education and health services. The ripple effect of all this cannot be emphasized strongly enough. For example, Measure 5 affected higher education in a profound and irrevocable way. *The Oregonian* newspaper reported that public higher education has lost more than $100 million in state funding and raised tuition 80 percent since Measure 5 was enacted.

Twenty-First Century School Reform

State-mandated school reform began in 1991. The Oregon Education Act restructured student learning and teaching strategies and also instituted site-based management, which isolated each school library, resulting in funding disparity, reduced staffing, and lack of district-wide coordination.

The Technology and Information Explosion

As the amount and availability of electronic information increases, all libraries are struggling to keep up. Consider the special circumstances of the school library media center. Unlike most colleges and universities, the schools have not had a steady influx of technology. The machines arrive all at once and are frequently placed in the library media center, which is usually staffed by one person responsible for all aspects of library service (reference, instruction, circulation, interlibrary loan, shelving, and administration). Now she/he must also provide support and training in the new information technologies—after she/he's learned to use the systems. As one colleague in the school district put it, "It's like trying to build an airplane in flight."

SOLUTIONS—THE SCHOOL DISTRICT AND THE PUBLIC LIBRARY

Much of the public library-school district collaboration was inspired by the involvement of the public library director and the school district superintendent in Yes For Kids. This state-mandated program identifies children's needs, then coordinates the activities of over twenty-five county agencies which provide services for children in our area. The public library director and the school superintendent have been active in this organization, and their discussions of school library service led to the creation of a joint committee to offer creative solutions to the problem of underfunded and understaffed school libraries.

Because the Corvallis-Benton County Public Library provides resources for the entire community through its collections and services, the school community is an important part of our mission to "bring people and information together." When financial constraints resulted in reductions in school library service, we felt an immediate impact on our services. Since funding is unlikely to increase in the near future we felt it imperative to collaborate with the schools on ways to improve their libraries.

The public library benefits when improved school libraries support student learning through adequate collections and staffing, and provide information literacy training. Students are more likely to use public library resources when they have positive experiences in their school libraries. Interaction with the schools strengthens our programming, services, and collection development. To facilitate collaboration, the joint committee of school and public library staff applied for federal grant funds to support our project, "Kids Need Libraries: Inventing a New Model of School-Public Library Collaboration."

Kim Thompson was hired as the School District-Public Library Liaison in August 1994 to build on the collaborative foundation already established between the public library and the school district. Her job was to facilitate a federal Library Services and Construction Act grant which had three objectives:

1. Market public library services in the school district, mainly our Assignment Alert program and library tours.
2. Establish Homework Centers in all of the system's libraries.
3. Create a mentor program to assist students with their homework and with basic information literacy skills.

Kim was able to spend all her time building collaborative relationships and opportunities. The district put her on its e-mail network, arranged for the district courier to stop at the public library, provided her with time at staff meetings, and encouraged her to attend district training and in-service programs.

The public library, in turn, offered tours for teachers, help with Assignment Alert, newsletters highlighting services, and professional advice on collection development and customer service. We jointly sponsored a seminar for parents called "My locker ate my homework." Because the district has no extra funds, we supplied the meeting place and the speaker fee; they provided the printing and district publicity and the refreshments from their self-supporting food service.

Once the Homework Centers were established, the district placed two of their workstations at the public library for use by students. News of the collaboration reached Hewlett-Packard, which responded with a gift of over $100,000 worth of computer equipment. This equipment not only benefited the library, but it also enabled the City of Corvallis to move ahead more quickly with its network. The result is that the library is the hub of technology for the city.

Many positive steps have been taken to improve school libraries. Here are a few examples:

1. The move to site-based management in the district meant that each school could establish its own priorities for service. Many schools slashed library staff and budget to the very minimum of service. One elementary school even tried to run their library with only volunteers, an experiment that lasted two weeks. Minimum staffing meant that personnel had no paid time to do any work outside their site. With encouragement, district library staff began meeting on a monthly basis—something which had not happened in four years because of the expense of release time. Meeting together soon became a priority and you can imagine the amount of information exchanged at these meetings after years of operating in isolation with severely slashed budgets. Since there are no certified media specialists at the elementary level, their meetings were especially productive as teaching sessions. Issues such as interlibrary loans could be discussed and policies decided. The public library and the university library liaisons attend most of these meetings and offer in-service training when requested. We also learn of deficits in service that we might be able to alleviate.

2. Jan Deardorff, the district's Library Media Information Services Coordinator, was promoted to an administrative level. This gave her accessibility to the principals—people

known to be a key factor in the success of school libraries. She was able to convince them of the need to support libraries and library staff as much as financially feasible.

3.   Jan was also instrumental in the creation of a new position in the district. The full-time "Information Literacy Specialist" will work with the classroom teachers and elementary library staff to plan the information literacy curriculum, and assist with library staff training and development. This position is unique in Oregon and is being acclaimed statewide as a progressive and optimistic step forward for school libraries.

4.   Beginning July 1, 1996, the district will subcontract for the public library liaison's services for one year. This offer on the part of the school district is intended to send a strong message that this collaboration is an important part of the school improvement plan and that partnerships are critical in a time of diminishing resources. This move also meant that federal funds could be used to hire a consulting team to evaluate the school library system and help build affordable models of collaboration.

Another area that we are collaborating on is technology. The library and the school district use the same online system for circulation, cataloging and card catalog functions. A recent district technology bond has greatly increased the computer equipment and training available in the schools and has also provided a fiber optic link to the library. Soon the district will place computer equipment in Homework Centers so that a student can begin an assignment at school and come to the library in the evening to complete it. Technology can be the link. We want to work together to create a seamless electronic environment; our director even volunteers as chair of the school district technology advisory committee. However, technology can also pose problems. For example, the elementary school library workers are often expected to oversee the use of the technology located in the library, which takes time away from the traditional tasks of running a library. There seems to be no time available for these staff members to be trained on this equipment.

SOLUTIONS—THE SCHOOL DISTRICT AND THE OREGON STATE UNIVERSITY LIBRARIES

Information and reference staff at the Oregon State University Libraries had come to dread school visits. They were a drain on staff and resources, particularly in the reference area. Competition for terminals in the CD-ROM Center increased, resulting in the need for imposing—and enforcing—time limits. Students were unfamiliar with Library of Congress call numbers, subject indexes, and bound periodicals. Information and Reference staff had to provide on-the-spot small group or one-on-one instruction. Many school teachers called and arranged for group instruction in advance, but we simply did not have the staff to provide the level of instruction that was needed. Compounding the difficulty was the unsuitability of the collection for the students' topics and, frequently, their reading and comprehension level. The visits were as frustrating for the students as they were for library staff.

Ironically, we also felt a great deal of guilt about school visits. OSU's Information and Reference staff are service-oriented: staff on the desks or working in the CD-ROM Center are there to guide and teach students to be independent, skilled researchers. It is our profession, and one to which we are highly committed. It did not feel good to gripe about noise, tell students they had to leave a terminal, or give only passing attention to any one student because there were so many others waiting with questions.

Library staff want all students to have successful experiences when they use the OSU Libraries, whether they are enrolled at OSU or at Corvallis High. Thus, the libraries need to have materials students can understand on the subjects they are researching. In addition, the students need to be prepared to use a library as complex and large as OSU's. To assure this, we had to work more closely with the schools. In 1996, OSU will institute a school visit policy that we believe will best serve the students in our community.

School Visits

School visits generally fall into one of two types: a field trip to "see" an academic library or a class visit to work on a research project. Each has a very different purpose and is treated differently. All, however, are coordinated with the school's library media specialist so that she/he is aware of class assignments and can determine if the OSU library is the most appropriate library for the class to use.

Field Trips

Any class, from preschool to college preparatory, is welcome at the OSU Libraries for several reasons. OSU is a land, sea, and space grant university charged with serving the citizens of the state. Such visits also have strong public relations value, which is especially important in a time when higher education is being asked to be more accountable to the public (and the legislators). We are also very proud of the library and want to show prospective students and parents the collection and state-of-the-art information technologies. The library is an important recruitment tool for the university.

Library tours are given by any OSU staff or trained students interested in participating in this program, the school's media specialist, or classroom teacher, or a classroom parent. OSU's Instruction and Training Team trains interested participants and provides handouts.

Class Projects

We encourage use of our library by junior and senior classes, especially college preparatory classes, and do provide them with instruction in the use of library resources. Instruction is given by OSU librarians and paraprofessionals or by the school library media specialist. This is a valuable opportunity for the students to gain experience using an academic research library before they attend college themselves. (We're not entirely altruistic in this. If they enroll in OSU, they'll be experienced users who we hope will share their knowledge with fellow students.) We do, however, ask that the students have prior library experience, either at the school library or the public library, and:

1. know that materials are organized according to a classification system,
2. know the difference between the kind of information found in books and in articles,
3. know the difference between a library catalog and a periodical index,
4. have used an online catalog and an electronic periodical index.

We do discourage elementary, middle-school, and freshmen or sophomore classes from using the OSU library to work on research projects and instead refer them to their school library and/or the public library. If they still choose to come to OSU, they receive no special instruction or assistance other than what is available at the Information and Reference Desks.

In-Service Training

The school's Library Media Specialists and Library Assistants are the key to successful coordination with OSU's library. They best know the students and their abilities, and they can best communicate with the teacher the strengths and weaknesses of the OSU library in relation to a given assignment. In September, library staff from OSU and the Public Library will participate in an in-service for school library media specialists and teachers to familiarize them with the services and collections available at each institution. OSU library staff will provide further training to school staff and interested parents in the use of the resources at OSU so they can, in turn, teach the students whom they serve.

Technology

OSU is looking to technology to link school library media centers with the OSU Libraries. Currently, our general periodical index is the same as that used by the schools and the public library, and our online catalog will be accessible on the school district's Z39.50 server. The Libraries' web site will include instruction on using the library and identifying resources in a subject area; thus, it can provide guidance for the school media specialist, teacher, or student in the content and use of our collection.

CONCLUSION

We believe that collaboration is essential in this information-rich but resource-poor society. We have different missions, but each of us has a piece of the responsibility of equipping children for the future and creating lifelong learning skills and attitudes. When one institution cannot adequately provide its piece, the others need to step in to help. Here are suggestions for a successful process.

1. Designate liaisons. It is important for liaisons to have decision making power and a broad knowledge of the institutions involved so that the collaborative process can move along fairly unimpeded. People who are truly committed to the idea of collaboration are the key to success.

2. Meet to identify and articulate common goals. Build trust. Leave the jargon at home. Be aware of differences in missions, experiences, needs, expertise, apprehension, turf issues, culture. Arriving at a collective purpose is a dynamic, time-consuming process that usually proceeds two steps forward and one step back. Just finding time to meet is a challenge!

3. Be willing to take risks. People are quick to say, "We've already tried that!" You need to forge ahead anyway. Try again. Involve new people who are not jaded by past experience, think "out of the box," and look at setbacks as opportunities.

4. Look for extended opportunities for collaboration. Build a web. Think about who else might benefit from collaboration. Tell the story to everyone who will listen and keep everyone informed of your progress. Telling the Hewlett-Packard Company about our collaborative efforts resulted in a generous gift of equipment to assist students with their school work. HP benefits from a better-educated work force.

5. Be open to different types of partnerships. Interaction can range from complementary to cooperative to collaborative. You might even decide that outsourcing is the way to go. Partnerships evolve slowly—be patient with the process. Learn as much as you can from each other as you proceed down the path.

6. Celebrate achievements. It is hard to remember to do this, but very important for morale.

Collaboration is not always a pretty process. We have been exasperated at one another and with our different cultures. We have had setbacks. We have drastically changed course in the middle of our new grant project. But our common thread has been our shared goal: to improve student learning by providing complementary library service in the schools, the public library and the academic library. Creating the information literate student is possible, but it cannot be done in isolation anymore.

TEACHING A NEW
ORGANIZATION NEW TRICKS

Laura Bender and Jennalyn Tellman

ABSTRACT

Librarians at the University of Arizona Library are initiating instructional partnerships with faculty to integrate new information technologies into the curriculum and achieve greater learning outcomes. In this paper we describe how the partnership project team, of which we are a part, determined what training and skills were necessary to equip librarians for this new work. We learned that the librarians needed skills in initiating faculty contact, teaching techniques, learning theory and technical skills. The authors embarked on the design and implementation of several workshops and other innovative instructional means to answer these identified needs.

INTRODUCTION

Librarians are initiating instructional partnerships with faculty for the purpose of integrating new information technologies into the curriculum and resulting in changing the methods of instruction to achieve greater learning outcomes.[1] This follows the University's goals and objectives: to transform educational activities to meet the needs of the learners of the twenty-first century—to improve student performance through a focus on learning and to capitalize on new and emerging technologies to enhance effectiveness.[2] This session will tell you how we are training librarians to integrate instructional partnerships. The partnerships are the Library's way of participating in these goals and objectives.

The purpose of forging partnerships is to integrate information literacy into the curriculum. The partnerships involve librarians and faculty members together designing and developing the research assignment/project or even curriculum. Instruction about finding information is an integral part of the material being taught in the class.

Our partnership project team consists of librarians who are all members of teams with public service responsibilities. We share our work with these teams and communicate our respective needs and issues to each other. To start the project work, the project team had to determine the needs of our colleagues. Part of our charge was to train library staff to be effective partners and to mentor the development of the partnerships themselves. The project team brainstormed to create a list of knowledge, skills, and abilities necessary to a successful partnership, and necessary to instill confidence and motivation in those who would be participating in this new work. We also asked members of the integrative services teams (those teams comprised primarily of librarians who are liaisons to campus departments and have reference responsibilities) to brainstorm skill areas and learning needs. We analyzed the results to design a questionnaire that covered skill areas in faculty contact, teaching techniques, learning theory, and technical skills (technology). To further refine our questions, we tested four volunteers who gave us more feedback and defined problem areas. We then distributed the finalized questionnaire, consisting of thirty-three questions, to the integrative services teams.

The design utilized a Likert scale which measured confidence levels from 1-6, with 6 being "very confident" or "capable of teaching." We chose an even number of possibilities to encourage participants not to choose the "neutral" middle number as a default. We also chose affirming verbs in our statements: I know how to...., I can use...., I recognize when...., and so on. Based on the results of the questionnaire, we determined that it was most important to develop training workshops on innovative teaching techniques, critical thinking and active learning, assessing learning needs of students, how to start the partnership process, and technology tools such as Ovid software training, HTML, Lynx, teaching the Internet, and how to use the World Wide Web for instruction. We created workshops designed to cover these technical topics. We also risked jumping out of the workshop mold, and held a contest to define Internet terms after our project had been in place for several months.

At the end of the questionnaire, we included an open question: In what other areas would you like training or assistance? The answers fell into two categories: more in-depth training in partnerships (the process), and training in specific software or technology applications.

Why are we doing this? Aren't librarians at the University of Arizona Library already proactive? Librarians have a history of providing library instruction, but we are going beyond this tradition. The old idea of a librarian or instructor as "sages on the stage" lecturing to students who hear, learn, and remember, is no longer valid. Based on the results of the questionnaire, we determined that it was most important to begin with teaching librarians about the actual partnering process. We sought buy-in and a commitment from our colleagues to participate in the various workshops we were to design based on needs identified by the librarians themselves. This required that we define what we meant by partnerships. Our definition is as follows:

> The purpose of forging partnerships is to integrate information literacy into the curriculum. As librarians, we bring expertise and experience to the collaborative effort. We know how information is organized; we understand how students approach research and try to find information; and we also know what resources are "out there." Partnerships are creative adventures which involve both the Library and faculty members together designing and developing the research assignment, project, or curriculum.

What is information literacy?

A. knowing when you have an information need
B. being able to state your information need
C. being able to formulate a strategy and find your information

D.   awareness of possible resources
E.   ability to identify, locate and evaluate resources
F.   ability to present and modify knowledge in new electronic
     formats

Several librarians had experienced success in setting up partnerships with faculty. The project team thought it would be a good idea to set up our first workshop featuring these successes, and have those responsible for the successes share what they learned with others. On December 11, 1995, we held a panel discussion and set up a poster session featuring the work of six librarians. During the panel discussion, the librarians pointed out how they made initial contact with faculty, what worked, what did not, how they negotiated assignments, how they evaluated assignments, and how they propose to make changes based on their evaluations.

Once each panelist had spoken, the audience was invited to ask questions. Audience members were asked to think of and write down one possible partnership they could develop with their own departments. We emphasized, as did the panelists, that partnering is a process. We cannot expect all contacts to turn into partnerships, nor can we discount the serendipitous possibilities inherent in a drop-in visit by a faculty member.

After audience members had thought of a possible partnership, we asked them to break into groups of three or four and share their partnership plan with others. They were encouraged to take risks and be as creative as possible. The groups then chose one of their proposed partnership ideas to share with the entire workshop. This audience participation provided a forum to work through the practical steps of partnership planning, as well as an environment that reinforced ideas and built confidence in those who had never tried the steps before. The steps for successful partnerships that came out of this workshop would hold for any organization aspiring to become a learning organization. We took notes from these presentations, and here is what we learned:

•   Get to know your faculty. Start building rapport as soon as
    possible.

- Be proactive. Make an appointment to introduce yourself.
- Find out all the information you can about courses: name, number of students, assignments, research needs, and so on.
- Find out if your faculty member has a Web home page. Check for assignments there too, and dialogue about aligning assignments with library resources.
- Ask if you can link their home page to the Library's home page.
- If your faculty member comes to you, take the opportunity to discuss assignment design and appropriate library resources.
- For faculty attending a workshop you've designed, help them see that there are Library resources to fit their needs.
- Negotiate participation. You are there to complement their role, not usurp it.
- Check lists of new faculty for possible contacts.
- Attend faculty brown bags, Ph.D. defenses, and departmental meetings when possible.
- Practice marketing library resources, yourself, and your skills.
- Check departmental mailings for information about research projects or Library coordination activities.
- If you do not really know where to start, ask colleagues or other faculty for the name of a pro-library faculty member with whom you could meet one-on-one.
- Sometimes opportunity knocks in the form of problematic assignments at the reference desk. Call faculty to clarify and offer to work with them.
- Stay in touch with your faculty—follow-up is very important.
- Keep library colleagues apprised of upcoming assignments to help them at public service desks.
- If the project will be complex or lengthy, solicit help from an intern or student assistant.
- Assignments/home pages will need to be updated. Check for resources to add or outdated information to delete.
- Remember: we may not be specialists in a subject area, but we know a heck of a lot about libraries!

To elicit more feedback from workshop participants, we asked participants to pair up with the person next to them and think about any tips or strategies that we may have overlooked. We asked them to discuss what they found most important about partnerships and the project so far. We then asked for volunteers to share their ideas with the group.

At the time this "LOEX" workshop on successful partnerships was given, there were fourteen partnerships in various stages of completion that had been formed by twenty-two librarians in the library.

Because of the identified need for improving skills on innovative teaching techniques, critical thinking, and active learning, we consulted with the University Teaching Center. This Center has professional educators who are experts in the area of how to teach effectively. We met several times to explore the types of training they could provide for our librarians, given that most instruction in the library took place as one-shot interactions or single class sessions. As a result of these discussions, the staff from the University Teaching Center delivered a workshop entitled "Is Learning Taking Place?"

They taught us cognitive principles and modeled different teaching and active learning techniques. The general cognitive principles that were covered include:

- Learners construct knowledge within contexts of existing knowledge
- Memory principles
- Learning involves conceptual change
- Cognitive overload

Because learners construct knowledge within contexts of existing knowledge or schema, it is important to engage the students and hook the new information onto material they already know. In an instruction situation, ask students questions that will engage their interest. Ask them what they would like to learn, or in what situation they hope to use the information being taught.

Memory principles include the fact that people remember most of what is presented at the beginning and end of the class. Therefore, an instructor must plan his or her presentation to emphasize the most important points at the beginning and the end of the presentation.

Cognitive overload is a significant problem. People remember between five to seven points. Therefore, it is necessary to focus teaching to the critical five to seven items being taught. This is very challenging for librarians who have only one instruction session for a given class. One way to deal with this is to present material in chunks. For example, telephone numbers are easier to remember because of the chunking of the number sequence. It is quite different remembering 520-621-6418 from remembering 5206216418. The same thing is true for Social Security numbers. Instructors should plan a presentation carefully around groups of related information.

Think of the learning stages of cognitive development that the students will be moving through, from simple black and white, dualistic thinking and memorization to learning how to analyze, synthesize and evaluate. One learns more by a combination of techniques, and one learns the most by teaching. Use the "think, pair, share" method to have students use several teaching methodologies. This is the technique that we just had you use when you shared with your neighbor your ideas about the tips we presented. This is a widely used "cooperative learning structure." To use this, the instructor poses a non-facile question that requires some thought. The students are given approximately a minute to think of a response. The students are then paired with another student or students to discuss their responses, and in the final phase several of the student groups are asked to share their responses with the group as a whole.

How do you find out if students are learning during the session? Check with the students at the end of the session. Review what has been taught. Ask the students to identify and state the most important factors or items that they learned.

We wanted to ensure that these concepts were incorporated into the librarians' teaching strategies. It is easy and stimulating to go to lectures or demonstrations. Actually practicing what has been heard or demonstrated is quite another matter. We decided to use active learning techniques and apply some of the principles that we had been taught within our integrative services teams to ensure that the librarians had successfully learned what we wanted. We had follow-up discussions about the workshop and its points in the various team meetings. We discussed what the librarians remembered. There was discussion and brainstorming about how they were going to use what they had learned in their own future teaching strategies.

As a result of positive feedback and team discussions, there was a second workshop given by two staff members of the University Teaching Center on "Creative Questioning." Librarians had asked for assistance in constructing questions that would help them ascertain if learning is taking place. The workshop explored the types of questions to ask in large classes or with students at different stages in their university careers. Strategies that are helpful with graduate students may not be effective with freshman. We also explored why and when students participate in the classroom and how to engage their participation.

Effective questioning can enhance student understanding. When questions are focused on a specific topic and presented in a clear and concise manner, opportunity for student response is maximized. It is best not to ask if there are any questions. This often elicits no response. Instead, ask what questions are there about the specific topic or point just covered. This implies that you expect the students to be thinking and asking questions. Educational researchers agree that most instructors do not wait long enough. It may take five to ten seconds to formulate a response, but instructors may only wait one to three seconds. Asking for clarification or support of a response stimulates a student's thinking. They suggested phrases such as "Tell me more," or "Can anyone give a specific example?"

Our needs assessment questionnaire revealed that many librarians wanted an opportunity to learn from more experienced librarians. Indeed, our whole partnership project was based on teaching and learning from others. As a result, we developed a questionnaire for people to use to ask for assistance. We called this our "buddy plan." It provides an opportunity for librarians to indicate the type of assistance, learning and modeling that they want or need from their colleagues and also indicates in what manner they might be assistants, teachers and models themselves. This questionnaire also used a Likert scale in which we offered six choices so that people could not take a neutral stance. Questions covered the following areas:

- Working with a librarian while she/he is designing an instructional session or a library-related assignment.
- Observe a librarian teaching subject resources on the Web.
- Observe a librarian using active learning in an instructional session. Here we are talking about all of the techniques that we learned from the staff at the University Teaching Center, such as using creative questions, the think-pair-share technique, or hooking the students' interests to something they already know.
- Observe a librarian teaching ways to use particular Internet resources.
- Invite a librarian to observe your session and give constructive feedback.
- Sit in on a collaborative session between a librarian and faculty member while they are determining the information needs of the students and planning an assignment.

Our final workshop on teaching techniques was an all-day workshop with Dr. Diane Nahl, from the University of Hawaii, entitled "Innovative Approaches to Teaching Electronic Searching." Dr. Nahl has done extensive research in the area of how learners learn to use electronic tools and how to teach others to use them, using different techniques to match different learning styles.

She emphasized the importance of the affective, that is, the emotional component, noting that students drop classes rather than do research. Given the same skill levels, searchers with higher self-confidence usually perform better than searchers with low self-confidence. Motivation is the key to learning, and when people feel anxious or fearful and dread the exercises, they are less likely to learn. Her research indicates that active learning seems to work best with the affective component of learning. This also is helpful because only about one-third of users read screens or instructions. This affective realm is not something that we covered in our needs assessment questionnaire and we may need to think further about future workshops and training in this area. Other areas that Dr. Nahl's program covered include:

- Instructional design models for teaching electronic searching
- Methods for teaching Boolean logic queries
- Common errors in searching
- Active learning models
- Active reflection techniques
- Information search process models

In designing instruction, it is important to focus on goals and objectives and to design evaluation tools for assessing outcomes. It is important, as we have done in the partnerships project, to start with some sort of needs assessment.

One active learning model that we incorporated into our discussions lets students begin with preliminary hands-on practice. This is followed by an explanation or demonstration of the system with invited questions and discussion. That is then followed by more hands-on practice. It is important for the students to be physically involved. This helps us discourage our inclination to do the search for the student.

With active reflection techniques, it is important to give users time to think. Pre-search activities include giving them time to think about their topic, the concepts that are involved, and which search terms to select. This helps students to develop criteria for analyzing, focusing, selecting, and choosing. While the students are searching, they need time to examine the screen instructions, explore the vocabulary in the records and examine the contents of the sets, as well as develop criteria for analyzing and choosing.

Dr. Nahl shared some solutions to counteract users' affective or emotional symptoms. They included reassuring and consoling to promote acceptance and support, affirming successful outcome and affirming the principle that the users are never at fault. She suggested advising and coaching, sharing convenient tips and giving feedback about different strategies and results. She encouraged constant feedback about how long searching takes, common errors we all make, acknowledgment of technical difficulty, and reasonable expectations.

The guidelines we incorporated into the planning of all our workshops were as follows:

1. Each workshop would be a model of good teaching; we would endeavor to apply as many of the techniques we learned as possible.
2. We planned follow-up activities; for example, we went back to our home teams to find out if learning had taken place, what further steps should be taken, and what our colleagues would use in their own teaching. We designed short evaluation forms for their use which also served as entries in a training/teaching portfolio.
3. We attempted to include activities that would be thought-provoking and aid attendees in their own planning.
4. At the end of each workshop, a project team member would provide a pedagogical summary of the methods used in the session.

REFERENCES

1. Karen Williams, *Interim Report on Faculty Development Partnership*, (Tucson, AZ: University of Arizona, 1996), p. 6.

2. University of Arizona Library Strategic Long Range Planning Committee, *Current Situational Analysis for 1996/97*, (Tucson, AZ: University of Arizona, 1996), p. 10.

IMPLEMENTATION OF INFORMATION LITERACY:
PROCESS AND POLITICS—A CASE STUDY OF LIBRARY 111 AT ULSTER COUNTY COMMUNITY COLLEGE

Larry Berk and Patricia Carroll-Mathes

ABSTRACT

This is a case study of the conception, development, and implementation of an information literacy initiative at a small, rural community college in New York State. The credit course is being taught by librarians and faculty from different disciplines. This collaborative approach is presented as one way of introducing information literacy concepts across the curriculum and reaching the goal of making certain that faculty and students are information literate.

BACKGROUND

This project really began the day Larry Berk interviewed for the position of Director of the Library and Patricia Carroll-Mathes recognized his potential to transform the library. The very same day, Patricia left to begin a six-month sabbatical devoted to reading and reflecting on instruction theory and practice, visiting libraries in various sections of the country, and attending LOEX (in Ypsilanti) and WILU (in Toronto). Larry brought a background which included teaching an early version of an online searching course, and Patricia had years of library instruction experience and was trying to find a better model to use. In July 1992, we began to work together to effect change—acquiring electronic resources, establishing information literacy as a goal, focusing on instruction—and the path we chose to pursue was credit instruction. That is, after all, how colleges traditionally do business, and it seemed to both of us the way to bring about real changes in the library and the college.

Ulster Community College is a small community college in a rural area in upstate New York. Ulster County lost its major employer and 6,000 jobs during the past few years; the college itself has been down-sizing as a result and this has been felt throughout the budget. The library operates by the management approach: "Ready, fire, aim." (Of course, the next step is to duck!) The basic premise: to plan, engage and then refine. What "ready-fire-aim" does is engage the field. Of course, readiness is everything. And yes, we've needed to recover from not having aimed, but remember, it is one thing to be fine-tuning a valid program, and another to be working it out on paper and at meetings with Talmudic precision until someone else does it before you (e.g., the computer center). We must be ready to deliver, and this unquestionably means we must continue to do more with less, do more with less and less, and do it enthusiastically. This philosophy recognizes that we are past the age of consensus and that the purpose of leadership is to communicate commitment to a vision. That said, planning is the keystone, and SWOT analysis was used as a technique to identify priorities by analyzing strengths, weaknesses, opportunities and threats. The library has operated with two priorities for the past several years; one is the implementation of our information literacy initiative.

In addition, the library operates with a flat organization, so people can function autonomously and independently. Without calling it that, we really have a library team as opposed to a hierarchical structure. With shrinking resources and staff, we've had to rethink and restructure, engage in staff development, and develop skills in support staff so they can provide reference help and backup in order for us to focus on and deliver instruction.

Our objective is to have an information literate faculty and student body. While there has been considerable discussion in the literature about what information literacy is and the role it must play in the information society, there is less attention to how to bring about these skills. The best way to understand a subject is to teach it. The best way for faculty to understand what is involved is to teach! Engaging the faculty in this process is, in fact, the only way in which change can really be effected—in the classroom, in assignments, in the curriculum. The goals of critical thinking and lifelong learning for students can never be reached without faculty not only on board but in the driver's seat. If you attempt far-reaching change on campus, faculty must be leaders in the effort. So it's really about librarians relinquishing control. We'd like to propose a definition of collaboration as the process of surrendering control.

This project could not exist without faculty such as Honey Fein, professor of nursing. A strong supporter of information literacy for our nursing students, she has helped build a sequential course-related information literacy component into Ulster's nursing curriculum. Honey is one of the faculty who responded when we asked for support in our curricular efforts, and she committed, not only to the training we offered, but also to teaching. She worked hard to become familiar with library resources. She sat in on Larry's section of the Information Literacy course the first seven weeks of the semester, and then taught her own section the second seven weeks, relying on our team-teaching support, our teaching an area with which she didn't feel completely comfortable, our reviewing strategies, assignments, and questions before and after class. After the first lecture, for which she prepared and prepared, she began to relax and absolutely loved the teaching and what she was learning. I found her exclaiming," I'm becoming information literate!" and feeling thrilled as she saw her students getting it!

Even before the course was over, she had so successfully promoted the benefits to be gained from the course to second-semester nursing students, that her section for the fall closed on the second day of pre-registration, and she initiated the first of our planned sections for health sciences students. As soon as the course was over, we sat together as a teaching team and decided how to improve the course and the assignments, which were tested in a summer session taught by a librarian. Subsequently, Patricia taught another section with revised assignments, and a restructured syllabus and sequence of topics which were tested on the students during the second summer session.

COURSE DEVELOPMENT PHASE: 1992-1994

Pursuing our initial idea of credit instruction to deliver information literacy skills, we proposed and gained approval of a two-credit elective course similar to those being offered at many institutions. We surveyed state initiatives through direct contact and professional organizations, and nationwide initiatives through the LOEX Clearinghouse. We identified the centers of power on campus and engaged in lobbying efforts with members of the college's curriculum committee and key faculty members. We gained the support of key administrators and used the opportunity of sabbatical reports to the board of trustees and the full faculty to define information literacy and the goals of our efforts.

By the time we gained approval of the curriculum committee, we were already at work on our one-credit Information Literacy course. We knew that if programs were going to require the course, it had to be one credit. Many programs are already at the upper limit with required credits. We also knew that librarians couldn't possibly teach several sections on top of their already full loads. And we didn't—and couldn't—and wouldn't—recruit qualified adjuncts. The point has always been to make certain that students, faculty, and staff are information literate. As a library director who has always been a part-time classroom instructor, and a reference librarian who has taught course-related sessions for faculty as well as credit classes, we felt that teaching faculty, once trained, could improve the course dramatically. Something else was also clear: once a teaching faculty member is comfortable with this material, her other courses will be transformed and her colleagues will be made aware of the need to become information literate and incorporate information literacy concepts into their curriculum. Librarians can never hope to be as persuasive with faculty as faculty can be with each other.

So we returned to the drawing board, enhanced the two-credit course content to meet three-credit elective requirements, and refined our objectives to focus on a one-credit course which could fit into a variety of career and transfer programs. Political reality required pursuing the goal of individual department/program requirements rather than mandating a universal general requirement. Preparation involved personal contact with faculty supporters, using LOEX to compile examples of courses offered elsewhere, and developing a competency-based final. The documentation included student evaluations of the existing course and their presence at the curriculum committee meeting. Despite some resistance, the groundwork and lobbying efforts resulted in approval and some measure of enthusiasm.

COURSE PROMOTION AND TRAINING PHASE: 1994-1995

Problems to be faced in implementing the new course were formidable: faculty did not understand electronic information or the need for such a course, staff development was required both within the library and across campus, and equipment was needed to secure a minimal level of support, including an additional networked classroom, projection panel and laptop. With the support of the academic dean and the sponsorship of the Teaching/Learning Center, we put together two eight-hour training sessions for faculty and staff. The goal of the training was to help faculty and staff acquire knowledge of and experience with electronic resources. This would enable the faculty to teach sections of the Information Literacy course and encourage incorporation of new information resources into existing courses and programs.

We recruited faculty and staff for the training by collaborating with the Teaching/Learning Center whose director, a chemistry professor, was committed to teaching a section of the course. A joint letter to all faculty was followed by personal contacts and persistent follow-up. The sessions were collaboratively developed and team-taught by three librarians. The course was compressed into an eight-hour sequence delivered over four days. The text for the course, *Introduction to Library Research,* by Carla List, was supplied as a resource. The absence of hands-on practice was a severe limitation. Conditions were not ideal for the training because the participants did not have computers at their desks. We taught the course, a compressed and modeled version of the fifteen-hour one-credit course, with one PC and a projection panel; the faculty were then on their own for practice. This is not the ideal way to do this, but these were the only tools we had, and we did the best we could. Faculty/staff participation was impressive: 36 percent of the full-time faculty, 15 percent of the professional staff, 5 percent of the part-time faculty. While more than a third of full-time faculty participated in the training, a significantly smaller group was interested in teaching Information Litcracy. However, it only takes two or three to begin.

COURSE IMPLEMENTATION AND REVISION PHASE: 1995-1996

Library 111, Information Literacy, was first taught in the spring of 1995 by Larry Berk. The first faculty section was taught by Dennis Swauger, professor of chemistry, in the fall of 1995. Three additional faculty members from different disciplines taught sections in the spring 1996 semester. Teaching faculty and librarians met as a team for development and evaluation sessions. Patricia, who serves as coordinator, provided team teaching when appropriate, content support, and lecture/demonstration help as well as hand-holding. Teaching team members received regular e-mail with selected postings from EduCom and the bi-l listserv as well as other communications. The definition of collaboration again: the process of surrendering control. As faculty began to teach Information Literacy, they began offering suggestions for revision. Among other things, the philosophy of "less is more" was very helpful in improving the course. The course content was revised and restructured on the basis of experience and faculty involvement. More emphasis was placed on search strategy and evaluation, and assignments were restructured and resequenced.

In the meantime, promotion efforts continued with faculty advisors and were aimed at encouraging students to take the course. These promotional efforts took the form of letters, meetings with department chairs, and personal contact with individual faculty members. With Teaching/Learning Center collaboration, ongoing faculty development efforts include workshops offered in Internet basics, e-mail, lists, search strategies for those using the World Wide Web, and FirstSearch. Faculty are encouraged to continue using tools for professional development. Additional faculty who participated in the training sessions have committed to teaching the course: a business professor will teach it for the first time this fall, and a professor of foreign languages will teach a section in the spring semester. Two programs have adopted the course as a requirement: Human Services and Chemical Dependency Counseling. A proposal to require it in Criminal Justice awaits action. Nursing students are strongly encouraged to enroll, so we can offer several targeted sections taught by a nursing faculty member.

RESTRUCTURING THE COURSE FOR LIBRARIANS: LSCA INITIATIVE 1995-1996

A proposal to adapt the "train the trainers" course was developed in collaboration with Southeastern New York Library Resources Council, a New York state regional organization. LSCA funded the development and delivery of three fifteen-hour sessions to librarians from school, public, and academic libraries who will, in turn, develop training sessions for their staff or for the public.

The grant enabled the acquisition of a projector unit and laptop to implement the program. Goals for the Electronic Information Literacy course were to inspire and empower other librarians to undertake information literacy initiatives in their own libraries, to encourage librarians to gain competency in using electronic tools and understand the basic information literacy concepts, and to promote the library teaching role for all types of libraries. Thirty-four librarians from this relatively rural, eight-county region participated in this training the (librarian) trainers course.

RESTRUCTURING FOR THE WWW: 1996

Interest in the information literacy initiatives undertaken led to a grant from the State University of New York Office of

Educational Technology to redesign the Information Literacy course for delivery on the World Wide Web. Consistent with our approach to collaboration, faculty member Honey Fein is chairing the content development team as we transform it. We are also collaborating with and looking for evaluation and feedback from librarians, faculty, and staff from other SUNY institutions, including librarians from SUNY Albany, faculty and graduate students from the School of Education, SUNY Albany, and staff from the SUNY Learning Network. This Web-based information literacy course currently in development is projected to debut in 1997. At the annual meeting in May 1996, the SUNY Council of Library Directors agreed to use the course as a model for use at other SUNY campuses.

THE FUTURE OF LIB 111

On our campus, we continue to work to get this course adopted as a program requirement. Teaching faculty members carry their enthusiasm to other colleagues and can effect changes throughout the department. The nursing faculty are redesigning their curriculum and plan to adopt Lib 111 and a computer literacy course as prerequisites or corequisites to nursing courses. The business faculty member teaching the course plans to propose its adoption as a requirement for business students in the transfer program. A science seminar being offered for the first time this spring will incorporate information literacy concepts, and faculty will encourage students to take Lib 111 as well. When presented to the curriculum committee for adoption, the science seminar will include Lib 111 as a prerequisite. With the science department supporting the course, we will be able to offer targeted science sections. An English faculty member is currently taking the course and we plan to continue efforts to persuade the department to recommend it, or better yet, require it along with English 102.

Tenacity and patience do work. Tenacity, patience, and a strategy for action, that is. There are a number of strategies we are using to achieve the goal of students, faculty and staff becoming information literate. The central element in the strategy is for faculty to engage other faculty, but there is more. We have a strong support system in place for those faculty who are interested in teaching Information Literacy but who don't feel as comfortable as they want with the material. Librarians provide teaching materials, technical support, and will even team teach specific lessons or the entire course with a first-time teacher.

This initiative is an ongoing work-in-progress. The only possible completion will occur when the course is no longer needed on campus, that is, when information literacy is woven throughout the fabric of the curriculum. In other words, if we are completely successful and all faculty become information literate and all students are required to use a variety of information resources as part of their class assignments, and the students receive the message that being able to locate, evaluate, and effectively use information is critical to learning, then this course becomes superfluous. Until then, this project is one way to make collaboration between librarians and teaching faculty a reality.

COLLABORATION ACROSS CAMPUS:

THE GATEWAY TO GLOBAL BUSINESS

Carolyn R. Johnson, Lisa Kammerlocher, and
Diane Gruber

ABSTRACT

The Library and Center for Writing Across the Curriculum at
Arizona State University West were involved in a collaborative
effort with the School of Management to integrate research and
writing skills into a new undergraduate gateway course in global
business. In reporting on this program the authors would like to
emphasize that while each collaborative situation is unique, there
are some issues that are universal to faculty-librarian collaboration. In response to these issues, personnel in writing centers and
in libraries can use similar strategies to work with faculty and
students.

BACKGROUND

In 1995, the Arizona State University West School of Management initiated its new global business curriculum through a pilot
run of a course entitled Gateway to Global Business. The Gateway course was created by a curriculum committee with campus-wide representation, including the business librarian and the

director of the Center for Writing Across the Curriculum. Successful course implementation would depend on the quality of collaborative efforts from the faculty, librarians, writing center personnel, information technology personnel and other individuals across the campus, since all would be involved in the course content and instruction. In a setting with ambitious goals and a diversity of ideas about how to best ensure achievement of these goals, collaborative skills would be tested.

One of the primary goals of the Gateway course was to raise to the same skill level a number of students who began their academic careers in the local community colleges or were returning to school after a lengthy hiatus. This often meant that the students had widely-varied backgrounds in terms of writing, library, and computer use, as well as in terms of their understanding of basic business concepts. Success for the students would be measured by their ability to meet the following objectives: (1) to become familiar with ASU, ASUW, and the School of Management (SOM) environment, (2) to become familiar with the SOM specializations and curriculum, (3) to view all functional disciplines as integral parts of the total business system within the global environment, (4) to learn performance expectations, student responsibilities, and code of conduct, (5) to develop basic skills in library research, business writing, computer literacy, online communication, teaming and presentation skills, and (6) to develop career management strategies.

The expectations for the Gateway course were high. From the library perspective, the course was an incredible opportunity to implement an ongoing information literacy initiative, based upon the Earlham model. To date, the library had had isolated success in implementing information literacy in other curricular areas. The presence of research and writing skills as a critical course objective meant that the library and writing center were major stakeholders and had a significant role to play in the implementation of the course. The Gateway course represented the potential for a model that could be used campus-wide. Yet, as the fall 1995 semester approached, the library faced a crisis situation. Nearly a third of the professional staff, including the business librarian, had taken other positions. The social sciences librarian assumed interim responsibilities for the School of

Management. By the time she took over as business librarian, six assignments had already been developed by the faculty, thus placing the interim librarian in a reactive mode. Fortunately, an additional interim librarian was soon hired to assist with the School of Management program.

ISSUES

As the fall 1995 semester got underway, several issues quickly emerged. The first of these resulted from the actual design of the student assignments. For example, the first assignment required the use of a large number of business concepts, many of which were insufficiently defined. This problem was only exacerbated by the inadequate amount of classroom instruction time allotted to collaborative faculty and librarians. For example, two hours of library instruction time negotiated early in the planning process was now reduced to forty-five minutes in the interest of covering more course content. Moreover, students were not required to attend additional library instruction workshops that were being offered outside of class time. Consequently, the ability of students to successfully complete their assignments was compromised.

The primary place where assignment confusion, lack of instruction, and student frustration converged and then exploded was, of course, at the reference desk. The types of questions reference desk personnel received from the Gateway students centered around four areas:

- Use of computers (downloading and uploading, questions about computer access on campus and remote access);
- Library sources and use (staff had to go over information, students didn't bring library handbooks with them);
- Business concepts (students were confused about concepts such as top management team, product life cycle, corporate culture, state ownership, and social responsibility, so reference staff had to explain or look up information for them); and
- Critical thinking (reading between the lines, inferring information, reasoning, logic, evaluation, synthesis, analysis of information, common sense).

In many instances, not only were students unfamiliar with course content, they were also inexperienced in general critical thinking. For example, many were unwilling to say, "This is what I think," but would search for hours to find the "one correct answer." Some students would go from one staff member to another, trying to find the perfect source of information that was "out there" some place. It reached a point such that reference desk staff began to joke about hiding when Gateway students approached. The joking, however, raised serious concerns about the workload of the staff and the impact of assignments on the students.

At one level, these problems were attributable to the nature of any course being offered for the first time: simply put, there were still a number of unforeseen kinks that needed to be worked out and which could only be identified once the course was put into actual practice. At another level, however, both the library and the CWAC faculty began to wonder if certain problems were also due in part to a misunderstanding between management faculty and the various collaborating units concerning the extent of the role each was to play in the design of the new course. Whereas the collaborating units saw their role as that of bringing disciplinary expertise to bear on the creation of a new curriculum, management faculty seemed to view the collaborators in a more ancillary manner, that is, as occasional speakers or workshop facilitators who might contribute additional information and skills training to an already established course of study.

This misunderstanding seems to have stemmed from two possible sources. First, given the personnel changes that had occurred at the library, librarians had had only a limited amount of time over the previous summer in which to actually contribute to the assignment design. Second, it may simply be that any collaborative enterprise such as this requires the various participants to be working in a concerted and consistent manner over an extended period of time before the full range of talents each unit might contribute to the project becomes apparent. In other words, collaborative efforts require a sufficient amount of time for participants to build trust as well as a shared vision and set of values.

In an effort to increase the Management faculty's awareness of the additional disciplinary expertise that might be brought to bear on the course, library and CWAC faculty began meeting together, independent of management faculty, in order to identify the particular problems each unit was experiencing. In these meetings, we worked to develop mutual strategies for addressing these problems. This then meant that we were able to return to meetings with management faculty with drafts of assignments that had been designed in concert, presenting, as it were, a united front that demonstrated not only our willingness, but also our ability to contribute to the overall course.

STRATEGIES

The Library and CWAC developed similar short-term strategies to cope with the initial problems of course assignments. To take care of students and staff, handouts and special instructions helped stem the tide of individual consultations with each student. Special library handouts incorporated strategies and critical thinking skills that would help students complete the assignments. These included definitions of terms, best places to look for information, when to stop looking, working with teammates, and what to do when the "right" answer can't be found.

In the library, ideas and feedback were solicited from the reference desk staff by means of a survey and informally through conversations, memos, and e-mail. This helped staff vent frustrations and offer suggestions that would help the situation next time. This strategy was also the beginning of a feedback loop for continuous improvement and collaboration within the library.

In preparation for a meeting with the School of Management at the end of the semester to evaluate the success of the course, both the library and the writing center began to develop long-term strategies to move from a reactive mode to a proactive mode. Several of the tools used to begin the transition to a proactive stage were facilitation, critical thinking, assessment and marketing skills, in order to clearly define issues and better communicate with the School of Management. For example, there were a substantial number of issues that the librarians were attempting to address over the course of the semester. The issues and potential solutions had to be articulated in a condensed fashion during the semester-end meeting. To gather all issues and ideas, the brainstorming technique was used and the resulting information was clustered into specific categories. These categories were analyzed to reveal existing patterns and identify areas for future collaboration. The writing center and library reported the same conclusion to the School of Management: the integration of critical thinking skills into the course assignments was essential if the students were to have a successful learning experience in the second semester of the Gateway course. While the faculty understood the need to integrate critical thinking, they were unsure of how to apply it to their curriculum. The writing center and the library could offer expertise in course integration of critical thinking skills and so the meeting served as a turning point because the faculty began to recognize the enhanced role that the library and the writing center could play.

Library and CWAC faculty then turned their attention to the actual assignments and their redesign. First, while the assignments had always been modeled to offer students real-world writing situations and tasks (e.g., writing a memo to a company CEO summarizing information gathered on the company's public image and suggesting recommendations for its improvement), there was a general consensus among management, library, and CWAC faculty that there were simply too many of these assignments for students to adequately handle in a single semester. For that reason, the collaborating units began the process of prioritizing the skills and information they believed the students most needed to master. After this prioritizing process, various assignments were then combined or trimmed down, resulting in a series of four more-manageable assignments.

While the desire to teach critical thinking skills to students had been expressed from the outset of the course planning, it was clear that this goal was not being adequately met, given the current course load and assignment design. Management faculty found themselves in the difficult position of being responsible for the teaching of both extensive course content and the variety of cognitive skills students would need in order to handle the types of tasks required of them in the business world.

While students were generally successful at grasping some concepts contained in the actual course material, they were still having difficulty generating and judging the relevance of their own research materials, as well as analyzing and then synthesizing those materials into their actual written work. For this reason, the collaborating units began redesigning the assignments with an eye toward slowly but successively introducing students to a variety of critical thinking skills. Rather than overwhelm students with thinking tasks they would have to ascertain intuitively, the new assignments explicitly stated the discrete thinking skills required to successfully complete the task at hand. Subsequent assignments then built on the previously-mastered thinking skills while introducing more complex ones at each stage. To construct these assignments, each unit brought to the table a variety of critical thinking models that had previously been successful, among them Bloom's classic taxonomy and those of the Sonoma Center for Critical Thinking.

It quickly became apparent, however, that the various units would have to agree on a common vocabulary, since each of the models employed slightly different terms to describe similar tasks. For example, well-intentioned efforts to clarify the thinking process would only result in greater student confusion and frustration if the professor was using the term "evaluation," while the writing center staff was talking about "judgment," and the librarians were referring to "critique." After agreeing on common terminology, it was decided that each assignment would contain a section entitled Key Terms which would provide definitions of each of the required thinking skills. Along these same lines, in order to further break down the assignments into a series of discrete and manageable tasks, the assignments were reorganized under a series of headings labeled Purpose, Thinking Critically, Researching, and Writing, each of which attempted to lay out in explicit detail the connections between the various stages (see Appendix I).

OUTCOMES

The collaborative revision of the Gateway course assignments resulted in a more positive experience the second semester. As the primary focus of the collaborative effort, students acquired more skills than usual in research and writing, and learned how to network and collaborate with a variety of University staff and students. Similarly, the School of Management recognized the value of campus-wide contributions to the Gateway course. The School has since begun discussing an expansion of the course from three to four hours to better provide opportunities for integrating research, writing, computer and other skills.

In working together with the faculty, the library and the writing center recognized a common agenda for working with curricular programs: to teach practical and cognitive skills that require subject content and the cooperation of faculty. We can, in concert, provide assistance in the development of assignments that integrate critical thinking, research, and writing.

SUGGESTIONS FOR COLLABORATION

Cross-campus collaborations are simultaneously frustrating and rewarding endeavors because they bring together a variety of wide-ranging disciplinary outlooks and cultures. Our own experience suggests that successful collaborations result when the various groups involved find a way to both identify the common ground shared by the various disciplines, as well as create the conditions that make it possible to still hear the specific expertise of each unit. Our experience also suggests that such understandings are best reached if collaboration is understood as an ongoing process—one in which the various players may need to meet again and again, reiterating their concerns and expertise in a variety of ways, until they are truly heard and true collaboration can begin.

There are a number of levels to the collaboration process, and we have attempted to provide a series of specific, tangible suggestions for dealing with each in Appendix II. Generally speaking, however, we suggest entering any collaborative undertaking with several things in mind. First, as concerns the actual meetings with collaborators, be prepared not only to teach them, but to learn from them as well. Second, don't go it alone when you do enter a collaborative enterprise. Rely on the input and assistance of other members of your unit. Third, given the large number of people involved in any collaboration, be prepared to document everything in order to avoid misunderstandings later concerning the various suggestions that were made and the decisions that were reached. Fourth, always remember that the end goal of the collaboration is to assist of students, not to win of disciplinary battles. Finally, at the level of personal attitude, remain flexible and patient; while the opportunities for frustration are great, the end results of a successful collaborative enterprise demonstrate what is possible when university cultures, split for historical and organizational reasons, come back together to provide the means for students to excel.

APPENDIX I

Spring '96 Version of Assignment #1

GLB 300 Assignment #1—Company Profile (individual)

Key Terms

- *research*: collecting information about a particular subject
- *organize*: arranging elements according to some principle, for example, time, priority, and so on
- *evaluate*: judging the value of materials or methods
- *analyze*: determining the relationship among component parts
- *synthesize*: putting together elements to form a whole

Purpose

This assignment will familiarize you with some of the basic company information and reference sources at the ASU West Library. You will be seeking primarily *factual* information which is typically developed *internally* and disseminated *by the company*. This assignment will also begin to familiarize you with the types of writing used in the business world.

Thinking Critically

Like many of the assignments in this course, Assignment #1 asks that you:

- *organize* research questions, information sources, and the information you gather
- *evaluate* similar information found in multiple sources to determine the best information to use
- *analyze* the information in order to understand it, which may require drawing inferences from it that aren't immediately clear ("reading between the lines")
- *synthesize* the information in order to present it in a clear, concise, and well-organized manner

Researching

Using the sources suggested in your Library Handbook, collect the following data about your company:

Part 1.   *The Who, What, Where, When, and How of Your Firm*

- Company name and address of headquarters
- Top Management Team
  — Name(s) of CEO and/or President
  — Names of Vice presidents (limit to five names)
- Names of up to three products/services
- Primary four-digit SIC codes (limit to five codes)
- Annual revenues (or sales) in 1994
- Most recent stock price and ticker symbol
- Year-end stock prices, 1990-1995
- Foreign countries in which company operates (limit to five)
- Names of divisions and subsidiaries
- Historical information
  — Company founder
  — Year of incorporation
  — Original name
  — Key events in company's history (two or three)

Part 2.   *The Why of Your Firm*
While the above questions require factual information that can readily be obtained, this question may require more analysis of information that is not so clearly stated.
Obtain and read the company's Annual Report to determine the following:

- What seems to be the company's mission or purpose(s)?
- Whom does it serve?
- How does it serve its clients?

Writing

Now that you have completed your research, you need to present it. The format for this first assignment is divided into three parts:

1. a one-page list of factual information based on your findings in Part 1 above;
2. a paragraph which provides a summary of the company's history; and,
3. a paragraph that gives your initial impression of the company based on your findings

Audience for the report: your professor

While we encourage you to regard this first assignment as a rather informal one, we also want you to *write clearly and concisely*—two highly prized business communication skills.

APPENDIX II

Suggestions for Collaborative Projects

Working with Collaborators:

- Allow yourself to learn from your collaborators.
- Listen and observe carefully to determine collaborators' attitudes, assumptions, and vocabulary.
- Avoid disciplinary jargon; be deliberate and selective about language; clarify the terminology you use.
- Be sensitive to others' levels of expertise. Tactfully bring them up to speed on technology and information in your area.
- Focus on commonalities.
- Establish models and strategies that can be adopted for other programs.

Working Within Your Own Department/Program:

- Don't be the only one from your department working on the collaborative effort; two heads are better than one.
- Seek the input and advice of administration and staff.
- Keep your administrator and staff well informed of developments.
- Keep this feedback loop intact.

Documenting Progress:

- Write down everything and save all memos, e-mail notes, drafts, and so on.
- Offer concisely written, well-designed reports.
- Use assessment tools.

Keeping the Focus on Students:

- Focus on how students will benefit from each aspect of the program.
- Back up suggestions with examples of students' questions and problems in completing assignments.
- Communicate about teaching issues: share copies of articles, conference announcements, workshops, pedagogical techniques, and so on.

Keeping Your Sanity at All Levels and at All Times:

- Remember that collaboration is a *process*.
- Go in thinking you can do anything…given enough time.
- Allow things to occur incrementally.
- Be flexible and willing to "give ground"; others will reciprocate.
- Be tenacious, but tactful, on the truly important issues.
- Be creative: think of 3 options or strategies for everything.
- Be ready and able to say the same thing and present the same information in several different ways; for example, provide multiple examples.
- Identify opportunities and act on them.

- Always have multiple points of access for sharing information.
- Keep your sense of humor.

PARTNERSHIPS AND SHARED RESOURCES:
DEVELOPING A COMPUTER AND INFORMATION LITERACY COURSE FOR UNDERGRADUATES

Susan Waterman MacLean

ABSTRACT

In response to significant staff and funding cutbacks, collaboration between academic departments has become an area of great interest at the University of Guelph, a mid-size university in south-western Ontario. In keeping with this new environment, the Library pursued a collaboration with the Computing and Information Science department to provide a course in computer and information literacy to incoming undergraduates. An evaluation of this collaboration indicated that partnerships between internal and external stakeholders and the sharing of both physical and staffing resources were of crucial importance. The factors identified in the evaluation can serve as a template to guide the development of future collaborative programs.

INTRODUCTION

In the fall of 1995, the Department of Computing and Information Science (CIS) and the Library at the University of Guelph began a collaboration to develop a credit course titled Computer and Information Literacy. Although the library is substantially involved in subject-specific instruction in many disciplines, this was the first experience with a credit-bearing course and the first instructional contact between the library and CIS. This paper describes the development of the course, with an analysis of the role of various internal and external partners and the necessity of sharing human and physical resources.

The Dean of the College of Physical and Engineering Sciences provided the initiative for the project and brought together CIS and the library. The Dean was aware both that CIS was actively restructuring its introductory first-year courses which focused on basic computer literacy and that the library was committed to information literacy and desired to reach a larger portion of the incoming undergraduate population. In addition, the newly-completed Strategic Planning Commission (SPC) report recommended a common first-year course and had identified collaboration as a strategic direction, creating an atmosphere that encouraged co-operation. Therefore the Dean arranged a meeting between the Chief Librarian, the Head of Reference Services, the Library Education Co-ordinator, and the Chair of Computing and Information Science. By the end of this meeting, CIS promised to devote three of the twelve course weeks to information literacy and the Chief Librarian contributed the funding required for software development. A proposal outlining the content in the three information literacy modules was due to CIS in one week.

THE DEVELOPMENT PROCESS

There was little time to prepare the course outline. Especially critical was the issue of staffing the module development groups, as it is in any understaffed and underfunded library. Since we had earlier incorporated Donna McCool's recommendation to broaden our instruction model by including library reference associates as instructors thereby "utilizing the skills and talents of others,"[1] it was logical for us to use this same inclusive model when creating a team to develop a proposal. Unfortunately, we had less than a week to form a team and prepare a proposal.

Members of the team were appointed with an attempt to have each subject section of the library represented.

THE COURSE

The basic outline of the CIS computer literacy course consisted of eight modules:

1. Introduction to computing, including e-mail, the Internet, and introduction to Windows
2. Operating systems, including DOS, Windows, and file organization
3. Word processing
4. Spreadsheets
5. Using a database

The remaining three modules were to deal with information literacy in an electronic environment. The course instruction consisted of three one-hour lectures and one two-hour laboratory session per week. Each module would include an assignment and students would also write a final examination. The expected enrollment in the course was approximately 1,500 students.

THE INFORMATION LITERACY MODULES

A review of the literature revealed very little that was directly relevant to our specific situation. Although there were excellent examples of credit courses on information literacy,[2,3] core courses that had a highly integrated information literacy component,[4] or specific subject courses which included a substantial introduction into discipline-specific research methods,[5] we could find nothing that dealt with a discrete series of information literacy modules in partnership with computer and information science.

Although the target group for this course was incoming undergraduates, we had only the most general (and undocumented) information on this group. It became obvious that we needed detailed demographic and computer literacy information on this group if we were to develop a set of modules that would serve their needs. We turned to a small research group, the Student

Environmental Study Group, to provide this information. This group prepares an annual questionnaire for incoming students. The new student questionnaire provided us with all necessary demographic information to make informed decisions on the instruction style we should use and the materials we should cover. We learned that nearly 70 percent of the incoming class in 1995 was female and over 90 percent was in the eighteen to twenty age range. In addition to demographic information, the questionnaire also provided us with data on the students' computer expertise. Although 95 percent of them had used a personal computer, less than 20 percent of them had used the Web. This information allowed us to identify concerns to be addressed in the format of the course.

Of first and major concern was how we could service the estimated 1,500 students in the course. As with many campuses, spaces in computer labs were at a premium. Also, there was reluctance in our student population to spend time in isolated lab situations late at night and on the weekends, when facilities were fairly deserted. We decided to leverage our inadequate on-campus computer resources by taking advantage of the equipment that the students were bringing with them. The new student survey had indicated that 50 percent of the incoming class would have their own computers. Almost 90 percent of the incoming class was living on campus and all residence rooms had access to the campus computer network. The students would be able to connect to the network and complete their labs and assignments in the comfort and safety of their residence rooms if material was available online.

The format of laboratory instruction was based on this information, and we took advantage of the software and expertise existing within the organization. An earlier failed experience with the Toolbook software had demonstrated the steep learning curve needed for instructional software. Although the product resulting from Toolbook was excellent, the amount of time to become familiar with the software was prohibitive in our understaffed environment. However, many staff were experts in developing Web pages for departmental or instructional use. Since we needed a product that built upon our existing skills and that had a short learning curve, the Web would be our tool of choice.

Using the Web would reduce our overall development time and would require less management than a listserv. It also eliminated the need for the library to find and fund external programming skills. (We have since found Burke's discussion of the use of a list-serv as an instructional tool very interesting.[6] It would provide the forum for student discussion and interaction, which is lacking in the option we have chosen.)

The large number of female students in the incoming class presented another concern. Studies, notably one completed by Canada and Brusca,[7] have shown that females have a higher level of anxiety surrounding the use of computers and the electronic retrieval of information. Since the course is electronically based and deals with computer technology, we felt it was prudent to take this research into consideration when designing the course. As an initial solution, we decided to implement an e-mail help line for the course. We also knew from experience that one-to-one instruction was very useful in reducing user anxiety. In order to provide this instruction option, we decided that a small library computer classroom, previously closed except for scheduled library education classes, would be opened a pre-determined number of hours every day during the information literacy modules.

We were also able to identify some areas of little or no concern. For instance, with 90 percent of our incoming class between eighteen and twenty years of age, we were not concerned with the increased impact age has on anxiety for neophyte users.[8] However, at institutions with a large adult learner population, this information must be taken into consideration when assignments and lab exercises are being developed.

Now that we had determined how we would teach, we had to clearly define what we would teach. A cursory analysis of our reference statistics, coupled with the results of our library education evaluation forms, indicated a student-identified need for instruction in the use of the OPAC (an internally developed CD-ROM product), computer-based indexes (CBIs), and the Internet. Some concern was expressed with providing OPAC instruction, stemming from the fact that the library would soon be installing a new Web-based system, which was very different in nature and capability from the existing product. However the team was unanimous in the belief that the use of the CBIs and the Internet were crucial to any instruction on electronic information literacy.

After the initial outline of these modules was complete, the team set about creating module development groups. Hoping to take advantage of our significant non-librarian human resources, an open call for volunteers encouraged any interested staff member to participate. It should be noted that this call was only made after the full support of building supervisors and department heads had been obtained. Without administrative support of the initiative, staff would not be encouraged to volunteer. Response to the call for volunteers was enthusiastic. The teams were formed consisting of librarians and library associates and including representatives from three of the four library departments.

THE MODULES

Two modules were developed:

Using Computer-Based Indexes

1.   Periodical literature
2.   Abstracts and indexes
3.   Computer-based indexes
4.   Searching the indexes
5.   Evaluating search results
6.   Locating journal articles in the library
7.   Citing journal articles

Lab session: Questions based on completion of Web-based module of sample CBI searches.

Using the Internet

1.   Internet overview
2.   Using different search engines
3.   Evaluating search engines
4.   Evaluating search results
5.   Citing the Internet

Lab session: Questions based on completion of Web-based module of recommended Internet searches.

The modules reflected the concerns expressed by students in their library education evaluations and by staff at end of term library education town hall meetings. The lecture portion of the course was planned for a five-hundred-seat hall and presented via LCD panel and laptop with live CBI demonstrations. Because of the difficulties in gaining timely access to the Internet, the demos featuring Net searching would be "canned," as would parts of the lab sessions. Time in the library education classroom would be allocated on a first-come, first-served basis. This system is the result of the library's poor experience with sign-up classes. This would be reviewed if found to be ineffectual. Students would be encouraged to take advantage of this classroom only if they did not have another way to access a computer or if they required hands-on assistance.

STAFFING

The Library Education Coordinator is responsible for maintaining the program after development. This maintenance function includes general co-ordination of the program, organizing staff involvement (as lecturers, classroom assistants, and markers), preparing and monitoring training for these positions, publicizing the program, and developing and administering evaluations of the program. Lectures presented by librarians would be based on materials prepared by the module development teams. This teaching opportunity would be open to any librarian. Library education classroom assistants would be drawn from the broad base of library staff. Staff working from a standardized answer sheet would grade assignments. The library has found this method to be highly satisfactory in the past.

THE COLLABORATION

Communication difficulties between the library and CIS appeared almost immediately. Repeated attempts to schedule a meeting between a library representative and the CIS Curriculum Committee were frustrated. When the meeting was eventually held, it was obvious that the two groups had very different goals and very different perceptions of their respective roles in the process.

The library education program had, for the most part, enjoyed a very positive relationship with the faculty. Our experience reflected the results of Nowakowski's research, that faculty believe that students should know how to do library research and that librarians are partners in the process.[9] It was therefore quite a shock to encounter what Hardesty has referred to as "faculty culture."[10] This set of attitudes, which places little emphasis on the process of learning, was firmly entrenched in the CIS department. The library proposal, due to a lack of communication and explanatory discussion, was seen as an intrusion on their initiative.

This misunderstanding was corrected through lengthy discussions with the Chair of the Committee, who became an active supporter of our involvement, albeit for two rather than three modules in the course. Since only two of the modules were crucial to our goal, this change was acceptable to us. Further difficulties with the CIS proposals had been encountered at the Board of Undergraduate Studies Curriculum Review Committee, resulting in the necessity for further course restructuring and further delay. Any possibility for implementation, even on a pilot basis, for spring of 1996 was ruled out. After several more months of development work, it became obvious that there was another challenge to be faced. At the request of CIS, the implementation date was moved from fall 1996 to winter 1997. It was then indefinitely postponed, due to a funding shortfall that cancelled hardware upgrades essential to CIS' implementation of the course. With the implementation date of the project uncertain, it was decided to provide the instructional materials as part of the library Web site. Although this was not a result anyone had foreseen, it was accepted as an alternate way to provide the students with the instruction they needed until the course is implemented.

EVALUATION

As this was our first team-based collaborative endeavor, it was important to evaluate the process in order to create a template that would assist us in developing future co-operative initiatives. We initially worked to identify two major facets of the collaboration: internal and external partnerships, and new approaches to resource use. We felt that their identification would increase our understanding of the underlying elements of an effective co-operative initiative.

Time was spent analyzing the roles played by the various internal players. We realized that the initiative would not have been possible without the active involvement or support of each group. The Chief Librarian made the project a priority and made available the budget resources necessary to realize the project. His support encouraged the agreement of the department heads and supervisors, which freed staff resources to develop the project. Librarian time necessary to develop and eventually present the course had been released by the inclusion of the library associates and assistants in the core library education program.

We also had a number of external partnerships. The Dean of the College of Physical and Engineering Sciences provided the initial suggestion and impetus for the collaboration. The CIS Chair was instrumental in the initial development of the project and the Chair of the Curriculum Committee has provided the ongoing support that has kept the initiative alive. Although not directly involved in the collaboration, the Student Environmental Study Group was invaluable in providing information that allowed the library to structure its modules on hard data, rather than conjecture.

Resource sharing in the electronic age has come to focus on the challenges of new technologies and shared data and information resources. Our resource concerns were much more mundane. How could we share and therefore leverage our existing human and physical resources in order to develop the new initiative? Through redefinition of roles, interdepartmental co-operation and the willingness of staff to learn new skills, we were able to develop a technology-based initiative in a chronically understaffed library. By being creative in scheduling and redefining the acceptable use of a facility, we gained an open computer classroom. By taking into account student equipment and network access on campus, we were able to take advantage of existing technology.

The evaluation process also identified a number of general issues of central importance to the process. The early sense of urgency (which we realized in hindsight was false) led us to hurry into the process and appoint our core organizing group, rather than form this group through a more open process. Although this problem was not repeated in the development of the actual module groups, having the core group identified through a more open process would have been more inclusive and sent a more positive message to staff in the library.

Problems could have been prevented if communication links between the two major partners in the collaboration had been developed earlier in the process. This failure to develop strong communication was, in our opinion, a direct result of the lack of adequate time at the start of the collaboration to become familiar with our partners in CIS, their goals, and their concerns. We did not know or understand the people we were dealing with. Although these communication links were eventually developed, the earlier process could have been much more productive with more communication. Of course, this situation could have been avoided if the recommendations on developing effective liaison relationships, as outlined in Wu et al.[11] had been implemented before the collaboration took place. Regular communication and attendance at departmental meetings and functions would have introduced the partners to each other and prevented some of the misunderstandings. We would also recommend that, whenever possible, the collaboration should be the result of a joint proposal, with both groups involved in all steps of development. Entering discussions after the original proposal has been formulated can be difficult for both partners.

Positive results were also found. The decision to form the module development groups in an open, inclusive way had a number of positive impacts. Because team members came from different departments, interdepartmental collaboration and communication were encouraged. This increased interaction continued after the development process was complete. The teams and the Library Education Committee benefited from hearing alternate perspectives on library education. It also provided all team members with a greater understanding of and appreciation for the ideas and experiences of others. All team members developed a new suite of skills.

CONCLUSION

Although at first appearance the project appears to be a failure because it was not implemented on the suggested time-line or in the way it was first envisioned, there have been many positive results. Solid linkages have been made with a department that had minimal contact with the library but which is now committed to collaboration in the eventual implementation of the course. Co-operation between library departments has been encouraged and individual staff members have developed new skills. The education materials loaded on our Web page will provide instruction and assistance for the student body at large. Our ability to turn lemons into lemonade, an invaluable skill in this challenging time of understaffing and underfunding, made this experience a positive one and has encouraged us to become involved in more faculty-library collaborations, albeit with a clear understanding of this experience and a willingness to use the lessons we have learned.

NOTES AND REFERENCES

1. Donna L. McCool, "Staffing for Bibliographic Instruction: Issues and Strategies for New and Expanding Programs," *Reference Librarian* 24 (1989), pp. 17-24.

2. Linda Alexander, "LME 101: A Required Course in Basic Library Skills," *Research Strategies: RS 13*, no. 4 (1995), pp. 245-249.

3. Rachel F. Fenske and Susan E. Clark, "Incorporating Library Instruction in a General Education Program for College Freshman," *RSR: Reference Services Review* 23, no. 3 (1995), pp. 69-74.

4. Paula Elliot, "The View from Square One: Librarian and Teaching Faculty Collaboration on a New Interdisciplinary Course in World Civilizations," *Reference Librarian* 24 (1989), pp. 87-112.

5. Robert B. Ridinger, "Uncharted Territory: Building a Library Instruction Course in Geography," In *The Librarian in the University: Essays on Membership in the Academic Community* (Metuchen, NJ: Scarecrow Press, 1990), pp. 117-121.

6. John J. Burke, "Using E-Mail to Teach: Expanding the Reach of BI," *Research Strategies: RS 14*, no. 1 (1996), pp. 36-43.

7.   K. Canada, and F. Brusca, "The Technological Gender Gap: Evidence and Recommendations for Educators and Computer-Based Instruction Designers," *Educational Technology, Research and Development* 39, no. 2 (1991), pp. 43-51.

8.   J. L. Dyck and J. A. Smither, "Age Differences in Computer Anxiety: The Role of Computer Experience, Gender, and Education," *Journal of Educational Computing Research* 10, no. 3 (1994), pp. 239-248.

9.   Fran Nowakowski, "Faculty Support Information Literacy," *College & Research Libraries News* 54, no. 3 (1993), p. 124.

10.   L. Hardesty, "Faculty Culture and Bibliographic Instruction: An Exploratory Analysis," *Library Trends* 44, no. 2 (1995), pp. 339-367.

11.   Connie Wu, et al. "Effective Liaison Relationships in an Academic Library," *College & Research Libraries News* 55, no. 5 (1994), pp. 254, 303.

A NEOTERIC APPROACH TO BIBLIOGRAPHIC INSTRUCTION:
"IF YOU CAN'T TREAT ME RIGHT, YOU CAN'T TEACH ME RIGHT"

Calvin Williams

ABSTRACT

An increased commitment to building an ethically and culturally diverse community at Bowling Green State University involves creating a many-layered support network. The bibliographic instruction program contributes to overall university efforts to increase retention of students of color. This paper shares one librarian's insights into his role in the success of minority students.

MY PERSPECTIVE

A young person's life is filled with choices. As a child I assumed that the natural course of circumstance was to graduate from high school and go to college. Yet deciding where to matriculate, selecting a course of study, and figuring out how to pay for it was something I had not considered. As I was to find out, these decisions were very difficult and at times frightening. I doubt I could have made the right choices without help from individuals who provided me with support and guidance. It is through introspection of my experiences that I hope to help other students, particularly students of color, become successful in the pursuit of a college education. I believe I can do this by serving as a mentor to students who are looking for direction, and also by sharing the results of a pilot project implemented at my institution. It is my hope that you, as library professionals, will critically evaluate what we are seeking to accomplish at Bowling Green State University (BGSU) through the Libraries and Learning Resources Consultant Program pilot project. I also hope that our experience will encourage you and your institutions to begin the process of enhancing, altering, or creating a bibliographic instruction program that focuses on the needs of students of color.

Making the decision to attend college requires a level of maturity and insight about one's individual needs, wants, and aspirations that is often absent when high school ends. A study that looked at how students make the transition from high school to college by Patrick T. Terenzini et al., found that most students did not belabor the question of going to college because it was something they simply never thought about.[1] It is disconcerting to realize that many college students are still faced with this reality, but have little if any support to sort through these issues when they set out to get an education.

Once I arrived at college, I found that making decisions was even harder. At the outset, like other students on campus, I had no idea what I wanted to do, where to begin, and whom to talk to. I had been given the freedom to make my own decisions, but was unclear how to make them. After four-and-a-half years, when my institution told me I was ready to graduate, I discovered I had also earned the privilege of suffering the consequences of several of my decisions. Despite my interest in fields such as human kinetics, economics, and law, I had deliberately avoided pursuing any curriculum I felt might be too difficult for me to pass. Did I miss my potential? Sixteen years later I still am unable to answer this question. But as I talk to students, my advice to them is to follow their dreams, despite being aware that, statistically, one-third may not obtain their goals.

EVOLUTION OF THE PROJECT

Despite my uncertainty and indecision, I earned a degree in communications (public relations and advertising) and a masters degree in library studies. My success provided me the opportunity to help other students achieve their academic goals. Graduating from college with two degrees was a monumental task and was significant to my development as a human being. Learning how to solve problems, make judgments, analyze information, and communicate ideas has given me a solid foundation to be a contributing member of society and to librarianship. Today my goal is to help other students, especially students of color, achieve these core competencies. This goal serves as the inspiration behind a pilot project at BGSU that seeks both to expose students of color to the traditional bibliographic instruction process through non-traditional methods and to help them achieve in an academic system that is often foreign to them.

DIFFERENTIAL GRADUATION RATES

Students of African and Hispanic descent graduate from academic universities at a rate of 50 percent over five years, compared to students of European descent who graduate at a rate of

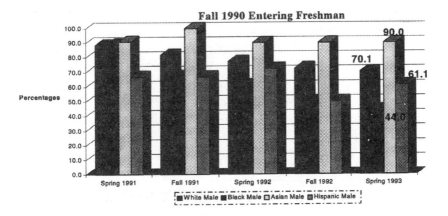

Figure 1. Retention Rates for BGSU Males by Race Fall 1990 Entering Freshman

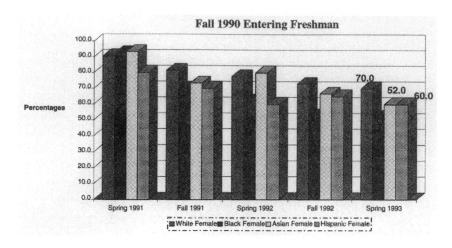

Figure 2.   Retention Rates for BGSU Females by Race
Fall 1990 Entering Freshman

84 percent over the same period.[2] National data confirms that
African-American and Hispanic-American student matriculation
rates at universities across the country continued to decline
steadily in the last decade. A disturbing report provided by the
Admissions Office at BGSU indicates that 35 percent to 45 percent of multicultural students leave the institution between the
first and second year of college.[3] The retention rate for males
and females entering their freshman year in the fall of 1990 is
depicted in Figures 1 and 2.

Figure 1 shows that 44 percent of African-American males and
61 percent of Hispanic-American males were still enrolled by the
beginning of their fourth semester.

Figure 2 shows that 52 percent of African-American females
and 60 percent of Hispanic-American females were still enrolled
after four semesters. Conversely, 70.1 percent of white males and
females were retained during this same period.

A NEW VISION FOR THE UNIVERSITY

In September 1995, Sidney A. Ribeau became the ninth president
of BGSU, and its first African-American president. With his

arrival came an increased commitment to improve relationships between faculty, staff, students, and the surrounding community. President Ribeau outlined five aspects he believed to be at the heart of an ideal university community:

- The university as a learning community where the intellect is challenged, the spirit is nourished, and creativity is allowed to seek its many forms.
- The university as a collaborative community where informal and formal boundaries can be lifted to promote flexibility and creativity, two of the most important virtues required in the contemporary workplace.
- The university as a diverse community where our full resources, perspectives, talents, or experience are made a part of the equation.
- The university as an outreach community, where we can broaden our access to education and develop partnerships with government, businesses, and other institutions.
- The university as a caring community, where every individual feels affirmed and valued.[4]

Using these themes as a backdrop, the president invited faculty, students, and staff to participate in a campus town meeting where ideas and opinions could be shared through dialogue. The president established a University Task Force on Building Community to promote a spirit of collaboration among faculty, staff, and students; evaluate the current campus climate; and make recommendations for improving work life and study life for all. To carry out this charge, the president appointed members to the task force who were representative of every campus constituent group.

Out of this effort came an ad hoc steering committee made up of administrators from various departments on campus committed to determining how a structured mentoring program for students of color might help improve retention rates. The committee decided to form a Multicultural Mentoring Program (MMP) where faculty and staff could serve as mentors to any student of color who wanted to participate in the program. The program goals are defined as:

- To provide an easily-identifiable structured support group for students of African and Hispanic descent, with the primary purpose of equipping students with the necessary information that would empower them to become active participants in their development;
- To provide positive avenues for students and faculty/administrators to interact outside the classroom;
- To promote the sharing of collegiate and other experiences between students and their peers, in order to enhance the students' personal development;
- To provide students with opportunities to network with professionals from a variety of career fields.

My participation with the MMP group led me to recognize the vital role the Libraries and Learning Resources (LLR) could play in enhancing the educational experience of the students participating in the MMP. Since traditional librarians have had tremendous success in teaching and instructing undergraduates, graduate students, and faculty throughout LLR's history, I believed that our bibliographic instruction program could be the conduit to this end.

Working with the Multicultural Librarian (who was also serving as the interim Library User Education Coordinator), I developed a plan to seek library faculty and staff who would be interested in volunteering to serve as library consultants for any students in the MMP program who wanted library-related assistance. A meeting was held with the library faculty to see if there was interest in developing a mentoring program in the library and to define the role librarians could play as consultants. Of the twenty-five faculty within LLR, ten volunteered. A diversity workshop was arranged through the Multicultural Affairs Office for all the volunteers, designed to evaluate factors that have influenced student retention rates over the last five years, and to discuss what students believed they needed from a mentor. We found that four factors heavily influenced students of color at BGSU:

- Lack of viable support systems
- Lack of culturally relevant activities
- Lack of minority role models
- Lack of meaningful relationships with university personnel

SUPPORTING BELIEFS

Judith Kleinfeld of the Center for Cross-Cultural Studies at the University of Alaska documented that pedagogy without an inter-personal dimension did not enable the teaching and learning process. She evaluated teachers in a cross-racial situation (white teachers, Native-American and Eskimo students) and analyzed the behavioral attributes of effective teachers, those who brought about positive student outcomes both in and out of the classroom. Kleinfeld found that the relationship between teacher and stu-dent was the key to how successfully students learned in the class-room. Two primary characteristics of effective teachers were defined: they (a) communicate personal warmth using nonverbal communication cues like smiling, touching, and eye contact with their students; and (b) demonstrate personal concern for each student's success and achievement and set high expectations.

Kleinfeld used the term "affectivity" to refer to qualities of empathy, closeness, interpersonal relationship, and the estab-lishment of high expectations that were required if learning was to take place.[5] Her research supports the belief that pedagogy that is sensitive to cultural diversity is an essential component to delivering effective instruction. If the LLR's bibliographic instruction program was to be effective for the purposes of sup-porting the MMP, it would have to make a priority of building relationships with students.

The African proverb introduced in the title of this essay emphasizes the value of relationships to culture. Both Hispanic and African cultures utilize relationships in their learning processes. By understanding the value of personal relationships in culture and the positive effect they can have on the educa-tional experience, librarians can reach and teach minority stu-dents the skills needed to understand and use the complex information technologies that are available today.

With the understanding that this new approach to instruction was just as important to the success of the program as the end result itself, I worked with the Multicultural Librarian to deter-mine whether any paradigm shifts would be needed. How should this new understanding change the way librarians interact with students of color? We were determined to develop proactive pro-grams specifically designed to reach students as individuals and to help break down the institutional barriers that alienate students. To achieve this outcome, the project focused on building relationships with the students before trying to involve them in the learning process. This approach transcends the teaching models used by many academic libraries and invokes revolutionary change in the pedagogical paradigm that has been the traditional model for teaching in our academic culture.

ORGANIZING THE PROGRAM

The library consultant's role would be to serve as a contact for individual students in the MMP who wanted assistance with information technology. Each librarian consultant was assigned to assist one student, but understood that these students had mentors from disciplines outside the library. The library consultant's role would be to instruct the student in several areas including understanding and using the OPAC, online searching techniques in research databases, searching the WWW, using e-mail, and gaining access to library materials. Consultants were also encouraged to develop a relationship with the student that went beyond the traditional student/librarian association.

Each of the students in the MMP was asked if she/he wanted to work with a librarian throughout the semester. Students who chose to participate in the program were invited to a luncheon to meet with their library consultant. The librarians were asked to greet each student at the luncheon and to arrange a second meeting where they could become better acquainted. A total of seven of the twelve students participating in the program were able to attend the first luncheon and only five were able to attend a second luncheon. Conflicts in scheduling were the primary reason for the lack of attendance.

MEASURING THE OUTCOME

An assessment instrument was developed to measure the student's understanding of library resources (see Appendix I). The instrument was used as a pre- and post-test survey, so that comparisons could be made to determine if there was any improvement in the student's use of library resources. Each librarian contributed to the questionnaire and reviewed it for content and consistency. A doctoral student in the higher education department with expertise in the collection of quantitative data was consulted on the design of the survey instrument and on the use of a database management tool to quantify the results.

WHAT WE LEARNED

There is no magic formula for developing a relationship with another human being, perhaps especially if the person is a student of color. Reaching minority students requires a total commitment on the part of the educator. The process is at times tedious and time consuming. A high-tech, no-touch approach using e-mail, memos, and flyers to make contact with the student will not in most cases result in an effective personal relationship.

I found that a personal approach, for example, a timely phone call when the student is likely to be in the dorm room, or recognizing and acknowledging the student during an unplanned encounter on campus, is necessary for forming a friendly relationship. Plans for holding meetings and social gatherings should be made well in advance of the events. Finally, setting high expectations of the students at the beginning of the program is vital, if an appeal for student commitment is to be honored. To be successful, the library consultant will have to be the aggressor in forming the relationship until the student believes that the consultant has his or her best interest at heart and that the consultant can be a supplier of valuable information.

MAKING A DIFFERENCE

A pre- and post-test survey was instrumental in determining if our goals were realized. Did the student gain a comprehensive understanding of the library's information resources? Did the student make a concerted effort to periodically meet with the assigned library consultant? Because of time constraints, all of the participants have not been able to complete this evaluation, so a full report is not available at this time. However, preliminary results have been both promising and informative.

CONCLUSION

Clearly, a focused intervention not limited to mentoring by faculty is necessary to increase the retention of multicultural students at BGSU and other institutions of higher education. It is imperative that students also come to view library staff as supportive and actively interested in the students' academic progress. Collaborative programs between university departments and the library offer the opportunity to develop a social support system for the student, with both adequate materials and qualified professionals. As the areas of teaching, learning, and technology emerge to facilitate a diversity of learning styles, the intellectual roots and theoretical heritage of our profession, which has traditionally been inclusive of all ethnicities, will play a vital role in the continued dissemination of information.

The retention of students of color and their integration into our society is one of the most worthwhile undertakings librarians and institutions of higher education can strive for, especially if we are going to establish a learning community where we have a diversity of cultures. Librarians must learn to find alternative ways of supporting and involving students of color in bibliographic instruction programs. Just as the industrial revolution affected the expansion of capitalism and entrepreneurship in the twentieth century, so will information and information technology in the twenty-first century. If this nation is to rise up and live out the true meaning of its creed, we will have to find more productive ways of involving students of color in the learning process. We can no longer ignore the important role libraries and librarians must play in their development. As John Gardner wrote:

> A nation is never finished. You can't build it and then leave it standing as the pharaohs did the pyramids. It must be re-created for each generation by believing, caring men and women. If we don't care, nothing can save the nation. If we do believe and care, nothing can stop us.[6]

APPENDIX

Your Name:_____ PO Number: _____
Your Mentor's Name: _____

   1. What is your current academic status?
      Freshman _____   Sophomore _____   Junior _____   Senior _____

2. How many semesters have you been at BGSU? _____
3. What kind of library did you use **most** in the last two years?

   High School _____ Public _____ College _____ Other _____ None _____

4. What kind of call number system did that library use for its books? Please check one.

   Library of Congress _____ Dewey _____ Don't know _____

LB	327.77
2386	K72c
B69	

5. Using the scale below, please answer each of the questions that follow:
   1. Always 2. Most of the time 3. Sometimes 4. Not often   5. Never

   _____ I feel confident that I can use BG'S OPAC to find relevant books on my topic.

   _____ I feel confident that I can find my books on the shelves of Jerome or Science Library.

   _____ I feel confident that if BGSU does not have the books I want, I can borrow them through Ohio LINK.

   _____ I feel confident that I can identify a journal index that will help me find relevant articles in magazines and journals.

   _____ I feel confident that I can find copies of the articles that I want in the library or online.

6. What statement best describes how you feel about using the BG'S OPAC system?

   _____ I like using BG'S-OPAC and generally can find the information I need.

   _____ I like using BG'S-OPAC but have trouble finding the information I need.

   _____ I find BG'S OPAC difficult to use.

   _____ I never used BG'S-OPAC.

7. Excluding use of materials on reserve, in how many of your courses were you required to use the library this semester?

   8. hardly any
   9. about one fourth
   10. about one half
   11. about three fourths
   12. nearly all

8. Indicate how often you use each.

   9. once a week or more
   10. two or three times a month
   11. a few times a semester
   12. hardly ever
   13. never

   _____ Study in the library.
   _____ Read books and periodicals for my own enjoyment in the library.

_____ Meet my classmates to work on projects.

_____ Meet my classmates to discuss or study subject.

_____ Obtain material from the reserve desk.

_____ Use the government documents collection.

_____ Use non-book items such as videotapes, sound recordings, etc., in the Instructional Media Service.

_____ How often do you use the BGSU Libraries on campus?

9. Use the scale below to rate the items below

1. Strongly agree   2. Agree   3. Disagree   4. Strongly Disagree

_____ The library staff is generally approachable and makes it easy for me to ask questions.

_____ My Professors in general do not give a high priority to knowing how to use the library.

_____ I avoid courses that require library assignments.

_____ Learning to use the library is an important part of my education at BGSU

_____ Use of the library will eventually contribute to success in my career.

10. How would you rank your skill level in each of the following resources using the scale below.

1. Very Comfortable   2. Somewhat Comfortable   3. Uncomfortable

_____ World Wide Web

_____ Email

_____ Research Databases on BG'S-OPAC

_____ Microfilm/Microfiche

_____ Reserve Room

11. If you were looking for information on diversity in corporate America, which of these databases would you choose to look at first? Please check one.

_____ ABI Inform

_____ ERIC

_____ HANNAH

_____ Library Literature

12. Using the scale below, please answer each of the questions that follow:

1. Very Easy 2. Somewhat Easy 3 Sometimes Easy / 4. Somewhat Hard
                                   Sometimes Hard   5. Very Hard

_____ I can find materials using the Libraries BG'S OPAC.

_____ I am able to make the distinction between popular magazine articles and scholarly journal articles.

_____ I understand how to locate periodical journals in the Jerome or Science library.

_____ When I am looking for a magazine, journal, or newspaper article, I know which part of BG'S OPACs to search.

_____ Once I find a citation to a magazine or journal article that I need, I know how to determine if BGSU libraries own it.

_____ Once I find a call number for a book in the BGSU Libraries Catalog, I am able to find it within the library.

_____ I understand the difference between keyword searching and subject searching.

_____ When I find that the BGSU Libraries do not own the book I am looking for, I know how to find if it is available in another OhioLINK school and request that it be sent to me.

_____ I am comfortable and somewhat confident when learning to use a new electronic database.

NOTES AND REFERENCES

1. P. T. Terenzini, et al., "The Transition to College: Diverse Students, Diverse Stories," *Research in Higher Education*, 35 (1994), pp. 57-73.

2. Bowling Green State University, Multicultual Affairs Office.

3. Bowling Green State University, Multicultual Affairs Office.

4. Bowling Green State University, excerpt from "Building Community at Bowling Green State University," [Online]. Available: http://www.bgsu.edu/offices/president/community/speech.html (November 22, 1995).

5. J. Kleinfeld, "Effective Teachers of Indian and Eskimo High School Students," (Institute of Social, Economic and Government Research, 1971) ERIC document, ED 068246.

6. R. Andrews, *The Columbia Dictionary of Quotations*, (Columbia University Press, 1993).

REMOTE POSSIBILITIES:
A DISTANCE-BASED ACADEMIC LIBRARY OUTREACH PROGRAM FOR SECONDARY SCHOOL STUDENTS

Keith Gresham

ABSTRACT

This paper discusses the process used to design a successful library instruction outreach program initiated by the University of Colorado at Boulder Libraries, that has, since its inception in 1994, reached more than 2,000 secondary school students, teachers, and librarians throughout the state. Amid renewed calls for shared responsibility in statewide education efforts, the outreach program makes use of the expansion of statewide electronic networks and Internet access in public school libraries and classrooms to provide on-site course-related instructional sessions and workshops which introduce high school students and personnel to the conceptual and practical processes of information access, selection, and evaluation using the OCLC FirstSearch system.

INTRODUCTION

As the largest academic library in the state of Colorado, the University of Colorado at Boulder Libraries is a busy research environment. More than 1,500,000 people enter the University Libraries each year, and more than 13,500 contact hours of library instruction are provided to University students, faculty and staff. Like many major academic libraries located near urban metropolitan areas, University Libraries policy has long recognized that secondary school students are a small but important clientele covered by our service mandate. We feel that we have a fundamental obligation to ensure that visiting school groups who turn to us are adequately served and that they receive the best possible research experience that our resources can allow. Typically, this experience has included extending circulation privileges to student groups and offering brief instructional sessions targeted directly at the visiting students' research assignment, followed by actual research time in the library.

About three years ago, our library began to see dramatic increases in the number of visitation requests by Boulder- and Denver-area high school classes who wanted to make use of our research collections. About that time, Colorado public schools were under heavy political fire to upgrade their educational programs. While attempting to reform their curricula, Colorado teachers were discovering that their traditionally underfunded school libraries were inadequate in meeting the research and curriculum needs of their students. As a result, many teachers felt they had no choice but to turn to nearby academic libraries to meet their students' educational needs. The requests from area high schools to use the University Libraries were so heavy during the autumn semester of 1993, however, that many of us in the library who offer instructional services felt an urgent need to review our existing policies and programs for these visiting groups.

As instruction coordinator for the Central Reference Department, I began to think about issues related to why and how public schools make use of academic libraries; issues related to the changing nature of research information and the information process; and issues related to time and place of need for instruction for these visiting groups. Upon reflection, it seemed to me that what high school students really needed was not so much a visit to our academic library specifically but rather access to the research tools and research information that a large academic library just happens to provide. Might there be other ways, more efficient and more effective ways, for these students to receive that access rather than arriving in large groups to our physical library building? In other words, rather than having high school students come to us, I felt that there must be a way to take the research tools and research information out to them.

One possibility, it occurred to me, was to make use of the OCLC FirstSearch system. FirstSearch was already widely available from within our campus library buildings, and I realized that there was no reason why the easy-to-learn electronic system couldn't also be accessed directly by high school students via network connections that were being placed throughout the state's public schools. If the University Libraries could provide schools with FirstSearch passwords and search blocks and instruct school librarians, teachers, and students in the use of the FirstSearch system, the students could complete the most difficult and time-consuming steps of the research process—the steps that also have the greatest impact upon library facilities and public services—from within their own schools. Furthermore, with full-text database options beginning to appear in FirstSearch, students need not necessarily make a visit to the campus library building at all.

PROGRAM OVERVIEW

What has since emerged from these thoughts, beginning in early 1994, is the Secondary Schools Outreach Program, a collaborative effort between the University Libraries, the University of Colorado at Boulder administration, and Colorado secondary schools. Since its inception two and a half years ago, the program has provided more than 2,000 students, teachers, and librarians from twenty-two partner schools with process-oriented hands-on instructional sessions that take place from within the students' own school library. With the growing presence of network access in Colorado public schools, the outreach program has been able to include rural schools from Colorado mountain and prairie communities who have always considered themselves geographically isolated from the resources of the state's flagship university. Through their participation in the outreach program, students and teachers in Colorado are discovering that information technologies—and especially instruction and application in the use of these technologies—are liberating tools that make physical distances to information irrelevant.

What I wish to provide in this paper is an overview and description of the process I went through in developing the Secondary Schools Outreach Program. What I want to show is that academic library instruction programs for secondary school students don't have to require large amounts of professional time or money to be effective. Even more important, outreach programs for secondary school students can be designed in such a way as to increase the accessibility of research information for high school students while decreasing the physical impact student visits have upon academic library personnel and collections.

TRADITIONAL SCHOOL AND ACADEMIC LIBRARY PARTNERSHIPS

The journal literature of the past twenty years includes numerous descriptions of instructional partnerships between academic libraries and secondary schools.[1] As described, these partnerships typically fall into one of four primary types:

- cooperative borrowing agreements in which academic library circulation privileges are extended to high school students;
- referral agreements, in which school librarians and media specialists are granted the authority to refer their students to an academic library on a case-by-case basis;
- coordinated student visits to academic libraries for selected groups; and
- coordinated outreach visits to secondary schools for selected groups

There is some research to suggest that academic libraries can affect the educational and intellectual development of secondary school students[2] and that the impact of academic library instruction programs for college-bound students seems to relate to the present and later academic success of these students.[3] A planned program of instruction in information access, use, and evaluation for high school students can not only provide the students with the specific skills needed to complete their research assignments, but also prepare and encourage the students to become effective lifelong users of information and information sources.

OUTREACH PROGRAM CREATION PROCESS

The process I went through in creating the Secondary Schools Outreach Program can be described in a series of practical, sequential steps.

Identify Existing Policies and Programs

The first step in designing the outreach program was to identify the existing University Libraries' visitation policy for secondary schools. The policy already in place for visiting secondary school groups requires school teachers and librarians to schedule visits a minimum of two weeks in advance and requires each visiting group to attend an instructional session taught by a campus librarian prior to beginning their research. The policy also allows for circulation privileges for certain groups, places limits on the size of visiting groups, and prohibits visits during certain busy times of the academic year. Only by possessing a clear understanding of the existing visitation policy could a program be created that would not work at odds with already established instructional efforts.

Develop Program Components

Once existing policies for visiting secondary school students had been identified, I began to develop core outreach program services and activities that would encourage and allow high school students to complete as much research as possible within their own school libraries or computer labs. As I conceived the program, a successful outreach program to high school students would provide:

- in-school access to electronic research databases, both bibliographic and full-text;
- on-site classroom visits and instructional sessions that provide the conceptual foundations and practical experience of electronic information access, retrieval, and evaluation;
- technology training workshops for teachers and school librarians;

- research assignment consultations for teachers and students;
- in-service programs to assist teachers with the integration of research technologies into the teaching process; and
- optional follow-up visits to the University Libraries.

Identify Research Technologies

To carry out the envisioned program components, I needed to identify an appropriate electronic research system that could be used by students, teachers, and librarians in the public schools. The information technology needed to be easy to teach, learn, and use, as well as easily portable and affordable. It also needed to provide multiple access options, comprehensive subject coverage from a mix of academic and scholarly sources, and some degree of administrator control.

The OCLC FirstSearch online system met each of these criteria. The standard search interface allows beginning researchers to easily search a wide variety of general and subject-specific periodical indexes. The online nature of the system means that no out-of-the-ordinary computer equipment or search software is needed by schools. Most schools in the state already possessed some sort of network access via modem in their school libraries. Depending on the setup of each particular school, FirstSearch could be accessed via direct telnet, via the World Wide Web, through the Colorado Alliance of Research Libraries (CARL) network, or through the statewide ACLIN network of public, school, and research libraries. Because the University Libraries already subscribes to FirstSearch on a per-search basis, I was able to purchase additional FirstSearch passwords for outreach program schools for approximately $40 each and purchase as many searches as needed for each password at approximately $0.50 each. In addition, the FirstSearch system provides remote administrator control over a variety of system functions, including passwords, per-search counts, database access or blocking, full-text availability, and e-mail and document delivery options.

```
┌─────────────────────────────────────────────────────────────────┐
│                                                                   │
│          Secondary Schools Outreach Program Budget                │
│                                                                   │
│  Assistance:                                                      │
│                                                                   │
│      Outreach Coordinator: 30 weeks @ 15 hours/week @ $10/hour    $4,500 │
│                                                                   │
│  Supplies and Expenses:                                           │
│                                                                   │
│      4 FirstSearch passwords @ $37.50 each                  150   │
│      2,000 searches @ $0.50 each                          1,000   │
│      long-distance telephone calls to schools              150   │
│      paper and photocopying costs                          500   │
│      postage and other mailing costs                       320   │
│      general office supplies for program assistant         200   │
│                                                                   │
│  Travel to Participating Schools:                                 │
│                                                                   │
│      2,000 miles @  $0.20/mile                             400   │
│                                                                   │
│                                                                   │
│  TOTAL  ANNUAL  COST                                     $7,220   │
│                                                                   │
└─────────────────────────────────────────────────────────────────┘
```

Figure 1.   Annual Program Budget

Develop Program Budget

With the development of program components and the selection of an information system that could be introduced in the schools, I next created an annual budget for the outreach program. Three major budget areas were identified: hourly assistance (someone to coordinate the program and travel out to the schools), program supplies and expenses (FirstSearch costs, long-distance phone charges, paper and photocopying costs, and postage), and reimbursement for travel costs associated with visits to participating secondary schools (twenty cents per mile for gasoline and automobile wear-and-tear, as allowed under university regulations). The total budgeted cost for the first year of the Secondary Schools Outreach Program was $7,220, as shown in Figure 1.

Locate Source of Funding

The annual budget of the University Libraries did not include money for the creation or implementation of an outreach program, so I next began a search for outside sources of funding. I located a University of Colorado at Boulder outreach grant program that provides a maximum of $7,500 per year for campus projects that "enable Colorado citizens not normally served by the University to access University of Colorado at Boulder expertise, programs, and activities in their own communities." The project I was developing clearly fit within the scope and guidelines of the campus outreach grant program, which is administered by the University of Colorado at Boulder Office of Academic Affairs and the Division of Continuing Education. One month after submitting the required application materials, I received word that my outreach program had been accepted for funding.

Potential sources of campus funding abound on most college and university campuses. Sources to investigate on campus include:

- friends of the library organizations
- public/community relations offices
- academic support services offices
- undergraduate affairs office
- academic affairs office
- schools of education and/or library science
- continuing education offices
- instructional technology services
- computing services
- alumni associations
- parents associations

A wide variety of off-campus grants are also available to academic libraries and librarians.[4] Potential sources of off-campus funding include:

- school district media center coordinators
- school district gifted/talented coordinators
- state and federal educational grants
- state libraries or state departments of education
- statewide library resource sharing boards
- private and corporate foundations

Hire an Outreach Program Coordinator

Having secured funding, I next concentrated on locating a qualified person to coordinate and administer the outreach program activities. The ideal candidate would be a highly self-motivated graduate student in library science or education with an interest in information technology and prior public school teaching experience. A complete description of the outreach coordinator qualifications and responsibilities is provided in Figure 2. The individual eventually hired for the position was a graduate student in the School of Education with twenty years of Colorado public school teaching experience.

Outreach Coordinator Qualifications:

- highly professional, self-motivated, and responsible individual
- strong interpersonal communication skills
- prior academic library research experience
- teaching experience at the secondary school level
- experience using online research databases, the Internet, and statewide networks
- experience/coursework in critical thinking and active learning pedagogy
- commitment to the role of library instruction in student academic success
- interest in instructional outreach services to rural and inner-city populations
- valid driver's license and private transportation/insurance

Outreach Coordinator Responsibilities:

- identify specific target schools
- initiate contact with target schools
- assess instructional needs of individual schools and classes
- schedule and conduct outreach workshops and instructional sessions
- instruct students in the use of electronic research tools via the Internet and other networks
- develop instructional materials and handouts
- coordinate, schedule, and host visits to the University Libraries
- promote University Libraries resources, services, and programs

---

Figure 2.   Outreach Program Coordinator Qualifications
and Responsibilities

Create Instructional Objectives

Once the outreach program coordinator was hired, we began the process of designing key components of the outreach activities. Using the ACRL Model Statement of Objectives for Academic Bibliographic Instruction as our guide,[5] we developed seven key instructional objectives that provide the instructional context and structure for all outreach visits and instructional sessions with high school students.

- students can identify useful information from information sources or information systems;
- students understand that individuals or groups identify themselves as belonging to specific areas or disciplines and use specific methods to communicate;
- students understand that there are a variety of information sources whose primary purpose is to identify other information sources;
- students understand how information sources are bibliographically structured;
- students understand how to construct an approach or strategy appropriate to the anticipated result of the research process;
- students understand how to manipulate access points to identify useful information; and
- students understand how to evaluate retrieved citations or full-text documents.

Publicize the Outreach Program

To publicize the outreach program to various secondary schools around the state, the outreach program coordinator relied upon pre-semester mailings of an outreach program brochure to specific target schools that had been chosen to be part of a pilot group. The outreach coordinator also made use of library and campus public relations offices to provide further publicity for the program.[6] The coordinator conducted follow-up telephone calls to the various schools to speak with school media specialists and teachers about how and when the program

Secondary Schools Outreach Program
Participating Schools, 1994-1996

Boulder High School	Boulder, CO
Eagle Rock High School	Estes Park, CO
Evergreen High School	Evergreen, CO
Fairview High School	Boulder, CO
Golden High School	Golden, CO
Horizon High School	Thornton, CO
Independence Pass H.S.	Longmont, CO
Longmont High School	Longmont, CO
Louisville Middle School	Louisville, CO
Manual High School	Denver, CO
MLK Middle School	Denver, CO
Middle Park High School	Granby, CO
Mullen High School	Denver, CO
Nederland Jr./Sr. H.S.	Nederland, CO
New Vista High School	Boulder, CO
Niwot High School	Niwot, CO
Ponderosa High School	Parker, CO
Steamboat Springs H.S.	Steamboat Springs, CO
Steamboat Springs M.S.	Steamboat Springs, CO
Thornton High Schools	Thornton, CO
West Grand H.S.	Kremmling, CO
West Middle School	Littleton, CO

Rural (mountain and plains communities):	36%
Urban (city of Denver):	21%
Suburban (Denver/Boulder metro area):	43%

Figure 3. Outreach Program Participants, 1994-1996

might be used or implemented within their own school buildings. Through the success of the various publicity efforts, more
than twenty Colorado schools have now taken part in the
Secondary Schools Outreach Program. A list of participating
schools is provided in Figure 3.

Choose Instructional Content

Although governed by the core instructional objectives of the
program, specific instructional content of each outreach session
varied according to student level, academic subject area, and specific research and information needs of the students taking part
in the outreach program. In all instances, however, a concept-

and process-based instructional approach was used, covering seven primary areas:

- creation and transmission of information;
- structures of information;
- construction, application, and revision of a search strategy;
- access to information;
- structure of electronic information;
- electronic searching concepts; and
- evaluation of information.

To illustrate these core concepts and provide a hands-on practical research environment for students, the outreach coordinator provided school librarians, teachers, and students with access to and instruction in the use of a variety of FirstSearch databases, both bibliographic and full-text, appropriate to the students' research needs. Outreach participants were also taught how to access statewide information networks that provide access to most of the state's online library catalogs to identify where certain printed information sources could be obtained.

Conduct a Program Evaluation

A final step in the creation process, that of conducting an evaluation of the Secondary Schools Outreach Program, is currently underway. Following an evaluation strategy proposed by Mignon Adams,[7] the following steps are being carried out:

- conduct needs assessment;
- establish program goals;
- determine evidence needed to assess goals;
- identify types of evaluation instruments that will yield needed evidence;
- develop evaluation instruments;[8]
- administer instruments; and
- analyze results.

Although detailed results of a strategic evaluation of the program are not yet available, there is clear anecdotal evidence to suggest that the Secondary Schools Outreach Program, through the creation of educational partnerships, has achieved results that are mutually beneficial to both the University Libraries and the secondary schools who participate in the program. As a model, the Secondary Schools Outreach Program has demonstrated to the students, parents, teachers, and residents of Colorado that the University Libraries, and by extension, the University, is:

- an active and willing partner in the education of all students in Colorado;
- committed to providing public access to University services and resources;
- serious about increasing in-state recruitment and retention; and
- determined to provide a return upon the taxpayers' investment.

NOTES AND REFERENCES

1. For an in-depth look at the variety of academic library/secondary school partnership programs over the past two decades, see Nancy M. Davidson, "Innovative Bibliographic Instruction: Developing Outreach Programs in an Academic Library," *South Carolina Librarian,* 29 (Spring 1985), pp. 19-20; Angie LeClercq, "The Academic Library/High School Library Connection: Needs Assessment and Proposed Model," *Journal of Academic Librarianship* 12, no. 1 (1986), pp. 12-18; Donald J. Kenney and Linda J. Wilson, "Developing a Partnership in Library Instruction," *College & Research Libraries News* 47, no. 5 (1986), pp. 321-322; Noelle Van Pulis, "School/College Cooperation: Building BI Bridges in Ohio," in *Reaching and Teaching Diverse Library User Groups*: *Papers Presented at the 16th National LOEX Library Instruction Conference Held at Bowling Green State University, 5 & 6 May, 1988* (Ann Arbor, MI: Pierian Press, 1989); Cathryn Canelas and Lynn Westbrook, "BI in the Local High School," *College & Research Libraries News* 51, no.3 (1990), pp. 217-220; Margaret Hendley, "Community Cooperation in Reference Service via a Librarians' Liaison Committee," *Reference Librarian no.* 33 (1991), pp. 191-205; Jay R. McNamara, "High School Students and Libraries in Public Universities," in *Academic Libraries in Urban and Metropolitan Areas: A Management Handbook,* ed. Gerard B. McCabe (New York: Greenwood Press, 1992), pp. 55-65; and Barbara J. Ford, "All Together Now," *School Library Journal* 42, no. 4 (1996), p. 48.

2. See Kathleen W. Craver, "Use of Academic Libraries by High School Students: Implications for Research," *RQ* 27, no.1 (1987), pp. 53-66; and M. Elspeth Goodin, "The Transferability of Library Research Skills from High School to College," *School Library Media Quarterly* 20, no 1 (1991), pp. 33-41.

3.   See Connie J. Ury, "Prepping for College," *School Library Journal* 42, no.1 (1996), p. 48; Mary M. Nofsinger, "Library Use Skills for College-Bound High School Students: A Survey," *Reference Librarian no.* 24 (1989), pp. 35-56; and Ronelle K. H. Thompson and Glenda T. Rhodes, "Recruitment: a Role for the Academic Library? Creating a Good Impression for Visiting High School Students," *College & Research Libraries News*, 47, no. 9 (1986), pp. 575-577.

4.   See American Library Association, *Big Book of Library Grant Money, 1996-1997* (Chicago: American Library Association, 1996).

5.   Association of College and Research Libraries, Bibliographic Instruction Section, "Model Statement of Objectives for Academic Bibliographic Instruction: Draft Revision," *College & Research Libraries News*, 48, no. 5 (1987), pp. 256-261.

6.   For an overview of publicity and management ideas for library outreach programs, see Marcia Trotta, *Managing Library Outreach Programs: A How-To-Do-It Manual for Librarians* (New York: Neal-Schuman, 1993).

7.   Mignon S. Adams, "Evaluation," in *Sourcebook for Bibliographic Instruction* (Chicago: Bibliographic Instruction Section, ACRL, 1993), pp. 45-57.

8.   For a representative sample of the numerous evaluation instruments developed at libraries around the country, see American Library Association, *Library Instruction Round Table, Research Committee, Evaluating Library Instruction: Sample Questions, Forms, and Strategies for Practical Use,* ed. Diana D. Shonrock (Chicago: American Library Association, 1996).

USING AN ABILITIES MODEL IN LIBRARY INSTRUCTION PROGRAMS:
IMPROVING TEACHING, ASSIGNMENT DESIGN, AND DISCIPLINARY CURRICULA

Kyzyl Fenno-Smith and Debra Gilchrist

ABSTRACT

The abilities model of library instruction focuses on measurable objectives for student learning. These objectives are integrated into the cross-disciplinary campus-wide curriculum at Pierce College. Three questions guide the process of structuring an ability-centered curriculum: What does an information-literate person need to be able to do? What does a student need to learn to gain these skills? And how will we know when the student has succeeded? The abilities model brings library instruction closer to the goal of an information-competent student.

INTRODUCTION

Our focus for this workshop is student ability; what are our students actually able *to do* following course-integrated instruction and a library research assignment? This focus is a result of two concurrent conversations we had about our instruction program. The first was about outcomes assessment, and the second concerned bringing the student to the center. With outcomes assessment, we initially focused on accountability; with student-centered learning we spoke of better delivery and what we *as instructors* could do to improve student learning. So, we were not concentrating on the student in either case. When the irony became clear to us, we transitioned toward a model we believe does position the student at the center of the educational conversation. We refer to this as an abilities model of library instruction.

We realize in most workshops the theory is presented first, after which participants are asked to apply that theory. In this workshop, we would like to save the theory for last, and instead use the workshop to model with the participants the processes we went through and the questions that we asked as we developed this model of library instruction. There are several guiding principles that have developed out of our work:

1. The process is *not linear*. We continually revisited topics and the process was never the same from one course to the next.
2. Specific words are less useful than *concepts*. We encourage you to think broadly and not become mired in language.
3. *Many* rather than one. A solid foundation will need to be applied in many different ways; one solution may not work.
4. Know *in order to do*. The application of the knowledge is where the emphasis should be.
5. *Whole* student development. There are very few divisions that can be drawn between disciplines, ideas, and theories.
6. You can teach to abilities as an *individual*. Even though we are developing a whole program, you can incorporate key concepts in your own library instruction.
7. Write *everything* down. You never know what will become important.
8. Nothing is permanent. *Keep going*.

In the experiential part of this workshop, participants worked in groups to quickly brainstorm answers to three questions that we've used in our work at Pierce College to structure the ability-centered curriculum design process. Each question is related to some part of the instructional process, be it learning objectives, instructional design, or student and teacher evaluation. Simply stated, the three questions are:

- What do we want students to do?
- How will we teach this?
- How will teachers and students know when learning is done well?

Question #1

What does an information literate person need to be able to do? Or, more specifically, what does the student need to be able to do to successfully complete the assignment at hand?

We asked each group to brainstorm a list of everything an information literate person is able to do. These lists included broad, general concepts like "knowing when information is needed" as well as specific issues regarding search strategy and controlled vocabulary. Next, we asked each group to select one item from their list to work with in the next question.

Example: One group of participants responded that a student needs to choose from available resources those which are most useful in resolving her question. In other words, she must evaluate information.

Question #2

What does the student need to learn in order to do this? Or to use the example above, what does the student need to learn in order to evaluate information?

We again asked each group of participants to create a list. Again, each group selected one idea to work with in the next question.

Example: The student can identify differing points of view.

Question #3

How will you know when the student is doing this? What evidence will be observable in the student's work?

Example: The student seeks material on additional points of view during the research process.

THEORY OF ABILITIES

The three workshop questions are central to our development of an abilities-centered curriculum. They flow from a philosophy of resource-based and inquiry-centered learning. This type of learning assumes complexity and transferability. It is our goal for students to see the applicability of information competency to other aspects of their lives. This curricular focus on abilities uses the student's performance to evaluate effective instructional design and teaching.

We articulate what students need to be able to do and express this in learning objectives. These objectives guide instructional design, inform teaching, and are made explicit to the student as criteria for evaluation. The Information Competency criteria developed by the library faculty are blended with the criteria the course instructor developed and given to the student at the time the assignment is made. This means the research process and the student's progress toward information competency is evaluated in addition to the specific course content.

Pierce College has identified five abilities for cross-disciplinary, institution-wide curricular integration. These are: Information Competency, Critical Thinking and Problem-Solving, Effective Communication, Responsible Citizenship, and Multiculturalism. We believe that these abilities and disciplinary course content are complementary foci in the curriculum; that they are central to whole-student development; that our purpose as educators includes developing information competent, critical thinkers who communicate effectively and thrive as responsible citizens in a multicultural world.

APPLICATION

The way in which we bring this theory and the question development series back to the student is through an expression of what we refer to as criteria. Students use these criteria in assignments to incorporate information competency concepts that the library faculty believe are accurate measures of accomplishment. These criteria are public—the student receives them at the time the assignment is made. And they are also explicit—giving the student direct guidelines to work from and a complete picture of how they will be evaluated. This gives the students a new level of understanding and adds a new dimension to their learning.

The final step is to express the ability and criteria as a student would see them. Example criteria to include with an assignment could be: identify key concepts of this article, or analyze information for its relevancy or irrelevancy. Potential criteria for questions #2 and #3 are: include citations in your bibliography, or include ideas in your paper that demonstrate you sought varying or opposing viewpoints in your research.

Including specific information competency criteria paints a picture of a whole assignment and delivers to the student specific benchmarks upon which to base their project. We believe that students who receive and understand criteria not only understand how they will be evaluated, but can ask distinctly different questions than if they had only been told to write a research paper for content and correct bibliographic format.

The format of this workshop followed the general approach we took in developing our learning objectives and criteria and this model of library instruction. We asked ourselves these three questions repeatedly, each time refining our answers until the criteria took shape. Our initial concentration on what an information-literate student should be able to do focused us on student ability and performance, not only on their knowledge. From there, we concentrated on our presentation of the information to the student—what does a student need to learn to be able to perform in the ways we had articulated in question #1, and what did we need to do in the classroom to ensure that learning? Finally, we examined how to recognize student achievement so that we could then articulate that to the student.

Abilities have provided us with a new framework for teaching, and a way to structure our library instruction program that we believe brings us closer to our goal of an information-competent student.

INTEGRATING INFORMATION LITERACY SKILLS INSTRUCTION INTO THE CURRICULUM:
COMPARISON OF TWO APPROACHES

Buhle Mbambo and Ann Roselle

ABSTRACT

A unique feature of the curriculum at the University of Botswana is that undergraduates select a specific identifiable major from the beginning and take core classes with the same group of students during the same year of study. This structured form of class scheduling provides librarians at the University with options for incorporating an Information Literacy Skills Program into the curriculum. This paper evaluates two different approaches that were adopted: the First Year Approach, instruction incorporated within the first year only; and the Staggered Approach, instruction incorporated across all academic years of study. Although analysis shows that each approach has its own strengths and weaknesses, general conclusions are reached on how best to incorporate information literacy skills into the curriculum.

INTRODUCTION

The University of Botswana, established in 1982, is a relatively young university. Its origins date back to the days of the University of Botswana, Lesotho, and Swaziland.[1] Between 1965 and 1972 this single university, based in Lesotho, serviced all three countries. In 1972, instigation by nationalists in Lesotho led to the withdrawal of Lesotho from the tripartite arrangement. Two separate institutions were thus created, the University of Botswana and Swaziland (UBS) and a separate National University of Lesotho (NUL). Eventually, in 1982 the University of Botswana and Swaziland also divided into two separate institutions, the University of Botswana (UB) and the University of Swaziland (UNISWA).

The University of Botswana consists of five faculties—Faculty of Education, Faculty of Engineering and Technology, Faculty of Humanities, Faculty of Science, and Faculty of Social Sciences. The academic year is divided into two semesters, each fifteen weeks long. Courses, for the most part, are year-long. The University offers a variety of bachelor's degrees. The duration of study for the bachelor's degree is usually four years. However, the duration of work for the bachelor's degree in those departments requiring students to have previously attained a diploma in that field of study is for three years only.

Academic study is structured, with a few exceptions, in such a way that students proceed from the very beginning with a specific identifiable major to be studied throughout their three or four years at the University. Students do not, therefore, spend the first years at the University exploring different faculties to determine a major. Due to this more structured arrangement, core classes are taught to the same groups of students during the same year of study. The example below of the three-year B.Ed. course structure in the Department of Adult Education (A.E.) illustrates the concentration of a major subject throughout all years of study.

YEAR 2	YEAR 3
Historical & Philosophical Foundations of A.E.	comparative A.E.
Psychological Foundations of A.E.	Adult Literacy
Sociological Foundations of A.E.	A.E. and Women
Curriculum Theory and Design in A.E.	Psychology of Adult Learning & Teaching
Introduction of A.E. Research	Research Methods in A.E.
Audio-Visual Media in A.E.	A.E. Methods

YEAR 4
Urban A.E.
Issues in A.E.
Policy Studies in Lifelong Education
Political Economy of A.E. & Development
A.E. and Community Projects
Management of A.E.
Field Project (10 weeks, during long vacation)

In addition, most students studying for bachelor degrees at the University of Botswana are required to take a communication skills course which is taught by the Department of English.

USER EDUCATION PROGRAM

Over the years, the formal user education program involved two steps—an initial tour of the library at registration followed by a single bibliographic instruction session for first-year students in the required English communication course. The participating librarians all had strong criticisms of such an orientation program.[2] They felt that the instruction was shallow, badly timed, and ineffective for providing students with lifelong skills. Likewise, the students expressed dissatisfaction with the time spent on orientation. To compensate for these shortcomings, the librarians gradually worked with faculty to arrange for more and more bibliographic instruction slots. The fact that the library was introducing new information technologies like CD-ROMs and online catalogues precipitated an immediate need to instruct users on information technology.

While the library continued negotiating for more bibliographic instruction slots, the biology department was organizing a communication skills course which included an information skills component. With a recommendation by the University Librarian, it was agreed that a librarian would teach the information skills component. Thus in 1994-1995, the first library course was taught in the biology department by the science librarians.

The librarians seized this opportunity to market their willingness and availability to conduct similar instruction across the curriculum. The library took the biology course plan with some adjustments to the School of Accounting and Management

(SAMS), which was in the process of changing its teaching orientation from textbook-based to resource-based, and to the Department of Nursing, which already was utilizing bibliographic instruction sessions heavily. After several negotiations, the librarians and the departments agreed to introduce the Information Literacy Skills Program into their curriculum. The remaining portions of this paper will concentrate on the Information Literacy Skills Program within SAMS and the Department of Nursing.

INFORMATION LITERACY SKILLS COURSE CONTENT

The Information Literacy Skills (ILS) course is designed to empower students with lifelong skills which will be applicable in a variety of circumstances not necessarily tied to a specific library or information center. After the completion of the course, students should be able to conceptualize the types of information that exist throughout the world and access, evaluate, and synthesize the information. The course consists of the following components: Organization and Types of Information; Topic Analysis; Access Tools & Access Points; Controlled Vocabulary; Online Public Access Catalogues; Print Indexes & Thesauri; CD-ROM Databases; Boolean Searching; Research Cycle/Process; Evaluation of Information; and Preparing a Research Paper/Citation Practices.

Instruction of information literacy skills is done through a variety of teaching methods including lectures, practical sessions, and cooperative learning exercises. Students' achievements are assessed through take-home exercises and tests. The grades on these assignments factor into the students' final grades for the course, which incorporated the information literacy skills instruction. Students also complete a student assessment survey on the quality of the instructor and the course.

TWO APPROACHES TO INFORMATION LITERACY

The Information Literacy Skills (ILS) course began in the 1995-1996 academic year for both SAMS and the Department of

Nursing. While course content was for the most part identical for the departments, the way in which the ILS course became integrated into the curriculum did vary. Variation in the approaches was caused primarily by the immediate scheduling options in each department. For clarity purposes, this paper identifies these two different approaches as the First Year Approach and the Staggered Approach. Fortunately, having two different approaches provides the opportunity to make comparisons and learn more about curriculum incorporation for an Information Literacy Skills Program that is still in its experimental stages.

INTEGRATION OF ILS COURSE INTO THE CURRICULUM

The First Year Approach, with the bachelor's students in SAMS, formally integrated information literacy skills instruction within a first-year English communication skills course designed for business students. During the first semester, one hour a week of the English course was devoted to the Information Literacy Skills course, culminating in fifteen hours of instruction. Due to the large class size of 116 students, additional librarians assisted during in-class practicals.

The Staggered Approach, with the bachelor's students in Nursing Education, formally integrated information literacy skills instruction within the three-year degree program. To facilitate scheduling, the information literacy skills course was divided into three separate units:

- Unit 1. Organization and Types of Information; Topic Analysis; General Discussion of Access Tools & Access Points; Introduction to Specific Monographs & Journals; Controlled Vocabulary; and the Online Public Access Catalogue
- Unit 2. Print Indexes and Thesauri; Specific Indexes in Nursing Education; Specific Indexes in Related Disciplines; Evaluating Appropriateness of Access Tools
- Unit 3. CD-ROM Databases; Boolean Searching; Research Process; Evaluation of Information; and Preparing a Research Paper/Citation Practices

Table 1.   Integration of ILS Course
Through Staggered Approach

Year	Unit	Semester	Week	Course Integration	Hours of Instruction
2nd	Unit 1	First	5th & 6th	ENE 220 (6 hrs.)	6 hours
3rd	Unit 2	First	3rd & 4th	ENE 321 (3 hrs.)	9 hours
				ENE 324 (3 hrs.)	
				ENE 326 (3 hrs.)	
4th	Unit 3	First	1st & 2nd	ENE 420 (4 hrs.)	15 hours
				ENE 421 (4 hrs.)	
				ENE 424 (4 hrs.)	
				ENE 426 (3 hrs.)	

Integration of these units of instruction took place within select hours from eight separate courses starting from Year 2 to Year 4 (see Table 1).

The number of students in each year was approximately thirty. Many of the hours utilized were lab periods from the courses. Classes ranged from two to four hours long and were for the most part held at the normal venue for those nursing courses which were incorporating the information literacy skills units. These more lengthy classes account for an increase in the number of total instruction hours compared to the First Year Approach. These extra hours were simply used to reinforce lessons.

ADVANTAGES OF THE STAGGERED APPROACH

The first advantage to the Staggered Approach is that it strives to provide learning activities and opportunities that match: (1) perceived student information and research needs, and (2) student learning ability. Generally, students' use of the library becomes more complex as they progress through their academic career. The Department of Nursing, specifically, requires its students to utilize the book collection in the second year and begin to use primary information within the journal collection starting in the third year. Finally, fourth-year students are required to complete an original research project. The Staggered Approach matches this progression by providing information literacy skills instruction from simple to complex.

Table 2. Student Opinion on Course
Survey Statement—"This was a difficult course."

Year	Agree-Strongly Agree	Disagree-Strongly Disagree	No Opinion
2nd	12%	66%	22%
3rd	24%	33%	43%
4th	40%	21%	39%

The Staggered Approach is also based on the assumption that students' level of comprehension and synthesis will increase throughout the years of study and will, therefore, better correspond to the levels of complexity and difficulty of the Information Literacy Skills course. The perceived difficulty of the course increased from the second to the fourth year (see Table 2). This is not to say that fourth-year students were not capable of comprehending the material but rather that more complex issues were introduced in Unit 3.

The Staggered Approach aims to present information literacy skills that are new to each group of students as well as applicable to their present-day academic needs. When questioned about the material presented in the Information Literacy Skills course, 82 percent of the second-year students, 77 percent of the third-year students, and 74 percent of the fourth-year students responded that they found the course material to be new. More importantly, each class of students was able to see the applicability of their particular component of the course to their academic studies: 82 percent of the second-year, 87 percent of the third-year, and 100 percent of the fourth-year students felt that they were able to apply what they had learned in the course.

A second advantage to the Staggered Approach is that it automatically provides scheduled instruction time each year to: (1) update students on any changes in the library, and (2) repeat or emphasize those information literacy skills considered most important. Updating is especially important because libraries change so constantly, especially in terms of technological changes in information retrieval. It cannot always be assumed that the previous skills mastered in the first year will be enough to adapt to these changes. Likewise, certain information literacy skills, such as search strategies and evaluating information, can be stressed throughout all years of the course. This provides the students with continuity in critical thinking about library resources and information. Moreover, students themselves seem to want regular contact as reflected by the following students' comments:

> I would like this course to be held periodically to keep us abreast with the use of the Library. The student and the library cannot be separated.
>
> This course should be taught continuously so that students have time to practice what they have learned and then bring up questions about issues they have encountered while using the library.

The Staggered Approach integrates information literacy skills into the curriculum at every level of the student's academic life, thereby demonstrating to the student that learning to use the library is a continuous process.

Additional advantages particular to the University of Botswana context are also worth noting. The Staggered Approach, which is integrated into several different courses, took little instruction time away from any one lecturer. In fact, the Staggered Approach took advantage of lab and tutorial periods that are often not utilized by lecturers in the first couple of weeks of the semester. In addition, time-tabling during labs and tutorials allowed for information literacy skills class periods to last three to four hours. Unlike one-hour class periods as in the First Year Approach, these longer classes provided an excellent opportunity to break away from lecturing to incorporate cooperative learning exercises, student discussions, and in-class practicals. Indeed, many students commented that they felt they benefited from these active learning sessions.

DISADVANTAGES OF THE
STAGGERED APPROACH

The most significant disadvantage of the Staggered Approach is that it excludes specific information literacy skills within the second and third years of the program. There is no guarantee that students in the early stages of the Staggered Approach will not need the skills and knowledge taught during the advanced years of the Staggered Approach. There is also no guarantee that those students who need further instruction will seek out help from a librarian. While the better students are likely to seek assistance and guidance, others may be less likely to take such initiative and instead rely solely on their own skills and knowledge gained through the early stages of the Information Literacy Skills Program. It is, therefore, important that a strong relationship exist between faculty and librarians so that the latter are aware of the research expectations being placed on the students within each year of study. In addition, librarians must be extremely observant on their own, either through informal observations or formal surveys, to determine actual student information needs.

In order for the Staggered Approach to work efficiently, students must remember what they have learned from the previous years. A second disadvantage arises in assuming that all the students will have retained what was previously taught to them and that the instructor can, therefore, immediately proceed to build on this knowledge. In reality, the instructor of the Information Literacy Skills course will have to use class time to fill any gaps in students' knowledge and skills before proceeding to the next level. However, there is no certainty that these knowledge gaps will be the same for each student. The better students may be more ready to move on compared to the other students. There is the chance that the instructor may "lose" the better students by recapping too much or may "lose" the slower students by not reviewing long enough.

A third disadvantage of the Staggered Approach is the time-tabling. The Staggered Approach takes much more time and effort to integrate into the curriculum and requires cooperation from more than one faculty member. The Staggered Approach at the University of Botswana involved all lecturers in the Department of Nursing because the information literacy skills classes were incorporated into eight separate courses. Flawless communication and coordination between the library and the faculty were essential because classes were not always held at the same venue nor at the same time. Although a significant amount of time was required to coordinate the Staggered Approach, it did ensure that the entire Department of Nursing was actively involved in the Information Literacy Skills Program, which strengthened the partnership between faculty and librarians.

There are additional disadvantages to the Staggered Approach which are perhaps specific to the University of Botswana context. First, the University of Botswana Library relies heavily on staff who come from other countries. Therefore, there is a high rate of staff turnover. The ideal situation would be for the students to have the same information literacy skills instructor throughout their entire academic career. This situation is nearly impossible within the Staggered Approach at the University of Botswana. Communication between librarians (syllabi sharing, explaining previous lessons, discussing student skills/problems) is extremely important.

Second, the University of Botswana does not have a separate instruction unit within the library and the librarians participate in the Information Literacy Skills Program along with their many other duties. At that time, there was only one available instructor for the Staggered Approach and, in order to balance work responsibilities, that librarian could only teach students one year at a time. Unfortunately, this meant that all instruction could not begin at the same time. In effect, instruction was first conducted for the fourth-year students, then the third-year students, and finally the second-year students. The majority of the third-year and second-year students indicated on their course evaluation forms that they would have liked the course to begin the first week of school. They felt the need for instruction on information literacy skills earlier than when presented. It should also be noted that in order to get to the second-year students as quickly as possible, classes for both the third and fourth-year students in the Staggered Approach were scheduled as close together as possible. This in turn created another disadvantage, since the students did not have enough time to absorb what they had learned nor apply the skills and knowledge while studying information literacy skills. It is believed that this is one reason why most of the students, irrespective of academic year, indicated on the course evaluation form that the course should be longer.

ADVANTAGES OF THE FIRST YEAR APPROACH

Teaching information literacy skills through the First Year Approach has several advantages for the students and the instructor. First, the First Year Approach provides students with all of the skills and knowledge for their perceived information and research needs. Instruction is conducted in a logical sequence providing a solid foundation of information-seeking skills for students to fall back on in their four years of study.

Second, unlike the Staggered Approach, instruction sessions were easy to schedule. At the beginning of the semester the coordinator of the English communication skills course allocated one hour a week for information literacy skills instruction. The hour was scheduled at the same time each week in the same classroom, thereby preventing any confusion for the students or the information literacy skills instructor.

Third, because the course is conducted over fifteen weeks, the lecturers had time to prepare lesson plans, grade assignments, and meet with students outside the classroom. Instruction was conducted by librarians with other responsibilities such as collection development and subject classifying of materials. Therefore, preparing for one lesson a week was not as burdensome as it was for the instructor in the Staggered Approach, who at times conducted eight hours of instruction a week. On a related note, unlike the student experience in the Staggered Approach, students in the First Year Approach had time to absorb and digest the information received from one class to the next. The students were also given ample time to complete take-home assignments.

DISADVANTAGES OF THE
FIRST YEAR APPROACH

The most significant disadvantage of the First Year Approach is that instruction did not match students' immediate information needs as well as the Staggered Approach did. The students did not have the immediate opportunity to apply their new-found skills and knowledge. Although the rationale for incorporating information literacy skills into the School of Accounting and

Management curriculum was based on the department changing its teaching approach from textbook-based to
resource-based, in practice the change was not implemented.
The lecturers did not demand any extended use of library
resources from the first-year students. Most of their assessed
work required short answers and multiple-choice answers. It is
believed that the students also failed to see the relevance of the
instruction to their business studies. This impression is based on
the large number of absences from the class halfway through
the semester. At times up to 40 percent of the students did not
attend class. On the other hand, 100 percent attendance was
recorded in the Staggered Approach classes. In addition,
although examples were all drawn from business and business-related subjects, some students commented on their course
evaluation forms that they felt the course was more suitable for
library majors.

Second, unlike the Staggered Approach which has scheduled
class time for updating and recapping, the First Year Approach
has no scheduled time for reviewing in the future. It may be an
incorrect assumption that students will remember the skills
learned in the first year to be able to apply them throughout all
of their remaining academic years. On a related note, lecturers
may falsely assume that students are well equipped to do library
research because they have had the Information Literacy Skills
course. Faculty must be made aware that additional instruction
may be necessary, especially as information technology continues
to expand.

Third, a one-hour class period did not provide enough time for
alternative teaching methods. The tendency, therefore, was to
lecture rather than to include cooperative learning exercises and
practical sessions. Due to time limitations, a split between the lecture and practicals was required and this resulted in students for-
getting concepts before having the opportunity to apply them
the following week at the practical session. The Staggered
Approach, on the other hand, as scheduled in the Department of
Nursing, was able to provide students with active learning
sessions on a regular basis.

CONCLUSIONS

Three general concerns, challenging to librarians, arise out of the comparison between the First Year Approach and the Staggered Approach. The first challenge consists of determining students' actual and future information needs in order to properly construct an Information Literacy Skills Program. A detailed study of an academic institution's curriculum as well as specific course assignments is a prerequisite in determining students' immediate information needs. It should be noted that, if the Staggered Approach is used, the cutoff point of skills taught within each year will probably vary from one academic institution to the next. Providing information literacy skills instruction which can be applied by students when they leave the academic institution is even more conceptually challenging. The Information Literacy Skills course should, therefore, be integrated into the curriculum where it best matches students' needs.

A second challenge in terms of information literacy skills teaching is to teach in those ways that are most effective for the various learning styles of students. Probably one of the best options to control for varying learning styles is to utilize a variety of teaching methods. It should be noted that alternative teaching methods, such as cooperative learning exercises, often do require more than a one-hour period. The Information Literacy Skills course should, therefore, be integrated into the curriculum in such a way that allows for flexibility in teaching.

A third challenge involves the extensive cooperation between faculty and librarians required to develop a successful Information Literacy Skills Program. While cooperation is obviously required in terms of time-tabling, close partnership is also required to determine faculty expectations of the Information Literacy Skills course. That is, librarians need to ensure that the skills being taught reflect the research requirements being placed on the students by faculty. Likewise, strong partnership can help in encouraging faculty to in turn encourage the utilization of library resources and services by their students. The Information Literacy Skills course should, therefore, be integrated into the curriculum in such a way that requires cooperation between faculty and librarians.

One of the best ways to meet these challenges is for the librarian to be proactive. The librarian should identify appropriate courses to integrate information literacy skills instruction. The librarian should look for labs or tutorial times early in the semester that could be used for cooperative learning exercises. The librarian should instigate communication with faculty or administrators to integrate the Information Literacy Skills Program into the curriculum. Being proactive will help provide a suitable integration of information literacy skills instruction into the curriculum. This surely is an admirable goal.

NOTES AND REFERENCES

1.   *University of Botswana Calendar 1995-1996* (Gaborone: University of Botswana, 1996).

2.   Edwin Qobose, *An Evaluation of the First Year Orientation*, (University of Botswana Library, 1991); E. Asafu-Adjaye, *Orientation: A State of the Art Review*, (University of Botswana Library, 1993); and Fran Lamusse, "Learning and Library User Education Programmes at UB," *Higher Education Development Unit Bulletin* 11 (1994), pp. 12-13.

LEXIS/NEXIS, FOUR NIGHTS, EIGHT HUNDRED STUDENTS!

Mary Strow and Emily Okada

ABSTRACT

A routine "let's get acquainted" encounter between librarians from the Indiana University Undergraduate Library and staff from the IU School of Business Placement Office led to the planning and implementation of a highly successful program that taught students how to search the LEXIS/NEXIS system. Comprised of several components, the program incorporates the use of an online LEXIS/NEXIS tutorial available on the World Wide Web; a fill-in-the-blanks worksheet; a hands-on, real-time workshop; and a take-home assignment that asks students to do LEXIS/NEXIS searches for annual reports and various types of information related to business. Librarians and Placement Center staff collaborated to determine: (1) what kind of information students need to enhance their job search skills, and (2) the length, nature, and timing of the tutorials, workshops, and homework assignments. The program was assimilated into the syllabus of X220: Career Perspectives, a required course taken by approximately 800 business school students every semester. Librarians who conduct the workshops are considered guest lecturers. This paper provides a brief history of the development of this program. It describes selected instructional components, emphasizing how they work together to accommodate a variety of learning styles and teaching methods. The continuing evolutionary nature of the program and points to consider when contemplating such a large-scale instruction program are also discussed.

159

INTRODUCTION

Collaboration has never been a foreign concept to the Under-graduate Library at Indiana University. For many years, librarians have worked with the departments of speech communication, English, journalism, and psychology on a number of library instruction projects. When the LEXIS/NEXIS project involving the IU Undergraduate Library and School of Business Placement Office germinated in the spring of 1994, it seemed a natural, normal undertaking.

For the previous six months, two LEXIS/NEXIS terminals had been situated in the Reference area, receiving a moderate amount of use. UGL librarians believed, however, that this powerful tool was largely undiscovered by the multitude of business students who patronize the Undergraduate Library. UGL Head Lou Malcomb acknowledged staff concerns that the system was under-utilized and subsequently suggested that an orientation to business and career-related resources be organized for full-time staff from the Placement Offices as a first step in raising awareness. Our contact was accepted with delight and gratitude; shortly thereafter seven people, including the director, attended a special two-hour session in the library.

The orientation began with a brief classroom demonstration of LEXIS/NEXIS, and within a matter of minutes the value of the system became evident to our visitors. Later we walked the group throughout the UGL Reference area, pointing out print collections as well as other electronic business-related resources. At the end of the orientation, we informally brainstormed about how library technologies could be incorporated into the curriculum, and the Placement Center director suggested that we try teaching LEXIS/NEXIS as part of a new course, X220 Career Perspectives in Business, which would be offered in the fall of 1994.

X220 is a two-credit course required for all business majors and designed to help students develop skills and qualities which will enable them to be "highly successful in the workplace." It also familiarizes students with a wide variety of career options, and teaches important skills, including self-assessment techniques, resume-writing, and interviewing basics. LEXIS/NEXIS training clearly fit the scope. Yet there were many factors for the UGL to consider. During the orientation, the director had asked librarians point blank: could we provide training for some **800** students **each** semester? Yes! was the answer (a program involving twice as many students was already running successfully). Could the library provide **hands-on** experience for all 800? Sure, was the reply—creative scheduling was a UGL forte. Could basic LEXIS/NEXIS training be provided within the span of **thirty-five** minutes? Why not? (only the basics would be covered). And last, could all the sessions be taught in **four nights**? No problem! After the orientation, librarians looked at one another in shock, realizing the magnitude of what had just been agreed to. Now our own questions surfaced: first and foremost, were we out of our minds? Did we really think that we could pull this off? But fall semester was four months away, there was plenty of time to prepare, we were confident that we could do it, and the Placement Center staff was enthusiastic and willing to help us any way they could. We agreed to **try**.

The initial development and subsequent refining of the X220 LEXIS/NEXIS program was definitely a collaborative project for the entire staff of Undergraduate Library Services! Our in-house business information expert, Carolyn Walters created and tested specific searches which were taught during hands-on sessions. Hilary Jolly tested and refined the searches for the 1995 and 1996 hands-on sessions. The Librarian for Reference Services, Emily Okada, refined the 30-minute "script" and created a step-by-step list of the search commands. Samantha Skutnik, the Bibliographic Instruction Assistant and later the Electronic Systems Coordinator, helped write the original gopher tutorial and load it on the server in 1994. Jon Hansen, the Bibliographic Instruction student assistant, did the HTML markup and moved the tutorial from the gopher server to the World Wide Web in 1995. The Bibliographic Instruction Coordinator, Mary Strow, devised the schedule and served as liaison with the Business Placement Office.

THE PROGRAM

The X220 LEXIS/NEXIS program we devised incorporated three learning modules or activities that provide for different learning styles. These components were sequenced and built on the skills and concepts covered in the previous component. Each could stand alone and be used for different classes under different circumstances.

THE TUTORIAL AND TUTORIAL WORKSHEET

Prior to attending the hands-on library session, each student was required to read the LEXIS/NEXIS tutorial and complete a fill-in-the-blank worksheet (see Appendix). Creating the LEXIS/NEXIS Tutorial was one of our first ventures into cyberspace. Mary Strow and Samantha Skutnik developed the tutorial and had it loaded onto the Libraries' gopher server. It didn't take long to recognize the improvements that could be made to the tutorial by migrating to the World Wide Web and when the university announced it would no longer support the gopher server, that was all the impetus needed. Content did not change. The LEXIS/NEXIS tutorial as a WWW document was ready for use starting in the fall of 1995. Currently the URL for the tutorial is: http://www.indiana.edu/~libugls/tutorial.html. Objectives for this tutorial were:

1. to provide definitions and introduce terminology: provide an overview of the organization of the database and its contents;
2. to introduce Boolean logic;
3. to introduce the use of LEXIS/NEXIS dot commands and segment searching.

We looked at the LEXIS/NEXIS interactive tutorial (at that time it was available on floppy disk) and the company's printed guides and received permission to reproduce their graphics and use their wording whenever necessary. The final product was simple: the student connected to the gopher tutorial through the campus network and read through a series of screens.

Because this was not an interactive tutorial, it was important to give students a way to identify the most important concepts illustrated in the tutorial, and to test their understanding of the information. The fill-in-the-blank worksheet was developed to meet these needs and actually served two purposes:

1. The pedagogical purpose was to require the students to read the screens carefully and think about the concepts and strategies that were described. Universal concepts such as the importance of keywords, database organization, the

use of Boolean operators as well as information specific to LEXIS/NEXIS were incorporated into the tutorial worksheet.

2. The administrative purpose served by the worksheet was as a record of completion. Students were required to turn in the worksheet when they arrived at the hands-on session. This more or less guaranteed that they had done the tutorial prior to the session and we could assume a standard level of understanding. In fact, the Business Placement Office stipulated that if the worksheet was not handed in during the hands-on session, students could not receive full credit for the entire assignment, even if the worksheet was turned in later.

THE HANDS-ON SESSION

The second instructional module of the X220 LEXIS/NEXIS program was a hands-on session during which students reviewed the concepts and strategies introduced in the tutorial. Hands-on training for 800 individuals required monumental planning, especially with only two small clusters of terminals available in the library; one consisting of twelve stations, the other with six. Eventually we were able to use a large computer classroom in the School of Business with forty stations. The schedule was calibrated to the minute, a script was written and refined, and seven library staff were drawn upon to teach the sessions. Each semester there were over forty sections of the class. Each class held 90-minute labs in the evenings, Monday through Thursday; there were often as many as five simultaneous sessions. The LEXIS/NEXIS training sessions were part of these evening labs.

While all UGL librarians had received early training on LEXIS/NEXIS and used it regularly at the reference desk, few of us felt entirely comfortable teaching business majors how to use the system. Carolyn Walters was familiar with the system from her years as a corporate librarian, so she developed the specific searches taught in the hands-on sessions.

These hands-on sessions were a series of guided searches. Seven searches were carried out during each 30-minute session. The searches were sequenced to begin with a review of important concepts from the tutorial and then demonstrate search strategies including the modifying or focusing of a search, using segment codes, using proximity commands, limiting a search by date, and using dot-commands to move around in the database. Each librarian/instructor used identical searches; these searches were tested daily to assure predictable and desirable results.

These sessions were fast and furious. The instructors spoke loudly and non-stop, hoping to overcome the noise of anywhere from twelve to forty terminals. There were no guarantees that each station would stay connected to the database (and depending on the time of evening, response time became a real factor) or that every student would keep up with the searches even if there were no technical glitches. Roving assistants were necessary. Rovers—all of them were graduate students in the School of Library and Information Sciences pulled from the UGL reference desk staff and instruction assistant staff—assisted by walking up and down the rows of terminals helping students keep pace or clear up their mistakes.

At the beginning of the session, each student received a tip-sheet of LEXIS/NEXIS commands and sample limiters, and a search outline—a list of the exact searches as they were performed during the hands-on session (see Appendix). The search outline sheet was developed after the very first night of this program. With so many people trying to follow along, someone was bound to get sidetracked or fall behind; these sheets, along with the rovers, helped keep the students on track. Reference staff also noticed many students clutching the search outline sheet and using it to recreate the hands-on session on their own, or using it as a guide as they did the homework assignment a few weeks later.

We decided that it was important to make the students aware of two factors during the hands-on sessions: our educational contract with LEXIS/NEXIS, so that they understood the difference in cost and functionality between that and a corporate account, and cautions about down time and slow response times and the importance of starting early. We also spent time explaining the difference between a publicly-held and a private company, and what that difference means in terms of getting information about the company.

THE HOMEWORK ASSIGNMENT

In the fall of 1995, the third component, a homework exercise, was added to the program (see Appendix). This, like the tutorial exercise, was reproduced in the X220 workbook that all students in the class must purchase. The assignment was simple and straightforward: choose a company you're interested in, and use LEXIS/NEXIS to find recent news stories on the company or its field, one annual report, two consecutive quarterly reports, and general (directory) information about the company. Print off what you find, then do some rudimentary analysis of the information.

The assignment, then, served as a review of all the strategies and concepts covered in the tutorial and during the hands-on session. It also required that students analyze and evaluate the information they retrieved. This fed into the goal of X220, which is to give students a sense of business "culture" as well as to expose them to information they need as they prepare for job interviews.

At least one month was allowed for the students to complete the homework exercise. This was due to the limited number of LEXIS/NEXIS connections available throughout the libraries. The UGL has four stations, there are also four in our Research Collections Library, two in the Journalism Library, one in the Government Publications Department, and one in the Business Library. Twelve stations may be adequate for everyday demand, but when 800 students have assignments which require the use of this one database, staggered due dates stretched over a longer period of time was the only solution. Use of the LEXIS/NEXIS in the Undergraduate Library, in fact, became so heavy that a sign-up sheet allowing students only half-hour sessions when others were waiting had to be employed.

The only real modification made to the assignment over the semesters occurred after it had gone to press because we realized what it meant for as many as 800 students to print off, screen-by-screen, two news stories, an annual report, two consecutive quarterly reports, and directory information from LEXIS/NEXIS. Now students are required to print off just the first page of each document to turn in with the assignment. We also encourage downloading to disk and doing the printing and analyzing off-line.

One of the most significant aspects of the program was the fact that both exercises, the tutorial worksheet and the homework assignment, were graded. This gave an extra incentive to students to attend the sessions and turn in all paperwork. The associate instructors from the School of Business took charge of taking attendance at all the sessions and grading all the exercises. If the librarians had been asked to grade 800 x 2 papers, we would have seriously reconsidered our involvement in this program!

EVALUATION

Evaluation is an area in which we could have done more. The feedback which we received from X220 instructors, while informal, was that the students who handed in the homework assignment did well. We did not devise any pre- or post-tests to determine whether students really learned the concepts we tried to teach.

Over the course of the semester, students who came to the Reference Desk asking for assistance with LEXIS/NEXIS said that they found the instruction helpful, but simply can't remember it all. They usually need only a quick review to get the ball rolling again. Observation indicates that their searches are not sophisticated but they achieve the results they want in a reasonable amount of time. Since they are for the most part occasional users, this may be the best we can hope for. We do include a "debriefing" for all librarians and rovers, as well as Reference Desk staff who assist with the homework assignment. The overall consensus has always been positive.

"VOICE OF EXPERIENCE"

We have a few suggestions for those who might be embarking upon such a collaborative program. They are chiefly related to the hands-on sessions and surrounding technical issues. These, we discovered, are the most stressful areas.

For the hands-on sessions:

- *Use simple searches.* Identify a (publicly held) company that is not HUGE so that you can avoid the dreaded "your search will retrieve more than 1000 records" message. Big searches slow down response time.
- *Stick to the basics.* Unless you are doing an intermediate or advanced LEXIS/NEXIS workshop, keep it simple. We knew that we could not turn out expert or even intermediate searchers in just 30 minutes. Our hope was that we'd turn out informed end users.
- *Plan alternatives in case the system crashes.* We never completely crashed, but we did have some tense moments (20 out of 40 connections dumped). We didn't plan alternatives, we didn't even have overhead transparencies or the equipment to use them if we did. The instructors managed to get through the sessions by having students watch screens over someone else's shoulder. In the case of a complete crash we all agreed that a simple review of the basic concepts, along with the strong recommendation to try the searches on their handouts before attempting the homework assignment would be the best approach.
- *The later the better!* Depending on the time of evening, response time becomes a real factor. If you can control the time of day for a LEXIS/NEXIS workshop, remember that later is better! Later in the week, later in the day. (Unless you are east of the Mississippi where earlier-before noon-might be better.) It helps to search the database when the entire North American continent is NOT in the middle of its business day.

Any time you are using technology:

- *Check your computers!* Even if you're using your own computers, something could change. Make sure all your presenters and assistants know how to reboot, what the password is, and so on.
- *Check your computers!* Especially if you're using someone else's! The first time we used the computer lab/electronic classroom in the School of Business it took three technicians two days to figure out how to configure the files so that

we could log into our LEXIS/NEXIS training accounts. The next time we used the very same computer lab we were feeling secure with the knowledge that we'd worked out the technical kinks the semester before. Unfortunately, the computers had been completely reconfigured for security reasons and running the DOS version of LEXIS/NEXIS would have meant rewriting all those files. Of course, the lab managers refused to let us do that. In our smugness we didn't even check the computers until the Friday before the Monday that all the sessions were going to start, but we got lucky. The Windows version of LEXIS/NEXIS, which was already available in the lab can also be made to work like the DOS version, so we just improvised by telling the students "don't pay attention to the buttons on the screen, don't touch the mouse!" Why, you ask, didn't we just use the Windows version? Because in the library we were still using a few 286s to provide access to LEXIS/NEXIS and because the Business School's Electronic Classroom, although it has all sorts of great connections, is used for training sessions only, and is not available for general use.

- *Involve technical staff from the beginning*. We're lucky because our department's Electronic Systems Coordinators over the years have all been very interested in bibliographic instruction and have participated in all our instructional efforts. There is simply no way we could have undertaken this particular program without working closely with whoever is in this position. We've also maintained a good relationship with the library's Automation Office staff; this is especially important because the Electronic Systems coordinator in the Undergraduate Library, although a "techie" compared to the rest of us, has traditionally come from a library background rather than a computer background. He or she serves as a trainer and interpreter for us, but is not necessarily well versed in all the intricacies of computers or networks. Although they have not been able to "fix" everything for us, the technical staff have provided us with options and if policy and reality made something possible, they've done it even if it meant shifting their priorities to put our project on the top of the list. Keeping all the technical staff informed about what we're doing and why we're asking all those strange questions makes our project their project.

CONCLUSION

The LEXIS/NEXIS instruction project with the School of Business was a positive venture in a number of ways despite the fact that it will be ending, at least in the way which we have just described. Its success was due to the efforts and teamwork of a number of people working within both units. For those of us in Undergraduate Library Services, the project served as a team-building exercise which brought us together in new contexts and gave us a common goal in which we all had a stake. It also extended beyond our unit to include technical staff from throughout the Libraries. Countless hours were spent explaining to the technicians why certain things had to be certain ways, and they, too, began to feel a responsibility that we had not previously seen. To this day, we reap the benefits of their participation, and feel comfortable calling them at a moment's notice.

Another benefit of the project was that the staff learning curve for LEXIS/NEXIS was greatly enhanced by our need to quickly become proficient teachers of the system. Although all staff received training when we first made LEXIS/NEXIS available in the Undergraduate Library Reference area, there's nothing like having to teach something to make one learn it in greater detail. Prior to this project, only one or two of our seven-member staff felt comfortable on LEXIS/NEXIS. Now all of us do.

Yes, it was a lot of work. Yes, it involved meetings, phone calls, e-mails, and last-minute stress. But on the whole, we all learned far more than we anticipated, we made friends across campus and throughout the library, and we gained confidence in our ability to take on future projects with just as much success. The once-scary idea of teaching 800 students in four nights NOW seems as routine as working at the Reference Desk or leading a library tour—well, almost.

APPENDIX

LEXIS/NEXIS TUTORIAL EXERCISE

Name: _____ X220 Section:_____

Directions: The LEXIS/NEXIS tutorial may be accessed on any terminal that is connected to the campus network. From the main gopher menu select the following: 1) Library and Research Services, 2) IUB Libraries News, Hours, Directories, and Services, then 3) Getting Started: A Beginner's Guide to IUB Libraries. Select LEXIS/NEXIS tutorial and read each file. Then complete the tutorial.

Answer the following questions about LEXIS/NEXIS:

1. Name three LEXIS/NEXIS libraries.

_____ _____ _____

2. What file in the NEWS library is limited to articles from the last two years?

_____

3. List five KEY WORDS which you might combine together to search LEXIS/NEXIS for information about working for Proctor and Gamble.

_____ , _____ ,

_____ , _____ ,

_____

4. What does "full-text database" mean?

_____

5. What is the most common problem people encounter when searching the LEXIS/NEXIS database?

_____

6. What is the TRUNCATION symbol used in LEXIS/NEXIS? _____

(turn over)

7. What does the "W/10" mean in the following search?

    Interviewing w/10 candidates w/10 jobs w/10 microsoft

_____

8. What does "atleast10" mean in the following search?

    Atleast10(salary and nike)

_____

9. List three SEGMENTS used in LEXIS/NEXIS:

_____, _____, _____

On the line below, show how you might use one SEGMENT to construct a search for information about Hallmark Corporation.

_____

10. On the line below, construct a search for information on Martin Marietta Corporation and limit the date to September 2, 1994.

_____

11. What is the dot command to change a file? _____

    What is the dot command to go to the first page of a document?

                        _____

    What is the dot command to see the full-text of a document?

                        _____

12. How do you log off the LEXIS/NEXIS system? _____

TURN IN THIS COMPLETED EXERCISE TO YOUR X220 INSTRUCTOR.

Libraries

Bloomington, IN 47405 (812) 855-0100

Lexis/Nexis Online

Lexis/Nexis is an online, full-text database that covers news, and business, company, financial, and legal information.

The basic steps to searching are:

Steps   Examples: at flashing cursor, type precise name listed.

1. Choose a library: For list of libraries, ask at UGLS Reference Desk.
   NEWS (Library for newspapers, magazines, newswires, and newsletters.)
   GENFED (library for general legal documents, like <u>U.S. Code</u>.

2. Choose a file: **MAJPAP** (File containing major newspapers.)
   US (File of U.S. Supreme Court Opinions

3. Enter a search: [Note: Be as specific as possible by using segment searching and operators
   to narrow and focus the search. See information below about planning a search.]
   subject (police and teenagers) <—segment searching
   market share and laptop computers <—free-text search

4. Viewing and saving documents: Use appropriate dot commands (see reverse side of this sheet)

Hints in planning a good search:
Because Lexis/Nexis includes the fulltext of most documents, it is imperative that the search is as precise as possible.

Choose search words: What is the **market share** of **laptop computers** within the
computer industry?

Connect search words by using **AND, OR,** And **W/n** (n = any number 1 to 255):
Market share **and** laptop computer   physician **or** doctor
(bill **or** president) **w/3** clinton

Simplify words with universal characters (!) and (*):
libr!   **Finds:** librarians, librarian, libraries, library
wom*n   **Finds:** women, woman

Restrict a search by segment:
Hlead (bosnia and bomb!)   **Company** (Apple Computer)
Byline (sawyer)   **Subject** (teenagers)
Atleast10(generation x) Search terms must appear at least 10 times in the article

Restrict a search by date:
subject (television and children) **and date is 9/19/1993**
name (evan w/3 bayh) **and date aft 3/1/1994**
High definition television **and date bef 6/21/1990**
Wom*n and media and date (**aft 6/1/1992 and bef 12/31/1992**)

Lexis/Nexis Commands

Searching:	.ns	New search
	.cf	Change file
	.cl	Change library
	Alt<F10>	Stop Search
Viewing Formats:	.fu	Full text
	.kw	Kwic - 25 words around search terms
	.vk	Variable kwic - 30 words around search terms
	.ci	Citations
	.se	Segments
	.le	Lead
Reviewing Results:	.np	Next page
	.pp	Previous page
	.fp	First page of current document
	.fd	Display first document retreived
	.nd	Next document
	.pd	Previous document
Refining Results:	m	Modify search
	.fo	Enter focus feature
	.ef	Exit focus
	r	Review search strategy

Printing: Print screen by screen using the "print screen" key

Downloading: Press Alt<F2> to toggle on the downloading function

Service: .ss or shift <F1> Select Service
.es or shift <F2> Exit Service

Quitting: .so or Alt<Q>   Sign off
Alt<F10>   Stop search

[Hint: Before quitting Lexis/Nexis, type r to review your search.
Print this screen so you can quickly recall the library, file and
search strategy you used.]

IU-B 1/96 LM/CW

LEXIS/NEXIS Guided Search
X220 Hands-On Session
Spring 1996

Select a Library	**compny**
Select a File	**allnws**
Do a search, but limit it to a segment	**.se**
	hlead(at&t)
Edit the search	**and layoff!**
Modify the search	**m**
	and date aft 12/30/1995
Look at the list of citations	**.ci**
Look at the keywords in context	**.kw**
Look at a full-text document	**.fu**
Go to the first page of the document	**.fp**
Go to the next page of the document	**.np**
Look at the next document	**.nd**
Look at the first document	**.fd**
Try a new search **.ns**	
	hlead(telecom!) and telephone w/6 television and date aft 1/20/1996
Change the file **.cf**	

Select a file	**compny**	
Do a new search	**.ns**	
Do the search in the company segment		**company(williams-sonoma)**
Select group 2		**group2**
Look at the full document		**.fu**
Look at the first page of the document		**.fp**
Review the list of groups		**r**
Focus the search	**.fo**	
	hoover's	
Select group 3	**group3**	
Look at the full document		**.fu**
Page through the document		**.np / .pp**
End the focus		**.ef**
Review the list of groups	**r**	
Focus your search	**.fo**	
	form(annual report)	
Look at group 6		**group6**
Look at the citations list	**.ci**	
Look at the first document	**1**	
Look at the first page of the full document	**.fu**	
	.fp	
End focus	**.ef**	
Focus	**.fo**	
	form(10-q)	
Select group 6	**group6**	
Look at the citations list	**.ci**	
End focus	**.ef**	
Do a new search	**.ns**	
	company(microsoft) and form(10-q) and date is 1995	
Look at group 6		**group6**
Look at the citations list	**.ci**	

X220 LEXIS/NEXIS ASSIGNMENT

Name: _____   Instructor: _____

Due date: _____

Directions:

Complete this assignment using the Lexis/Nexis system. Terminals are found at the following locations on the Bloomington campus: 1) Undergraduate Library- 3 terminals, 3 printers, 2) Research Collections- 3 terminals, no printers, 3) Business/SPEA Library- 1 terminal, no printer, 4) Journalism Library- 2 terminals, 1 printer. **You may download from Lexis/Nexis onto a formatted disk, so be sure to take one with you when you do this assignment.**

Note: Lexis/Nexis is occasionally down; do not wait until the last minute to do this exercise!. You may sign up in advance for a Lexis/Nexis session. Sign-up sheets are posted at the terminals, and sessions are limited to 30 minutes when other users are waiting.

For this exercise, you must select a publicly-owned company and track it for a two-week period of time.

Name of company: _____

1. Print off a copy of the company's 1993 annual report. Write you name on it and turn it in with this assignment.

Answer the following questions:

How many shares are currently held for this company?

As of what date?

What was the source for this data?

2. Print off information regarding the company's ownership. Write your name on it and turn it in with this assignment.

Answer the following questions:

How many vice-presidents does the company have?

Who is the Chief Executive Officer and what is his/her address?

What are the subsidiaries of this company?

How many employees does the company have?

3. Print and analyze two consecutive quarterly reports for your company. Write your name on them and turn them in with this assignment.

Answer the following question:

What changes are noted between the two quarters?

4. Find a newspaper article about the company. Print the article, write your name on it, and answer the following questions in a brief paragraph:

a) What is the main theme of the article?

b) How does this theme relate to the quarterly reports you printed?

c) What major changes have been reported in the last two weeks?

5. Find a magazine article or wire report about the company. Print the article, write your name on it, and answer the following questions in a brief paragraph.

a) What is the main theme of the article?

b) How does this theme relate to the quarterly reports you printed?

c) What major changes have been reported in the last two weeks?

BE SURE TO TURN IN ALL PRINTOUTS WITH THIS COMPLETED ASSIGNMENT.

INTEGRATING LEARNING COMMUNITIES AND LIBRARY INSTRUCTION IN THE VIRTUAL ENVIRONMENT

Michael Bertsch, Randy Burke Hensley, and Margit Misangyi Watts

ABSTRACT

The emerging virtual environment for teaching and learning is providing new opportunities for collaboration and participation among students, teachers, and librarians. Computer technology is providing a platform for creating interaction among learners that harnesses information access, online discussion, and global Internet connectivity to concepts of learning communities, the power of personal narrative, and critical thinking. The University of Hawaii's Rainbow Advantage Program is an example of a new type of electronic classroom that uses a MOO, a multi-user domain (MUD) object oriented, to build skills in information use and evaluation as it links students to an environment requiring knowledge of database structure and navigation.

THE ROLE OF TECHNOLOGY IN ESTABLISHING THE RAINBOW ADVANTAGE LEARNING COMMUNITY

A recent posting to the Learning Communities listserv (learn-com@vm.temple.edu) suggested that three very basic criteria are at the foundation of a true learning community. First, learning communities are not boring. Second, no one in a learning community is out to teach anything because that would make it a teaching community. Third, if it is has been done before, it isn't a learning community. As with most statements made tongue in cheek, there is much truth to these criteria. A learning community should indeed be a place that offers a supportive academic environment which promotes a sense of belonging and shared values. It should be a place where students are actively engaged in education with their faculty. Students should be full participants in the educational process, and the educational environment should foster open-ended inquiry.

Thus, the focus of a learning community is on collaboration, and the image of the teacher as bearer of knowledge is replaced by the collaborative teacher/learner model. This model allows for an environment which encourages students to be creative, original thinkers who ask questions and continually analyze and evaluate their own learning. A learning community should do more than simply engaging students and faculty in a cooperative effort to learn content, pass a test, or do assignments. It should affirm the right of each student to succeed and be dedicated to personal education and development.

In light of the creation of this kind of environment, attention must be given to the driving "narratives" of the students. Neil Postman, in his recent work *The End of Education*, suggests that we no longer have an adequate narrative to inspire our educational process. To Postman, the historical narratives of creating good American citizens or consumers, or even education to serve the American dream, no longer work. He strongly suggests that we must find a new reason to believe in education. He is most dissatisfied with the "god of technology" as the new fix. Postman warns against educators flocking to technology as the savior of all the ills of education. After all, technology is but a tool and we must use it instead of being used by it.

For purposes of the project collaboratory within the Rainbow Advantage Program, technology has indeed been integrated as a tool on a number of levels. The philosophy of connecting students with each other, with the world, ideas, and life underlies the entire project. Students are encouraged to think globally and act locally. In order to do so, they are connected to the wider community in a number of ways. First, they link with K-12 students from around the Hawaiian Islands and work together on public museum exhibits. Second, the students participate in a year-long community service project. Third, students develop the ability to define information needs, assess information quality, and determine knowledge through a year-long series of integrated instruction and learning activities that involve library and Internet resources. A librarian is an integral member of the learning community. Finally, students become members of a virtual community on Walden Pond MOO.

THE ROLE OF MOOS AS VIRTUAL INSTRUCTION

A MOO is a Multi-User Domain (MUD) Object Oriented (see Appendix). This Internet platform is a programmable database of networked text files which, when taken collectively, create a virtual educational environment (VEE). The platform is based on software developed by Pavel Curtis and Xerox Corporation, called a MOO core. It manages each user's input and inserts the pieces of text developed by them. The smallest pieces of text help create the illusion that people are having a conversation instead of typing to each other. What is important about this kind of environment is the opportunity it offers for text immersion.

One way to understand the value of text immersion is to understand that fluency derives from facility and familiarity. Students participating on Walden Pond are immersed in many forms of text, sometimes following grammatical conventions and at other times allowing student creativity to determine form and content. The key aspect of student participation is that, at all times, students are practicing how to communicate ideas through text. Each language-use situation requires evaluation of the context at hand which further enriches a student's repertoire of context. The enrichment is magnified when used on a VEE because the responses to student-generated text are from peers around the world. The collaboration then becomes truly global. VEEs bring both students and experts together effortlessly in a virtual learning community.

While writing on Walden Pond, students acquire critical thinking, collaboration, and writing skills through dialogue. The opportunity to create a safe educational environment for learning about self and others through communication is perhaps the most dynamic benefit of a MOO.

INTEGRATING LIBRARY INSTRUCTION

Incorporating library information skills into a learning community and virtual educational environment is first accomplished by the incorporation of a librarian. The librarian changes his or her role from teacher to participant learner. As with all instructors who participate in learning communities, it is usually obvious that the librarian knows things, has mastered skills, and understands issues better than some students. However, it is not the knowing that is the proof of expertise but the ability to connect knowledge and skills meaningful to others. The librarian is not an occasional visitor to a group of students but is an ongoing resource in the actual as well as the virtual educational environment. The librarian regularly connects with students by means of e-mail and the MOO. Walden Pond has a virtual library where the librarian has established hours for online interaction. The librarian organizes seminars for groups of students to log on at the same time for instruction and discussion. The librarian also builds skills through presentation and practice in the actual classroom and in meetings with individuals and groups. The virtual avenues for participation with students assist the librarian in managing the increased time required to engage in a learning communities approach.

For the VEE the library skills built must be consistent with the course inquiry, and those skills must be built in a sequential manner. In fact, the participant learner approach facilitates the ordering of skills building into distinct components conducive to student-perceived relevance and learning readiness. Furthermore, course inquiry is regularly shifting because of the focus on student interests. The fifty-minute, course-related session model is irrelevant and damaging to the VEE approach. The students develop their own agenda for learning, and the librarian is ready to participate in skills acquisition by means of a number of mechanisms. Traditionally, instruction librarians approach library skills with a design that introduces broad information concepts linked to specific details of database system use. What is instead required in a VEE is dynamic instruction rather than central, standard competency-based instruction. Surprises and changes must be relished with the total repertoire of skills-building techniques held at the ready by the librarian.

Database as metaphor is the encompassing concept for library skills in a VEE. Throughout the learning process, the understanding of database structure and navigation inform student learning. The virtual environment can be understood as a database created for a purpose, functioning in particular ways, producing results in particular forms. The consistencies among purpose, function, and form are the linkages for use of specific resources. The virtual is a rendition of the physical. Illuminating for students how the virtual library database relates to physical library resources facilitates familiarity and competence. This illumination targets the relationship between record content, searching strategies, and the structure and form of the physical source. It does not strictly resort to the position of the call number in the record and where that item is on the library shelf as the sole relationship between the virtual library and the physical library. For instance, exploring the contents of a database to learn how the database is searched produces enhanced learning transfer among databases. Another strategy is providing a perception that the online catalog is a composite of sites in the physical library that can be recombined for specific needs just as one can retrieve books from a variety of shelves and reorganize them in keeping with a student's strategy for using them.

The World Wide Web offers dynamic examples for the use of database as metaphor. Working with students to see Web pages as records, Web links as additional key words, controlled vocabulary, or cited references can create a holistic understanding of the nature of information, the nature of discourse, and the relationship between the virtual and physical worlds.

A final piece of the overall approach to library instruction in a VEE requires integration of electronic technology skills. Creating relationships between e-mail, MOO, library online catalogs, and Web skills is vital. For students to see the common characteristics between these pathways on the Internet is to greatly facilitate learning and application to new information needs. It is the need to expertly apply previous learning to new situations that is the single most crucial element of the dynamic of a successful learning community.

Virtual education environments and especially the MOO component are being increasingly experimented with as platforms for virtual universities, electronic classrooms, and electronic schools. It is clear that some version of these experiments will become established as an aspect of the larger configuration of education. Libraries must begin experimenting with these virtual environments if they wish to become even more relevant as dynamic components of teaching and learning. Furthermore, the increased attention being given to learner-driven education requires that instruction librarians become learning librarians, entering into the educational process not as actual sages but as virtual participants.

APPENDIX

MOO Commands

Command	What Happens
Talking to Others	
"Hello	You say, "Hello"
to Sam Hello	You say [to Sam], "Hello"
page Sam Hello	You page privately with "Hello"
:smiles	(your character) smiles
Assessing Information	
look	Displays the room's description
look Sam	Displays Sam's description
@info Sam	Displays Sam's information file
@who	Displays people and locations
read note3	Displays contents of note3
@details	Lists room's details
look (detail name)	Displays (detail)'s information

| help | Displays help list |
| help (subject) | Displays (subject)'s help file |

Movement

Room 2 A	Move to adjacent Room 2 A
@go #364	Move to room #364
@join Sam	Join Sam

Virtual Educational Environments

Walden Pond MOO	telnet olympus.lang.arts.ualberta.ca 8888
Athena University	telnet athena.edu 8888
PSCS MOO	telnet speakeasy.org 7777

Web Pages

| Walden Pond MOO | http://www.ualberta.ca/~walden/walden.html |
| Athena University | http://www.athena.edu |

NOTES AND REFERENCES

1.   Branch, Katherine and Carolyn Dusenbury. *Sourcebook for Bibliographic Instruction*. Chicago: ACRL, 1993.

2.   Chappell, Virginia A., Randall Hensley, and Elizabeth Simmons-O'Neill. "Beyond Information Retrieval: Transforming Research Assignments into Genuine Inquiry," *Journal of Teaching Writing* 13, nos.1-2 (1994), pp. 209-224.

3.   Gardner, Howard. *Frames of Mind*. New York: Basic Books, 1983.

4.   Heatherington, Madelon E. *Outside-In*. Glenview, IL: Scott, Foresman, 1971.

5.   Leonhardt, Thomas W., ed. *"LOEX" of the West: Teaching and Learning in a Climate of Constant Change. Foundations in Library and Information Science*, v. 34. Greenwich, CT: JAI Press, 1996.

6.   Perelman, Lewis J., *School's Out: Hyperlearning, the New Technology, and the End of Education*. New York: William Morrow, 1992.

7.   Postman, Neil, *The End of Education: Redefining the Value of School*. New York: Knopf, 1995.

8.   Rawlins, Jack, The Writer's Way. Boston: Houghton Mifflin, 1987.

9.   Smith, Frank, *Understanding Reading: a Psycholinguistic Analysis of Reading and Learning to Read*. Hillsdale, NJ: Lawrence Erlbaum Associates, 1986.

10.   Solomon, Robert C. and Jon Solomon, *Up the University: Recreating Higher Education in America*. Reading, MA: Addison-Wesley, 1993.

USING THE INTERNET TO LINK STUDENTS AND EDUCATORS AND TEACH LIBRARY LITERACY SKILLS

Margaret R. Zarnosky and John W. Tombarge, Jr.

ABSTRACT

The World Wide Web provides an electronically-based learning environment to support library/information literacy instruction at the classroom level. Virginia Tech's University Libraries initiated a pilot program with the Department of Hospitality and Tourism Management to incorporate such literacy skills into the curriculum. An undergraduate survey course, HTM 1414-Introduction to the Hospitality Industry, served as the basis of this program, which included a library exercise and a research paper. This paper addresses each of the components of the program, from inception to initiation to evaluation, as well as the potential which exists to employ the concept in teaching advanced searching skills in higher-level subject courses.

INTRODUCTION

One of the challenges facing college students today is the pressure to effectively process information. As a result, many students rely on computers to facilitate the retrieval, reorganization and presentation of information. However, they often fail to make the connection about the interrelationships of the sources upon which they rely in an electronic environment.[1] To develop students' information literacy skills, teaching faculty and librarians are entering into collaborative projects.

Information literacy has been defined many ways. This concept has been viewed as being similar to the research process in which individuals successfully define, locate, assess, select, organize, and present information, thus filling an individual need.[2] Others scholars suggest that an additional important step is to employ critical thinking methods to integrate information gained through research into daily problem-solving efforts.[3] With the widespread use of computer technology in homes, workplaces and schools, the definition of information literacy takes on new meanings and greater importance. Shapiro and Hughes present the concept of developing an information literacy curriculum for higher education which involves seven dimensions of literacy. These dimensions range from *tool literacy* (the ability to understand, recognize and use the physical/practical elements of information literacy, such as computers and networks) through *research* and *publishing literacy*. They end with the concept of *critical literacy*, defined as "the ability to critically evaluate the intellectual, human and social strengths and weaknesses, potentials and limits, benefits and costs of information technologies."[4] We view information literacy as a combination of these things. To us, students who are information literate are able to identify, search and evaluate information resources (print or electronic), process the appropriate information, and present the findings in new and meaningful ways.

THE WWW AND ITS ROLE IN INFORMATION LITERACY AND INSTRUCTION

Colleges and universities are relying upon the Internet as a major means of locating and exchanging information. While faculty members have utilized FTP sites and e-mail to locate and exchange information, they are now using them to complement lectures and text materials. Faculty members are also using newsgroups and listservs as a communication vehicle in their courses. For instance, at Virginia Tech, professors have the option of having the campus Computing Center create class listservs

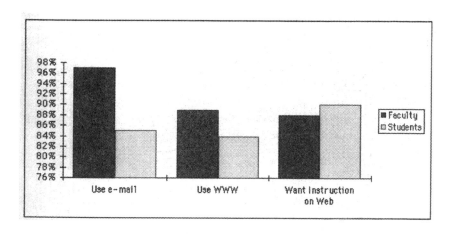

Figure 1. Internet Use

automatically from their class rosters. All students receive e-mail accounts as part of the matriculation process, which they keep throughout their studies at Virginia Tech. Thus, listservs become a standard way of continuing discussions outside the classroom.

In some cases, a major portion of the course is presented over the Internet, as a form of "Cyberschool."[5] Presenting courses or substantial portions of courses over the Internet is now a viable alternative for Virginia Tech faculty members. A recent study by the University Libraries at Virginia Tech found that approximately 85 percent of students[6] as well as 97 percent of all faculty[7] currently use e-mail (see Figure 1). The study also revealed that over 80 percent of faculty[8] and students[9] use the World Wide Web (WWW), and over 85 percent of faculty[10] and students[11] want to receive instruction on using information resources through the WWW. By placing instructional materials on the WWW, the University Libraries are able to make information conveniently available to over 90 percent of faculty who are connected to the Internet from their offices,[12] and over 80 percent of students who maintain computers in their place of residence (see Figure 2).[13] Internet access is also readily available in the library and campus computer labs.

Based upon the above data, we have found that the Internet is an attractive way of easily and effectively reaching large numbers

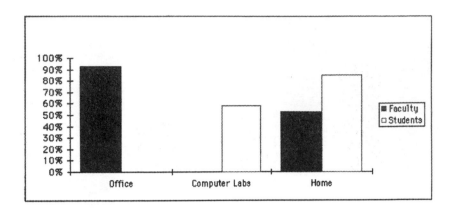

Figure 2.   Location of Computers

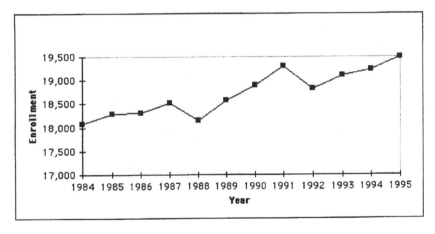

Figure 3.   Undergraduate Enrollment

of library users, and that both the students and faculty are comfortable with this technology. This is particularly attractive in
light of the fact that the student body has grown by almost 1,500
students since 1984, and the number of librarians serving these
students has dropped from over fifty to less than forty in this
same time period (see Figures 3 and 4).

Providing instructional materials on the Internet is not new to
libraries, and many excellent examples exist that can serve as

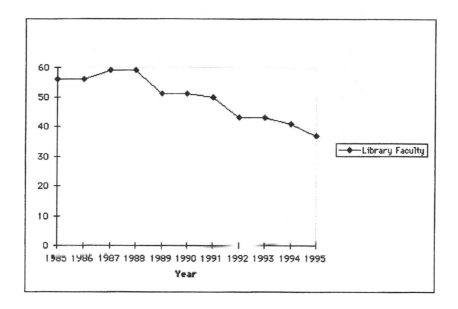

Figure 4. Librarians

models for the development of programs to meet the needs of the individual library or institution. Four programs currently available are:

1. Beginning Research On Any Topic from Stanford University Libraries.[14] This site provides a general overview of the research process, applicable to virtually every topic, and not dedicated to one specific course. Using the metaphor of preparing a gourmet meal from scratch (as opposed to ordering a prepackaged fast-food dinner), the pages at this site guide researchers through the information-seeking process, from start to finish.

2. Library Research at Cornell: A Hypertext Guide to The Seven Steps of the Research Process.[15] This site provides a general introduction to the research process at Olin*Kroch*Uris Libraries. Following a seven-step outline, students are introduced to a simple and effective strategy

for finding information for a research paper, writing the paper, and documenting the sources.

3. Introduction to Library Research for Psychology Class at MIT.[16] In contrast to the general overview available at Stanford, the MIT Libraries have developed a series of pages to support students in the Introduction to Psychology course. Students use an online form to register for a session with a library staff member, and information is provided in the HTML pages and course syllabus on how to contact the Library for assistance. The library assignment itself is available as an online form, which is sent to the librarian who taught the review session. The assignment directs students through the process of researching journal articles in the field of psychology, using *PsycLit* or *Psychological Abstracts*.[17]

4. CIStudio at Rensselaer Polytechnic Institute.[18] Rensselaer takes the concept of online instruction seen at MIT and takes it a step further. As noted in the course synopsis, "Chemical Information is a WWW-based required course jointly designed and taught by chemistry faculty and librarians...[and] integrates practical library exercises and 'hands on' experience at high-performance, networked workstations."[19] The program includes graded homework assignments, a final project, and classroom participation. The program begins with an orientation to the library, and builds from there. Course assignments are designed so that the students search both print and electronic tools, evaluate the results and save them to a file.[20] As at MIT, assignments are available as online forms, which the students submit for grading.

INTRODUCTION TO HOSPITALITY AND TOURISM MANAGEMENT (HTM 1414)

Evolution of HTM 1414

Hospitality and Tourism Management (HTM) is a relatively small department at Virginia Tech, with only about 250 full-time students. The introductory survey course, Introduction to

Hospitality and Tourism Management (HTM 1414), serves as a major recruiting device for the department. This course is offered fall and spring semesters with a typical enrollment of between 85 and 120 students every semester. By its nature, HTM is interdisciplinary, and many students take this class as an elective, particularly students from the human nutrition and business programs. However, it is a required prerequisite for upper-level courses in the department, and thus a good starting point for introducing students to the resources designed specifically for this field. The course emphasizes the practical aspects of HTM by incorporating field experiences and guest speakers, and the librarian is included as one of the guest speakers.

The initial invitation to speak in the class came as part of the evolution of a larger project to get the library more involved with the instructional mission of the university. The location of the librarian's primary office was then moved from the library to the college. Although the same librarian had been working as liaison with the department for three years, it was not until the librarian "moved in" that professors began to re-examine the role of research in their assignments. In the case of HTM 1414, initially the librarian was invited to come in and spend twenty minutes introducing students to library research. Since twenty minutes in the classroom was not long, most of the instruction about HTM sources was provided through a handout, while the class presentation focused on the process of finding articles in the library.

The professor noted an improvement in the quality of sources used by the students in their research papers, and was motivated to continue with the project given that one of the papers won an award from the Virginia Department of Tourism. Thus, the following semester the librarian and professor began discussing the problems students have in the research and writing process. Several key factors were identified as problems:

- recognizing sources by type of publication: popular, trade, or scholarly
- determining where to start looking for information from trade and scholarly sources and where the strength lies in each type of publication

- evaluating the content of the source and the author's credentials for writing the article
- understanding APA citation style
- understanding the library and its organization

As HTM 1414 is a prerequisite for upper-level courses, it was hoped that future instruction at the upper levels could focus on more complicated research tools used by students in the department without having to go back and teach the basics of library research in each class. This raised some concern about transfer students, who may not take this course, or returning students who took the course a few years ago, but are returning to complete a degree. The instruction would need to be available for these students as well. After examining many alternatives, the librarian and the instructor decided to use the WWW as the basis for the tutorial.

In the fall of 1995 the instructional materials were placed on the World Wide Web (see Appendix) and the class presentation time expanded to thirty minutes. The class presentation focused on how to get to the Web pages and retrieve the class handouts and library exercise for which they could earn extra credit. The Web pages allowed the students to easily contact the librarian through e-mail links if they had any questions about their library exercise or their research. It was found that by using the Web, students were much more likely to seek the librarian out or approach him when available, even at local stores or restaurants. An informal evaluation of the class revealed improvements needed for the next term.

The success of the class in the fall term resulted in the instructor allowing fifty minutes (one class period) for the library portion of the class. This allowed for instruction in the more complicated aspects of the assignment, as well as instructing the students on how to locate and use the Web pages. The library exercise became a requirement, rather than an optional extra credit assignment. A formal evaluation of the instruction was completed and results showed that the students believed that the Web should be used to deliver instruction of this type and that the instruction did prepare them for their term paper (see Figure 5).

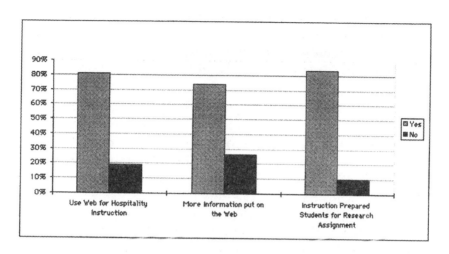

Figure 5. Student Recommendations

Goals of HTM 1414

From its inception, the HTM 1414 instruction program was designed to accomplish three goals; the first and most heavily-stressed was to provide an introduction to the research process. This goal was wide-ranging and included four facets. First, HTM 1414 was meant to provide an orientation as to how to use indexes, including the indexes that are designed specifically to support hospitality research, and how to interpret citation information found in these indexes. Second, the program was designed so students could learn how to use VTLS (the online catalog) to discover the proper location of the journals in the library. Third, as the physical layout of the Newman Library is not always intuitive to users, students learned how to physically locate journal titles. The fourth and perhaps most important facet, HTM 1414 was designed so that students could learn how to evaluate sources of information to see if they could be considered credible and/or reliable.

A second goal of the class was to introduce students to the APA style for citing their sources, as this was the format the department uses for all classes. A third and final goal of the program was to provide a general orientation to the Library, a challenge as the library component was normally taught at a location at least half a mile from Newman Library. Further, the syllabus for the course was structured so as to not allow for a second class session devoted to a physical tour of the facility.

Objectives of HTM 1414

The HTM 1414 program was designed to accomplish five objectives. First, upon the completion of the library assignment, it was intended that students could determine the appropriate indexes to use to find articles on their topic. This meant that not all of their research results could come from *InfoTrac* or *Readers' Guide,* but also from the specialized sources such as *Lodging and Restaurant Index, Hospitality Index,* and *Leisure, Recreation and Tourism Abstracts* as appropriate. Second, students would be able to locate journal articles in the Library, whether they were current or back issues, regardless of format (microfilm or print).

Third, HTM 1414 was intended to assist students in learning how to articulate the process of researching hospitality subjects. This included becoming familiar with the names of indexes focusing upon the hospitality industry, being able to interpret citations from these resources, and using VTLS to locate a call number for a journal title and determine its status and/or availability (what Shapiro and Hughes would call research literacy).[21] Fourth, after completing HTM 1414, the students were to be able to evaluate the information they were using in their research. This included being able to name the type of journal (scholarly, popular, trade) in which the articles appeared, as well as the credentials of the author. Finally, students were to be able to cite articles in the format specified by the *Publication Manual of the American Psychological Association.*

The Future of HTM 1414

When reviewing the past, present, and future of HTM 1414, two questions come to mind. The first question is "What will happen to HTM 1414 in the future?" Unfortunately, the true future of HTM 1414 as an instructional effort is unclear at the present time for at least three reasons. First, both librarians who were the most active in the program currently have new duties elsewhere. Second, the professor of the course left the department to assume new duties elsewhere in the college. Third, the college is undergoing a merger with another college in the university, which has consumed much of the faculty's time, efforts and energies, thereby making them less inclined to focus on integrating library or information literacy instruction into their courses.

While the course in its current incarnation may have an uncertain future, its modular nature as well as the concept behind HTM 1414 does have a future. This is evident in viewing where elements of the course have been incorporated elsewhere at Virginia Tech. One example of this is found in the Department of Clothing and Textiles and its survey class, CT 2604-Introduction to the Fashion Industry. The library component for this class was based upon a much simpler array of pages designed specifically to reinforce a class presentation on the steps in the research process and identify key resources necessary to complete the course assignments. Another area in which the experiences of HTM 1414 have affected library instruction efforts is visible in the business WWW pages that are used to support business research at Virginia Tech. One example of this is found in pages designed to support courses offered by the marketing department.

The marketing department at Virginia Tech developed a new required junior-level class, initiated in the fall of 1995 entitled "Marketing Skills." This class was designed to prepare marketing students for the classes they will be taking in their senior year. Skills learned in this class included using spreadsheets and presentation software, performing library research, accessing the Internet, and searching online and CD-ROM databases such as FirstSearch, Dow Jones News/Retrieval, and LEXIS/NEXIS. Four of these classes were taught by the librarian either in the library or in a computer lab and the students were required to complete assignments designed by the librarian in the use of the research resources. The WWW was used to provide the students with access to the handout materials on demand as they attempted to complete the assignment. Students always had easy e-mail access to the librarian if they needed personal help with the assignment. A class listserv was also used for students to communicate with each other and the instructor.

The second question regarding HTM 1414 is whether or not HTM 1414 can be determined a success. Certainly the program can be said to have mixed results, especially since it was not given the opportunity to develop to its fullest potential. However, the project was successful in that the concept worked on a variety of levels. First, the program was a true example of faculty and librarians working together to integrate information literacy skills into the curriculum, in a way not seen before at Virginia Tech. Second, the program provided an opportunity for librarians to team teach in both large and small-group settings. Third, through the utilization of e-mail, the program allowed the librarian for the College of Human Resources to keep in touch with students in the course, which may or may not have been as likely through one in-class session. An additional (although unplanned) benefit of the program is the example it provides other institutions across the world as a result of availability of pages over the Internet.

CONCLUSION

A large-scale project such as HTM 1414 requires commitment of the institution and project participants due to the time required for the program to evolve. As seen in this case, personnel changes and variable funding can impact an institution, and the true potential of a endeavor such as the HTM 1414 program may never be realized. We have found where there is some question of long-term commitment to such a project, a smaller-scale program, such as that seen in CT 2604, may be more likely to succeed. In the end, as librarians and educators, it is our responsibility to remain involved in the process of teaching information literacy skills. As we have seen, teaching such skills does not have to be limited to the library building or classroom, but can be done virtually anywhere at any time, thanks to the presence and opportunities afforded by the Internet.

APPENDIX

HTM 1414 Introduction to Hospitality and Tourism Management Spring 1996

Table of Contents

Library Workshops for HTM 1414 will be held in the second floor classroom in Newman Library at the back end of the Reference area.

- Thursday 1/25/96 5:00pm
- Monday 1/29/96 3:00

The Research Process

The research process should progress through several levels before you begin drafting the paper itself.

●**Defining Your Topic:**

Before you begin your research, it is often useful to clearly define what information you are looking for. Begin by finding background information on your topic from your textbook, almanacs, encyclopedias, and other general information sources for the industry. Use this information to focus your approach so that you can write your topic as a single sentence or question. This will help you to devise a workable research plan and to explain your information needs and research problems to your professor or the librarian.

Choosing and defining a topic can and should include consideration of:
- o Subjects or topics which are interesting to you.
- o The assignment requirements and time frame available for completion.
- o What Library resources are/might be available.

●**Finding Articles:**

*Use an <u>index</u> to find citations for articles on your topic, in <u>journals, periodicals and newspapers</u>.
*Use <u>VTLS</u> to find out if the Library has these articles and locate them in the Library.

●**Evaluating Articles:**

* <u>Evaluate</u> the articles you have found on your topic.
* For articles you expect to use in your paper, record the bibliographical information needed to provide proper <u>APA citations</u>.
*As required by your assignment, locate other sources of information.

Go to...

- The top of this page.
- The Hospitality and Tourism Management Page.
- The College of Human Resources Internet Resources Page.
- The Reference Services Home Page.
- The University Libraries Home Page.

Comments or questions can be directed to John Tombarge (tombarge@vt.edu),
Business Librarian
University Libraries,
Virginia Polytechnic Institute and State University

Last Updated: January 12, 1996
URL: *http://refserver.lib.vt.edu/refhtml/subjects/HTM1414.html*

**Using the Internet
To Link Students and Educators
And Teach Library Literacy Skills**

John Tombarge and Maggie Zarnosky
June 21, 1996

Information Literacy Defined

Process of successfully:
> **defining**
> **locating**
> **assessing**
> **selecting**
> **organizing**
> **presenting**

information to fill an individual's need

 To be "Information Literate,"
a student must know how to:

> Use libraries and other resources to find information effectively
> Evaluate the information found
> Apply theory learned in class to the information found
> Use computers to manipulate and present the findings in new and meaningful ways

 What the WWW Offers as an
Instruction Tool

> Communication!
  > E-mail to communicate with classmates, the instructor, and experts not immediately available
  > Retrieval of computer files (text, image, sound, video)
  > Electronic Discussion groups bringing people together who are interested in particular topics
> "Cyberschool" (virtual classroom) capabilities
> Access to online catalogs and other databases

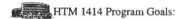HTM 1414 Program Goals:

> Introduction to the research process
  > **indexes that support Hospitality research**
  > **interpreting citation information**
  > **using VTLS to locate articles in Library**
  > **physical orientation to Library**
  > **evaluating the credibility of information sources**
> Review of APA citation style
> General orientation to the Library

HTM 1414 Course Objectives:

> Upon completion of HTM 1414 class assignment, students should be able to:
  > **select appropriate indexes for topic**
  > **locate articles in the Library**
  > **articulate process of researching hospitality subjects**
  > **determine the type of journal (scholarly, popular, trade) an article came from**
  > **evaluate the article and the credentials of the author**
  > **cite articles using APA format**

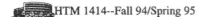HTM 1414--Fall 94/Spring 95

➤ **Class components:**
  ➤ In-class presentation using overhead
    transparencies to outline key concepts
  ➤ Overview of Hospitality-related indexes and
    types of journals
  ➤ Emphasis on using VTLS to locate journals

HTM 1414--Fall 1995

➤ **Class components:**
  ➤ First use of HTML Pages to reinforce in-class
    presentation:
    ➤ Library Exercise developed with instructor
    ➤ Hospitality Library Resources Handout
    ➤ Using VTLS
    ➤ Types of Periodicals--Scholarly, Trade, Popular
  ➤ Emphasis of E-mail and in-person contact with
    Librarian through office/desk hours

HTM 1414--Spring 1996

➤ **Class components:**
  ➤ Additional HTML Pages:
    ➤ Overview of the research strategy
    ➤ Process of evaluating sources
    ➤ Using APA Citation style
  ➤ Handouts covering use of Netscape to navigate the
    WWW
  ➤ Review sessions in the Library
  ➤ Varying presentation formats (offline and "live")
  ➤ Library Exercise Evaluation

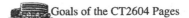Goals of the CT2604 Pages

➤ Introduce students to the research process
➤ Familiarize students with the University
  Libraries
➤ Reinforce information presented in
  classroom session

The Future of Internet-Based
Instruction

➤ HTM 1414 and related projects
➤ Using HTML/Netscape as a presentation
  medium

If not us, then who? If not now, then when?

Internet-Based Instruction

➤ For examples of Internet-Based Instruction
  at Virginia Tech and elsewhere, visit:

**http://library.nvgc.vt.edu/loexwest/
loexwest.html**

OR

**http://pam-library.cob.vt.edu/loex/
loexwest.html**

NOTES AND REFERENCES

1. Nancy Niles, "Integrating Information Skills into a Two-Year College Wildlife Technology Curriculum," In *Instruction for Information Access in Sci-Tech Libraries,* ed. Cynthia A. Steinke (New York: Haworth Press, 1993), p. 63.

2. Joyce Kirk, Barbara Poston-Anderson, and Hilary Yerbury, *Into the 21st Century: Library and Information Services in Schools* (Sydney: Australian Library and Information Association, 1990), pp. 2-3.

3. Hannelore B. Rader, "User Education and Information Literacy for the Next Decade: An International Perspective," *Reference Services Review* 24, no. 2 (1996), p. 72.

4. Jeremy J. Shapiro and Shelley K. Hughes, "Information Literacy as a Liberal Art: Enlightenment Proposals for a New Curriculum," *Educom Review* 31, no. 2 (1996) [Online]. Available: http://www.educom.edu/web/pubs/review/reviewArticles/31231.html (May 10, 1996).

5. College of Arts and Sciences, Virginia Polytechnic Institute and State University, "Welcome to Cyberschool!" [Online]. Available: http://www.cyber.vt.edu/ (August 28, 1997).

6. Virginia Tech Center for Survey Research, "Virginia Tech University Libraries Student Survey," (Blacksburg, VA: Virginia Polytechnic Institute and State University, 1996), p. 15.

7. Virginia Tech Center for Survey Research, "Virginia Tech University Libraries Faculty Survey," (Blacksburg, VA: Virginia Polytechnic Institute and State University, 1996), p. 15.

8. Ibid.

9. Virginia Tech Center for Survey Research, "Student Survey," p. 14.

10 Virginia Tech Center for Survey Research, "Faculty Survey," p. 19.

11. Virginia Tech Center for Survey Research, "Student Survey," p. 18.

12. Virginia Tech Center for Survey Research, "Faculty Survey," p. 14.

13. Virginia Tech Center for Survey Research, "Student Survey," p. 14.

14. Stanford University Libraries, "Beginning Research on Any Topic," [Online]. Available: http://www-sul.stanford.edu/depts/ssrg/adams/resea.html (October 1996).

15. Olin*Kroch*Uris Libraries, Cornell University, "Library Research at Cornell: A Hypertext Guide: Seven Steps to Effective Library Research," [Online]. Available: http://www.library.cornell.edu/okuref/research/tutorial.html (May 1996).

16. Massachusetts Institute of Technology Libraries, "Introduction to Library Research: Psychology 9.00," [Online]. Available: http://bion.mit.edu/depts/humanities/bi/900/ (November 1996).

17. Massachusetts Institute of Technology Libraries, "9.00 Library Assignment," [Online]. Available: http://bion.mit.edu/depts/humanities/bi/900/assignment.html (September 1996).

18. Folsom Library, Rensselaer Polytechnic Institute, "Chemical Information," [Online]. Available: http://www.rpi.edu/dept/chem/cheminfo/cistudio/ (March 1996).

19.   Folsom Library, Rensselaer Polytechnic Institute, "Synopsis," [Online]. Available: http://www.rpi.edu/dept/chem/cheminfo/cistudio/synopsis.html (January 1995).

20.   Folsom Library, Rensselaer Polytechnic Institute, "Homework Menu," [Online]. Available: http://www.rpi.edu/dept/chem/cheminfo/cistudio/assign/hmwkmenu.html (April 1996).

21.   Shapiro and Hughes. Online.

COLLABORATIVELY DEVELOPING AND TEACHING A MULTI-INSTITUTIONAL COLLEGE CREDIT INTERNET COURSE

Nancy Lombardo and Deleyne Wentz

ABSTRACT

This paper will explore the Internet Navigator, a one-credit college-level course developed cooperatively on the Web by academic librarians from each institution of higher education in Utah. This grant-funded project studied the potential for cooperation between institutions and tested the virtual environment for instruction. Most librarian-developers had little prior experience but evaluation showed that the five-module active learning class met its objectives and was well received by students. Many issues came up regarding administration of a virtual course and they will be covered in the paper as well as development, implementation and evaluation.

INTRODUCTION

The Internet Navigator course is a one-credit college-level introduction to the Internet delivered electronically over the World

Wide Web. It was designed, developed and implemented by a team of thirteen academic librarians, who represent each library in the Utah Academic Library Consortium (UALC). The proposal for the project was written in the spring of 1995 by Nancy Lombardo and Wayne Peay of the Spencer S. Eccles Health Sciences Library at the University of Utah (U of U). Project funding was awarded by the Utah State Higher Education Technology and Distance Education Initiative in May of 1995. In the year that followed, the course was developed and implemented. The course has now been offered at ten Utah institutions of higher education. This paper will describe the development of the course and will outline some of the issues associated with using a multi-institutional approach to implement a virtual college course.

The goals of the project, as identified in the original proposal, were:

- Implement a model for an electronically-delivered Internet course using current Internet technology
- Train students to use the Internet as a resource and equip them with the skills necessary to succeed in the electronic information environment
- Initiate an electronic, interactive learning environment that overcomes time, distance and location barriers
- Cooperatively create an electronic reference tool to be accessible statewide

The development team's intent was to create a course that would serve as an extension of library instruction so that enrolled students would learn to use the Internet as an information source. A strong emphasis was placed on presenting the Internet as a research tool. Rather than creating another course focusing on the mechanics of the Internet and its technology, the Internet Navigator concentrates on the information aspects of the Internet and encourages critical thinking. Students are taught research strategies, search techniques, and the importance of identifying criteria based on their own information needs. The need for, and the importance of, evaluation of information sources is emphasized. The class is offered as a self-paced independent study course, requiring the students to take responsibility for their own learning.

FORMING THE DEVELOPMENT TEAM

The development of the Internet Navigator began with the recruitment of volunteers from each academic library in Utah. UALC directors were very supportive of the project and the resulting development team was composed of thirteen librarians, including Nancy Lombardo as principal investigator. The members of this team were to cooperatively develop the course and serve as preceptors, or local instructors, during the first quarter or semester of implementation. A graduate student in educational psychology was employed to assist the team in project evaluation.

The preliminary outline for the curriculum had been designed for the grant proposal. Prototype documents following this outline were prepared in HyperText Markup Language (HTML) and presented to the group at the first meeting held August 25, 1995. This initial meeting presented the project goals and course outline to the development team. Discussion of goals ensued and revisions and modification were made to improve and expand the course outline and clarify the goals. A development schedule was outlined. The team's objective was to offer the course during the winter quarter beginning in January of 1996. At this first meeting, potential challenges were discussed, curriculum goals and objectives were determined, and team members volunteered to develop specific portions of the course. The afternoon was spent learning HTML techniques for effective Web page design.

A second meeting was held on October 25, 1995. The team assessed the progress of the project, examined course content, determined areas needing further development, and discussed details of course administration. By this time, the group had formed a congenial working relationship. The daylong meetings included lunch to provide an opportunity for the team members to get to know one another and better understand the varying resources at the different institutions represented.

After the first quarter of implementation, a third meeting was held to review the information gathered from student evaluations, to share observations and suggestions based on the teaching experiences of the librarians, and to discuss possible revisions and improvements. Serving as preceptors had provided the team with many insights into the benefits and problems of electronic course delivery. Issues relating to self-pacing were also discussed. Many administrative issues remain unresolved. These will be discussed later in the paper.

COURSE DEVELOPMENT

Development of the one-credit course proceeded on schedule, despite the highly variable degree of expertise among the team members. Some of the librarians involved had not been involved with course development and many were inexperienced with HTML. A mailing list was established to allow the development team to share ideas, ask questions and stay informed on the progress of the project.

The course curriculum consists of an initial student skills survey, five required course modules with assignments and quizzes, and a final project in the form of a web page demonstrating a working knowledge of the research techniques taught, and a final course evaluation. Developers took advantage of the forms capability of the World Wide Web. CGIEmail was utilized to automate most of the delivery of the student work to the appropriate preceptor. Quizzes were designed to be taken online and results displayed to the student for immediate feedback. Quiz results were automatically e-mailed to the preceptor for grading and recording. In order to implement the course at all the academic institutions in the state, technology requirements were kept to those which could be reasonably supported at all institutions.

Technical difficulties provided an interesting challenge late in the development process. The main server, which was to be the primary delivery mechanism, suffered a hardware failure and was completely unavailable for three weeks in November and December of 1995. All data on the server was lost. This crisis caused a reconsideration of the delivery methods and resulted in the course being mirrored on two additional servers. Providing access to the Internet Navigator course content on three distinct

Internet servers provided students with uninterrupted access and prevented catastrophic loss of data.

A PRECEPTOR'S VIEW OF THE PROJECT

Deleyne Wentz from Utah State University (USU) was first introduced to the project through reading the grant proposal. Although the project sounded interesting, Internet training was already available for no charge at USU, as was free online instruction. Her initial reaction was that there was not significant need and that her library would have a difficult time supporting the project due to short staffing. She was concerned about the time commitment and wondered how participants would be compensated. The proposal sounded exciting, but seemed as if it would require a full-time effort.

At the same time, Deleyne realized that librarians should be taking the lead with respect to cooperative curriculum development and in using technology to deliver instruction. She was interested in improving her HTML skills and in participating in an experimental project dealing with technology and a collaborative effort on the part of Utah libraries. The director asked her to volunteer for the project and she viewed it as an opportunity to improve her existing skills, gain new skills, and take part in a novel experiment. She brought a colleague from USU's Computer Services to the first meeting to ensure that the technical requirements of the project were acceptable for her institution. He proved a valuable resource and contributed to the project by creating a tutorial on VMS mail.

The initial meeting was very positive, and the orientation was well prepared. Essential material was presented in the form of a binder organized with information on the course curriculum and HTML techniques. Positive energy was generated and the team meshed well. Issues and challenges were clearly identified. As the meeting concluded, Deleyne had gained enthusiasm and had volunteered to develop glossaries, proofread modules and find a departmental sponsor for the Internet Navigator at USU. These were significant risks to take for a librarian with no course development and very little HTML experience.

Finding a sponsor turned out to be easier than anticipated at USU. The head of the Business Information Systems and Education Department enthusiastically agreed to sponsor the course. Developing indexed glossaries required some assistance from the Faculty Assistance Center for Teaching.

IMPLEMENTATION OF
THE INTERNET NAVIGATOR

For the targeted trial quarter or semester beginning in January of 1996, only eight of Utah's academic institutions had received approval and were able to offer the course. There was a great deal of variability in procedure at the various institutions. At the U of U and at USU, the preceptors were simply provided with a list of students enrolled. The preceptors had to find the students' phone numbers or e-mail addresses and contact each student in order to provide instructions for beginning the course.

During the first quarter, Deleyne printed all her students' quizzes and assignments. The second quarter she abandoned this practice and felt secure in grading the materials online and storing the assignments in e-mail folders. She made herself available to the students and enjoyed seeing their progress. One student started the first quarter by sending her a message saying, "BIS student needs you desperately. I am not a computer friendly person and this whole class is taking me forever to get anywhere." The same student was reluctant to join the class mailing list. When she did, she sent a message to the statewide student group saying, "Hi everyone that I have no idea who you are!" Another student signed a message saying, "Look forward to seeing you face-to-face or in cyberspace."

Grading was discussed at the development meetings. Some schools allow students to take the course Credit/No Credit, rather than for a grade. Students were encouraged to take the course for a grade to allow for more consistent evaluation criteria. Students were graded on a 100-point scale, with quizzes providing fifty, assignments adding thirty, and the final project making up the final twenty points. Preceptors agreed to grade generously during the trial quarter, as there was no precedent for this type of instruction and it was agreed that the students should not be penalized for flaws in the experimental design. Preceptors took different approaches to informing students of their grades. Some sent summaries after every quiz, while others sent scores less frequently.

Some quiz questions were ambiguous. Multiple correct answers on multiple choice questions were problematic. It was difficult to break down points into fractions. The quizzes were ultimately revised to be more straightforward and allow for more consistent grading.

Students generally seemed enthusiastic about the course. However, some students found e-mail correspondence with the preceptor to be slow. A question asked one day might not be answered until the following day, slowing their progress on the course. Some students would have liked more hands-on assistance. Other students believed the course required more time than was appropriate for one credit. However, when questioned on the actual number of hours spent, the median number was twenty-five and the mean was thirty, indicating that, in fact, students spent an appropriate amount of time for a one-credit college-level course. The independent study and self-paced aspects may have allowed procrastinators too much freedom.

There was some concern among preceptors that having the course accessible over the World Wide Web would lead to participation from multitudes of Internet users who were not registered for the class. Occasionally, unidentified quizzes did appear in the e-mail of one or another preceptor. These were generally posted to the preceptors' mailing list in case a student misdirected a quiz to the incorrect preceptor. Of the few cases of actual unregistered students submitting quizzes over the Internet, the all time favorite identified herself as Chris P. Lettuce! The chuckle was worth the bother of an extra quiz in the incoming e-mail.

There were variations in the actual administration of the course from one institution to the next. One preceptor saw all his students at registration and explained access to the course at that time. One college was required by the Continuing Education Department to hold a meeting of all students at the beginning of the quarter. Another preceptor offered four pre-arranged, optional labs for students to come together and receive face-to-face instruction and assistance with questions or problems. Preceptors spent an average of one hour per day answering the e-mail sent by their students, grading quizzes and assignments and assisting students with course work.

The traffic on the Navigator student mailing list can be heavy, but students are encouraged to use the list to chat with other students from around the state, to ask questions regarding the course and to share their experiences. The associated assignment only requests that students introduce themselves to the list. If the traffic is too much for them, they are allowed to sign off once that assignment is complete. The development team believed that this gave students a realistic idea of what to expect from mailing lists and how to deal with e-mail overload by simply unsubscribing, rather than through the use of extensive flaming.

At USU, the course started out open-ended, as it did at the other seven institutions. Four weeks into the ten-week quarter, it was noted by the head of the sponsoring department that the way the class had been configured, students needed to complete the course within the confines of the usual quarter schedule. While the change was not popular, the students adjusted their thinking and USU had more students finish the class during the trial quarter than any other institution.

The students enrolled in the first quarter of the course represented a broad range of majors. Computer fields did not dominate. Most considered themselves traditional, as opposed to non-traditional or off-campus students. A large number had little or no Internet experience, although about one-third of the students described themselves as regular Internet users. The vast majority were regular computer users, which was expected as this was an intended prerequisite for the course. The overall student rating of the course, based on the required student evaluations, was between excellent and very good. In general, the students seemed very pleased with the course and many commented on the convenience of the delivery method and schedule.

INTERNET NAVIGATOR GOALS ACHIEVED

The Internet Navigator course has been successfully implemented and has achieved the goals outlined in the original funding proposal:

1. Implement a model on-demand electronically-delivered Internet course. The on-demand course was offered and delivered over the World Wide Web using the latest Internet technology, including HTTP, HTML, forms, mailing lists, and CGIEmail. The development team met on March 29, 1996 to discuss the first quarter results of the Internet Navigator course. In general, the preceptors believe the course to have been a success. The reception by the students was very positive. The method of delivery was stated to be one of the most positive aspects of the course because of its convenience and flexibility.

2. Equip students for the electronic information environment. The students were extremely positive in their overall rating of the course. A majority found the method of learning to be convenient and claimed they were able to use their time more efficiently. Many students believed they performed better in this course because of the delivery method and the self-paced schedule. Many also believed that they performed better in their other courses due to the convenience and flexibility of the Navigator. All the modules were rated well by students and most students particularly appreciated the focus on searching, research strategies, and evaluation techniques. The final projects indicated that students did learn to adequately search and evaluate Internet information. The preceptors believe that these skills will transfer to research using other online tools and traditional resources.

3. Create a collaborative, interactive learning environment. A collaborative, interactive learning environment was created by the Internet Navigator course. The development and precepting team shared knowledge, skills and expertise to create the experimental course. These same resources were shared to teach the initial quarter or semester of the course. By collaborating and making use of

current Internet technology, the team was able to create an environment where instructors and students could talk to each other around the state, regardless of time, distance and location. Using the Navigator electronic mailing list, students were able to carry on discussions and ask questions at their own convenience. Preceptors and students could respond with answers, regardless of which student initiated a question. In this way, the statewide precepting team and student body were able to share in the responsibility for teaching and learning. When asked about their preceptor's role in the course, an overwhelming majority stated that the preceptor was very accessible and helpful.

4. Cooperatively create ad electronic reference tool to be accessible statewide. The course material serves as a teaching resource for all Utah academic institutions and all Internet users. It has been adapted for varying applications at Utah academic institutions, as well as other teaching institutions around the world. Two preceptors from Australia have joined the list of instructors. The moduclar format allows librarians to adapt segments of the course for subject specific training, as requested by academic departments or professors on campus.

ISSUES REQUIRING FURTHER INVESTIGATION

A host of issues were identified during discussion and implementation of the statewide course. It became clear over time that there were many issues that were not going to be resolved during the time frame of this project. Many issues will need to be examined by administrative entities with statewide influence. Many of these issues will be directly relevant to the planning and implementation of the proposed Western Governors University. If the virtual university is to integrate with existing higher education institutions, some of the barriers encountered by the Internet Navigator team must be resolved.

The biggest task assigned to the developers at the first team meeting was that of negotiating approval of the Internet Navigator at their respective institutions. In some cases, institutional territoriality prevented approval by curriculum committees.

Some institutions believed that existing Internet courses were adequate and that there was no need to offer an alternative, despite the experimental nature of the electronically-delivered course being proposed. Many institutions have a mechanism for offering experimental courses which allowed easy integration of the Navigator course. Other institutions found departmental sponsors. At some locations, the library itself is authorized to offer accredited courses directly. The variations in new course acceptance policies and procedures at Utah institutions is remarkable. As a result of these and other issues, the Internet Navigator was not offered during the trial quarter or semester at three of the state's colleges. A more unified and consistent approach to curriculum approval seems necessary.

A related issue for those institutions offering the course was that of variable course numbering and variable tuition. The wide range of departmental listings and course numbers made it more difficult for students to enroll at schools other than their primary institution. For example, when the course filled at the University of Utah, the logical solution for those wishing to take the course would be to enroll at nearby institutions such as Salt Lake Community College or Weber State University. The varying course numbers and departmental listings discouraged students, who believed that they would have difficulty applying the transfer credit toward their majors. However, variable tuition rates made the course more attractive at the smaller, less expensive schools. Students would naturally rather pay $50 than $220 for the same course. In a virtual university environment, this kind of inconsistency should be eliminated.

Preceptor Compensation

During the period covered by the grant funds, each preceptor was paid $500 for participating in the development process and another $500 for precepting the first quarter. Reimbursement practices were also found to vary dramatically from one institution to the next. Some institutions pay instructors $20 per student and other offer a flat fee of $400 per class. With the grant period over, the Internet Navigator continues to be offered at most of Utah's colleges and universities, but the future of the

Navigator is uncertain at institutions where no reimbursement is offered for teaching a course in addition to the librarian's regular responsibilities.

Class size was a factor in time spent precepting. The development team initially agreed that twenty to twenty-five students per preceptor would be an acceptable class size the first time the class was offered. In order to limit the time spent assisting students and grading work to an hour per day or less, this class size still seems appropriate.

Self-Pacing Issues

There was some concern over the students taking the class at institutions where it was an open-ended, self-paced independent study course. Questions arose over whether undergraduate students have enough experience and maturity to undertake self-paced independent study. There was a very high percentage of non-finishers at the institutions that allowed students to determine their own schedule. Many institutions allowed the students to take nine months or longer to complete the course if they desired. This leads to a heavy load of students as the procrastinators are added to those currently enrolled. Evaluations from those taking longer to complete the course indicate that those students appreciated the freedom to extend the course to meet their personal timetable. Those remaining enrolled in the course for nine months did not claim to have more difficulty with the material nor did they rate the course lower than those finishing in a more traditional time frame.

The course was not truly offered on demand. All institutions have rigid registration procedures that required students to register at or before the start of the quarter or semester. Grading options at some schools did not conform to an open-ended schedule. In many cases, students extending the course beyond the traditional quarter were issued incomplete (I) grades. This was not popular with the students, as it implied negligence on the student's part, which was not the case. Some schools issued a more appropriate In Progress (IP) grade, indicating that the course had not officially ended at the close of the quarter. This is another area where consistent policies and procedures across institutions would enhance the administration of multi-institutional classes.

SUMMARY

The Internet Navigator has succeeded in achieving the goals stated in the initial USHE proposal. The course was developed collaboratively by librarians representing all academic libraries in Utah and has now been offered at ten of those Utah academic institutions. Students completing the course have indicated very positive experiences and rate the class highly. Continuation of the course will be at the discretion of each institution. The Spencer S. Eccles Health Sciences Library at the University of Utah intends to continue indefinitely as the main server site for the course and Nancy Lombardo will continue to update and improve the course over time.

The preceptors and developers consider this type of library instruction to be feasible. The Internet continues to develop as a valuable research tool and libraries have the responsibility to provide Internet instruction along with traditional library instruction programs. It is believed by the development team that other kinds of library instruction could be adapted to this method of delivery in order to expand access and provide instruction to more users. Other libraries are encouraged to use the Internet Navigator course as a model for developing curriculum that is suited to the needs of their particular clientele.

REFERENCES

Internet Navigator Gateway Page: http://www-navigator.utah.edu
Grant Proposal: http://medlib.med.utah.edu/navigator/pdfs/grant.pdf
Final Project Report: http://medlib.med.utah.edu/navigator/intro/report.html

ORIENTING NEW STUDENTS USING A WORLD WIDE WEB TUTORIAL

Ann Scholz-Crane

ABSTRACT

This paper discusses the use of the World Wide Web to deliver orientation-level instruction. It focuses on the experiences of the Purdue Libraries' development of a Web-based instructional module, PLUTO (Purdue Libraries Universal Tutorial Online). It highlights cooperation among librarians, computing professionals, instructors and students during the development and implementation of the module. The general intention of PLUTO is to concentrate on a few essential skills such as beginning database searching and orienting students to the local online system. PLUTO contains an interactive tutorial and a quiz section which are integrated together through a series of hypertext links. Students complete the entire program online and orientation instructors later receive students' registration and completion information.

INTRODUCTION

In 1994, the Purdue Libraries began an effort to revamp the instruction program into a system-wide effort based on three instructional levels: orientation/beginning, middle, and subject.

In an effort to encompass more than just library skills into the program, the Libraries identified six information literacy goals for Purdue university graduates. The depth of understanding for each of the following goals depends upon the instructional level:

- User understands the role, value, and power of information in modern society
- User understands and is able to communicate his/her specific need(s) for information
- User understands that information varies in its organization, content, and format
- User can retrieve information from a variety of systems and in various formats
- User can evaluate information sources
- User understands how to organize information effectively

To achieve these goals, the Libraries began to develop the orientation/beginning level of the instruction program. Orienting the large number of entering students each year in an effective and efficient manner is one of the Libraries' greatest challenges. If these students receive a good grounding in orientation/beginning level information literacy skills, instruction at the middle and subject levels will be facilitated because students will have a solid foundation of basic knowledge on which to build the more conceptual understanding of the research process.

Given the vast number of students and the finite number of instruction librarians, not every entering student can be reached through individual class contacts. Even if this personal contact were possible, the question remains of addressing the varying levels of student knowledge in a single class session. Taking a proactive approach to improve library instruction at the orientation/beginning level, the Libraries have created a readily-accessible, interactive, learner-centered World Wide Web information literacy module, PLUTO (Purdue Libraries Universal Tutorial Online). Collaboration between librarians, computer professionals, classroom instructors, and students shaped the planning, development, and implementation of the PLUTO program.

The general intention of the Libraries' orientation/beginning level program is to concentrate on a few essential skills such as beginning database searching and orienting students to the local online system, THOR. The program is designed to whet the student's appetite by covering skills he or she is likely to use in the first year of college. A less-measurable goal at this level is to make the students more confident in their information-seeking abilities and comfortable in the academic library setting by providing an individualized, self-paced instruction experience in a non-threatening environment. PLUTO contains an interactive tutorial and a quiz section which are integrated together through a series of hypertext links. Students complete the entire program online and orientation instructors later receive students' registration and completion information.

ADVANTAGES

Easy accessibility of the Web was key to getting instructors to assign and students to use the program. The newness of the learning environment along with the ease of use built in to graphical Web browsers added to its initial charm for some instructors and students. Students do not have to invest a great deal of time becoming familiar with the software or computer hardware in order to complete PLUTO. Another great advantage is the learner-focused nature of the Web's hypertext environment. This is important at the orientation stage because of the varying levels of students' information literacy skills. Students choose their own learning paths according to their prior knowledge and experiences. In the hypertext format, testing instruments can be designed to encourage students by providing immediate responses and hypertext links to more information.

Each student's learning paths can be recorded to help the program's producers see how the program is utilized and thus how to make improvements. By recording each tutorial page accessed and the amount of time spent per page, the producers gain a better understanding of how the program is used. The information can also be used to generate statistics on the average amount of time needed to complete the program, error rates for quiz questions, and correlation between time, paths, and quiz responses.

DISADVANTAGES

As with any new environment, the producers of the PLUTO program invested a great deal of time initially becoming familiar
with how to design Web instruction, how to create Web graphics,
and how to program for the Web. Since the Web environment is
not static, producers have to constantly update their skills to take
advantage of new instructional opportunities.

For the students, one disadvantage of computerized instruction is a loss of face to face contact with librarians in the classroom. In surveying the students, some comments suggested that
while computer learning may enhance learning, it does not
replace the teaching skills of a librarian. A small percentage of
students unfamiliar with computers in general expressed frustration in accessing the program without outside help. To address
this problem, some evening help sessions were held in the
Libraries' electronic classroom. The sessions allowed students to
come and complete the program with a librarian available as a
guide to access the program and answer any questions that arose.

PLANNING

Planning for PLUTO began in February of 1995. During this
time, learning objectives were identified, program requirements
were outlined, partnerships were formed with the Libraries'
Information Technology Department and selected classroom
instructors, and funding for equipment and staff time were
secured. Interviews were conducted with Purdue librarians, classroom instructors, and student government organizations to
determine key objectives that orientation/beginning level
instruction should include. From this feedback, three primary
learning objectives were established. After completing PLUTO, a
student should be able to:

- define and formulate keyword searches on a given topic
- retrieve information on a topic from THOR, the Libraries'
  online system
- locate information from THOR within the Purdue Libraries
  System

Physical orientation to the Libraries would be available to beginning students through a number of existing programs including an audio tour of the Undergraduate Library and a videotape. Once learning objectives were identified, a basic structure for the program was outlined and program requirements were identified. Graphical software, file converters, and a color scanner were also purchased.

DEVELOPMENT

Prior to creating any PLUTO pages, an initial storyboard was created which outlined the learning concepts for each of the three identified learning objectives. In developing a basic structure and layout, the user instruction librarian took advantage of hypertext capabilities by including essential information at the top of the tree structure and providing more detail underneath. A great effort was made to keep the program self-contained and of a manageable size, focusing on only the identified objectives and avoiding the temptation to include everything students might need to know for the future. Hypertext links were provided in every portion of the program as menu links and internal text links to improve user control.

Using the storyboard created earlier, the user instruction librarian began writing the PLUTO tutorial pages and creating the format for the PLUTO quizzes. In designing each page, a basic design was followed which would ensure that each page:

- was no longer than one to two screens
- had a standardized layout
- included a navigation bar with links to menus and quiz information
- contained embedded links to other relevant portions of the tutorial

Further, the program was designed to run on its own within the Web environment and did not need any outside applications to work such as a Netscape plug-in. The user instruction librarian provided text, technical graphics, and HTML markup for all tutorial pages using a Macintosh-based text editor, graphics program, and several Web support programs such as a graphics transparency program. Tutorial screen graphics were designed by a student graphic artist employed by the Libraries.

After PLUTO's basic structure was identified, the user instruction librarian discussed the program requirements with the Libraries' network administrator and worked out a schedule for implementation of specific programs. The network administrator then selected a student programmer for the PLUTO project and began training and educating the student on programming in a Web environment. The student worked for three months during the summer of 1995. The network administrator and a student programmer now provide continuous support of PLUTO during the regular school year.

PLUTO teaches new users of the Purdue Libraries' system how to search for information in electronic databases. It focuses on keyword search concepts and methods.

Upon completion of PLUTO, the learner will be able to:

- Define and formulate keyword searches on a given topic
- Retrieve information on a topic from THOR, the libraries online system
- Locate information within the Purdue Libraries System

Learners may enter the PLUTO quiz section at any point by selecting the PLUTO quiz button located at the bottom of every tutorial screen. The quizzes included test understanding of the objectives listed above.

General Information

- About the PLUTO Project
- How to register & use PLUTO
- General information on Purdue Libraries

Enter PLUTO

Figure 1.

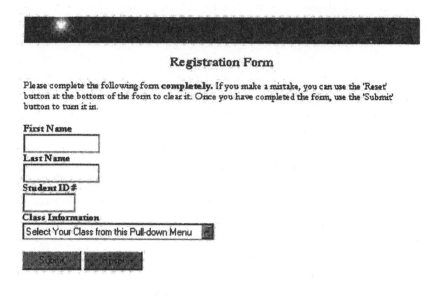

Figure 2.

The student programmers have created several CGI (Common Gateway Interface) programs which facilitate program use, tracking abilities, and instructor notification, including: online student registration; an interactive quiz with online feedback and links back to relevant tutorial pages; the ability to track students through the tutorial and quiz; and an easy method for gathering the names of students who have completed the program. Various test groups were used to work out possible programming bugs and linking errors and feedback was sought from all Undergraduate librarians.

PROGRAM

The PLUTO program is composed of two main parts: a tutorial and two quizzes. The tutorial uses the three objectives identified during the planning stages to form its primary structure (see Figure 1) and the quizzes test knowledge learned within the tutorial. Students may begin PLUTO by selecting any one of the stated objectives or by selecting to begin the quizzes immediately. In order to receive credit for completing PLUTO, students register online (see Figure 2).

Each of the three sections of PLUTO has sub-topics which the student can view within the PLUTO menu. The keyword section covers why students would use keyword searching, how to choose search terms, and how to combine keywords into phrases and concepts (see Figure 3). The online system section covers what an online system is, databases contained in the system, basic searches, and specifics on the mechanics of keyword searching in the system. The third section covers how to interpret information found on an online screen including differences between book and journal records, linking article information to holdings information, and basic view commands.

The two quizzes in PLUTO are programmed so that when a user selects a link to begin or continue a quiz, a question is randomly presented. Students must successfully complete a specified number of questions from each quiz and must complete the first quiz before the second. The number of incorrect responses does not affect the student's overall success.

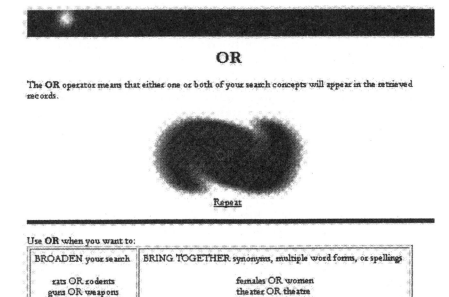

OR

The OR operator means that either one or both of your search concepts will appear in the retrieved records.

Repeat

Use OR when you want to:

BROADEN your search	BRING TOGETHER synonyms, multiple word forms, or spellings
rats OR rodents guns OR weapons	females OR women theater OR theatre

Figure 3.

The first quiz tests the basic principles of keyword searching which are explained within the tutorial. Students are provided with a topic and given three keyword search statements. From the three search statements, students choose the most effective search statement for that topic. Once the answer is selected, students are informed of their success. Regardless of the outcome, students are provided with an explanation of why search statements are acceptable, or not, with links back to relevant portions of the PLUTO tutorial. Once the student completes the specified number of questions successfully, they are informed of their success and are given the option of reentering the PLUTO tutorial or continuing to the next quiz.

The second quiz tests for comprehension of THOR screen information. Students are provided with a sample database screen and given a question about the screen information that appears, for example, which library would contain a copy of the article or book listed. The student then selects the appropriate area of the screen by clicking the mouse arrow on the piece of information which answers the question. Once an answer is selected students are informed of their success and provided with further explanation on the screen.

Upon completion of the second quiz, PLUTO prompts the student to inform his or her instructor. Students who have not already registered are provided with a link to do so. With the registration process completed, the student is prompted by a completion screen of his or her success.

IMPLEMENTATION

Getting PLUTO into the classroom is accomplished through joint efforts between the user instruction librarian, subject librarians, and course instructors. Orientation courses are the target markets for PLUTO although it has been used with a number of different courses. Subject librarians make the initial contact with the classroom instructors and arrange for the use of PLUTO. The user instruction librarian administers adding courses to the PLUTO registration information and the distribution of instructional handouts for students and instructors. Orientation instructors are encouraged to make PLUTO a regular class assignment for class credit. Some classes require a follow-up assignment after PLUTO to reinforce learning by having students find and evaluate articles on a particular topic. All courses assigning PLUTO are given instructional sheets describing PLUTO's objectives and how to access the program; in some cases a librarian will briefly introduce PLUTO to students during a regular class session or arrangements for an optional evening help session may be made. When arranging an evening help session, the user instruction librarian sets up a time when several classes can meet at once since the sessions are optional and the majority of students do not choose to attend.

PLUTO was first beta-tested by 200 students during the fall of 1995 and 200 students during the spring of 1996. This beta test gave PLUTO's administrators a chance to work through any programming bugs with a well-defined group of students. The first beta testers were first-year engineering students already familiar with using the Web. Selecting this group allowed us to see problems students had with the program and not with using the Web software.

EVALUATION

Preliminary results of a survey conducted in the spring of 1996 with over 160 senior level students indicate that over 80 percent of the students had a positive attitude towards instruction delivered via the Web. Ninety percent of these students, regardless of their previous experience in using the Web, indicated that written instructions were sufficient for accessing and using the PLUTO program. The majority of the students who completed PLUTO felt that the materials presented were clear and understandable (78%) while a slightly lower percentage rated the skills they gained by using PLUTO as good or above (65%). One reason for the lower percentage could be that since the students were senior level, many had already received some instruction, whether formal or informal, in the use of the Libraries' online system. In fact, some students made the remark that they wished PLUTO had been introduced to them earlier in their academic career. This seems to confirm the need for this type of instruction at the beginning level.

DEVELOPING AND ADAPTING A SUCCESSFUL LIBRARY USER EDUCATION PROGRAM TO MEET THE CHALLENGES OF TECHNOLOGICAL CHANGE

Fred Roecker

ABSTRACT

Confronted by the information explosion, declining budgets, reduced staff, and ever-changing technology, how does the library of a large public university educate students in information-seeking skills? Perhaps the efforts of one institution can be a guide for others seeking to meet this challenge. For twenty years, The Ohio State University Office of Library User Education has consistently reached between 25,000 and 30,000 students each year with course-related bibliographic instruction. This presentation details the key elements in developing this unique, multifaceted program and how the program continually adapts to the changes brought about by technology.

BACKGROUND

Each year approximately 50,000 students, including 10,000 new freshmen and transfer sophomores, face the challenge of finding information in the Ohio State University Libraries. The University Libraries consist of sixteen subject reading rooms in the Main Library, eighteen department libraries in separate buildings, and six regional campus libraries throughout Ohio. Altogether, the collection consists of nearly 5 million volumes, 4 million microforms, and 30,000 subscriptions to periodicals, making it the nineteenth largest research library in the United States.

To access these materials, the Libraries have installed public computers with hundreds of available information resources. OSU Libraries' users can search for locally-owned materials on OSCAR (the Ohio State Catalog for Automated Retrieval). For materials not held in our libraries, users can search the OhioLINK catalog (a statewide library consortium made up of thirty-five research, community college, and state-supported libraries throughout Ohio); the CIC catalogs (for holdings of the Big 10 University libraries); MELVYL, (the University of California); Library of Congress; and WorldCAT. For periodical articles, University Libraries' users may search over 150 networked and stand-alone databases with contents ranging from basic citations to full text journals. Public computers in all libraries also provide access to World Wide Web resources.

Not surprisingly, just the selection process can overwhelm novice users. If an electronic resource is chosen, the patron must understand which search commands to use. Currently, to search everything available a user would need to know many different sets of search commands. Beyond the challenges technology adds to a search, novice researchers need to acquire skills to identify, locate and evaluate information they find using this technology.

The complexity of technology is what spurred the development of the Office of Library User Education. Prior to 1976, bibliographic instruction in the University Libraries was handled by individual library personnel on their own initiative. This approach was serviceable until the early 1970s when the Libraries introduced the world's first online library catalog, the OSU Library Control System (LCS). This technology changed research techniques forever and greatly increased the users' demands for help.

It became the job of the User Education Office to simplify how the Libraries incorporated new technologies, first with LCS, then as the first CD-ROM network was introduced, followed by dial-up access to databases, and now, in the 1990s, the World Wide Web. Through brochures, workshops, audio tapes, in-class presentations, electronic tutorials and unique information systems, the office designed and implemented different strategies to achieve one goal: to help people in the University Libraries become successful, independent information users.

The Office of Library User Education developed in stages, mirroring in large part the complexity and demands of technology and the availability of resources:

1. build a foundation of support for its mission;
2. focus on primary bibliographic instruction needs (LCS instruction and freshman library courses);
3. expand services as resources and technology permitted;
4. promote user independence as staff resources diminished;
5. reach everyone as technology became cheaper and demand was greater (see Figure 1).

BUILD A SOLID FOUNDATION

LCS was created by IBM for the Libraries in 1972 to manage circulation procedures and help librarians identify and locate items on the shelves for users. Initially, LCS was not searched directly by the public. A user desiring a book would ask a librarian for assistance. The librarian would search LCS for the title and then page the item for retrieval by a staff person. The item then would be checked out on the LCS and handed to the user.

By 1976 LCS technology evolved from a system used only by staff into a system available on public computer workstations for nonprofessional (and thereby, untrained) users. University Libraries' researchers found many problems with trying to search this new technology. LCS had, among other challenges, an opening screen that was completely blank except for a cursor, a difficult search language (e.g., tls/ for title search, dsl/ to display records) and little on-screen help. OSU department librarians offered

Figure 1.   Stages of Development

their own LCS instructional guides and workshops, but there was
no central organization to this effort and therefore no consistent
approach to assisting users. Creating a centralized user education
office required a major effort. Three factors were critical to establishing such a resource: the support of the Libraries' faculty, an
administrative champion, and a visionary leader.

In 1976, a Committee on Library Instruction was appointed to
investigate and make recommendations about the existing user
education situation in the Libraries. This committee recommended a more active user education role be taken by the Libraries. In 1976, the Libraries' faculty voted in response to the
committee's report to create a tenure track librarian position for
Library User Education. Unfortunately, in 1976 there were no

funds available in the budget for this position. But in 1977, Dr. William Studer, a strong user education advocate, was appointed Director of the University Libraries. In 1978, he became the administrative champion for the user education office by appointing Virginia Tiefel, then head of the Undergraduate Library, to a new position: half-time Director of Library User Education. In 1985, she became full-time director of this new office.

Tiefel's focus for this office was to promote lifelong learning and help researchers become independent information users. The beginning of the information explosion and the increasingly complex nature of society required that users understand how to find and evaluate information successfully. Tiefel knew that the Libraries were relying on the Office of User Education to assist users with these and future challenges. The new Office of Library User Education had acquired a solid foundation in the support of the libraries' faculty, an administrative champion in Dr. Studer, and a visionary leader in Virginia Tiefel. Now it had the mandate and administrative backing to work on assisting library users.

ADDRESS CORE BIBLIOGRAPHIC INSTRUCTION NEEDS

The first years saw the office focus on the primary needs of the Libraries: instruct users with the technology of LCS, the search strategy, and the services available in the University Libraries. The office designed a standard print brochure for instruction on LCS available at all public computers. In addition, the office created a series of LCS workshops with lecture outlines and overhead transparencies for any OSU librarian to use. Other brochures were created to publicize and explain services such as interlibrary loan, circulation rules, and automated reference.

Department libraries no longer had to create their own instructional brochures. While still free to develop their own specific materials, librarians now worked with the User Education office as a partner to produce a superior product. The librarians supplied the content and the User Ed staff the hardware, software, and expertise to mold that information into a finished brochure that was consistent with Libraries' standards. Once the item was finished, the User Ed Office arranged for the printing, distribution and updating of the brochures as requested by the subject librarians.

The office collaborated with University College to address the more extensive instructional needs of freshmen users. University College (UVC) enrolled all new OSU freshmen and transfer sophomores (approximately 10,000 per year) in a mandatory one-credit orientation course to introduce students to the university policies and procedures. Students also heard presentations on current topics such as substance abuse, race relations, and women's issues. Virginia Tiefel, with the backing of Dr. Studer, persuaded the administrators of UVC to include class time for a section on research in the Libraries.

The purpose of this new UVC Library Instruction Program was to give students a "dry run" at a research project to acquaint them with the tools, both electronic and print, required by their OSU professors for future research projects. The program introduced new students to a search strategy to help organize a research project. All UVC students received an in-class presentation from a librarian, then completed the hands-on portion of the assignment in the library. During this assignment, students had to use print resources and LCS to identify, find, and evaluate relevant materials.

In fall 1978, the first quarter of the Library Instruction Program, 8,600 students received library instruction. Over 200 classes were taught by 25 librarians using the modern technology of overhead transparencies and, when projectors failed, oversized cardboard signs. Lectures and assignments covered instructions on using research tools as well as an overview of general services and policies of the Libraries.

The UVC program helped maintain support of the Libraries' faculty for the Office of User Education by providing an opportunity for librarians to be involved with students. So enthusiastic were librarians with this program they held a party at the end of that first fall quarter (and every fall quarter since) to recognize the contributions of the librarians with certificates and to tell stories about their UVC experiences. UVC classes provided a chance to fulfill the teaching requirements for promotion and tenure at Ohio State.

LESSONS LEARNED IN EARLY YEARS

The practical lesson learned in the early years of the program was that the only way to find out if an idea would work was to try it. Many library personnel doubted it was possible to instruct 8,000 students in one quarter, but it was attempted and it was successful. Librarians from technical services, cataloging, reference, department libraries, and the administration contributed their time and teaching skills to the UVC program. Without the system-wide support of the Libraries' personnel, the Library Instruction Program might have failed.

The early success of the User Education Office did not come easily. It required a tremendous amount of effort to plan and implement the programs. Large numbers of brochures had to be created and distributed. Most importantly, the Office had to work continually to inform administrators, librarians, and classroom faculty of the services available in the User Education Office.

Not every program attempted was successful. The original goal was to expand the Library Instruction Program to students of other grade levels. Phase II was envisioned for all students of freshmen English 110, incorporating an instructional workbook for more advanced information-seeking skills. Unlike the UVC administration, however, there was no support from the English 110 instructors. Phase II was abandoned, as was the planned Phase III, a bibliographic instruction class for sophomores and juniors. Despite these setbacks, the early years of the office must be considered successful in addressing core needs for users of technology in the Libraries.

EXPANDING SERVICES

By 1982, the Office was working in a variety of ways to expand its services. Course-related instruction and workshops now covered the new technology of stand-alone CD-ROMs available in the Libraries as well as LCS. Outreach programs were created for upper-division undergraduates, graduates, and classroom faculty. In 1982, instructional sessions were given to 1,000 communication department students, to continuing education students, and to classroom faculty on the OSU regional campuses.

Presentations were given in dorms, career offices, commuting centers, and to every other non-academic department possible.

To build support and bring bibliographic instruction to the OSU faculty, a Faculty Colloquium was created and offered yearly. The Colloquium was so popular that the president of the university, the provost, and the vice-president of Education Services each gave presentations to recognize the importance of user education. Their support increased the credibility for library instruction and added more administrative champions to the user education team.

Over 10,000 LCS brochures were distributed each quarter throughout the OSU Libraries. An internal OSUL newsletter *Comments on Library User Education (CLUE)* was created to keep all Libraries' personnel informed of developments in technology and bibliographic instruction. To relieve the teaching load on the librarians teaching UVC classes, the office created a highly-popular instructional video entitled *Battle of the Library Superstars*. This video, shown by librarians teaching their UVC classes, covered core library skills of searching LCS, finding journal articles, and locating items on the shelves. Using a Howard Cosell-like anchorperson, the video depicted two students racing to address specific library problems. The nasal drawl narration, the humorous misuse of information resources, and the appearance of current students and Libraries' personnel made this video very popular with UVC students. Made in conjunction with the local public television station, *Superstars* won a Public Broadcasting National Award.

LESSONS LEARNED WITH EXPANDED SERVICES

In the early 1980s, between 25,000 and 30,000 students received some form of library instruction yearly through UVC classes, course-related instruction, workshops, and tours. The support for user education was broadened to include non-Libraries' faculty through the Faculty Colloquia. Expansion of instructional services required additional resources. A new faculty position was created in the Office to oversee the expanded programs. More brochures had to be designed, updated, distributed, and stored, requiring more student help.

In addition, due to the increase in workshops and course-related instruction sessions taught, more members from the Libraries' faculty had to be recruited.

This expansion could not continue indefinitely Even if more workshops on technology were scheduled, there were not librarians available to teach them. More brochures could be created, but maintenance, distribution, and updating would soon be overwhelming. Finally, the Libraries' budget could not accommodate hiring of more user education positions. If the program was to grow, it would have to be done in a manner that did not require more resources.

CREATING INDEPENDENT USERS

Still, the program needed to grow if it was to reach more users. Although thousands of students attended a library instruction session, this figure represented only half the students at OSU. Most of these students only attended one session, insufficient to be considered information literate. Workshops began to show a decline in attendance, while reference desk questions rose. Users still needed help with technology and research, but seemed to prefer to ask a librarian for help at the time they needed assistance rather than attend a workshop to learn skills to be applied at a later time. Reference desks, understaffed due to recent budget cuts, were overwhelmed with users who continued to ask the same questions about how to search LCS and the new CD-ROMs.

For the next two years, one user education librarian explored ways to increase attendance in workshops. Workshops were offered at all hours, on different days, for a variety of relevant skills, in different locations and with different instructors. Still, attendance was poor. Virginia Tiefel reasoned that if workshops were not successful, the Office of User Education should use technology to help address this situation. If users wanted help at their time of need, they should be able to use an automated information system to get answers. Such a system would provide consistent answers to assist novice researchers identify, locate, and evaluate materials. It would simplify use of LCS and CD-ROMs by creating a common front end to those various interfaces. It could even answer other common user questions about hours, locations, evaluation of materials, and search strategy.

Such a system had to be easy enough to operate that first-time users could successfully address their information needs without needing instructional workshops, handouts, and staff assistance. The reference staff, freed from answering basic instructional and directional questions, could concentrate on more challenging research needs of users. This new system took shape under Tiefel's direction over the next few years. Using grants from FIPSE (Fund for the Improvement for Post-Secondary Education), Title II-D from the Department of Education, and from the William Randolph Hearst Foundation, Tiefel and her design team constructed The Gateway to Information.

Based on the search strategy concept, The Gateway guided users through HyperCard stacks to hundreds of relevant encyclopedias, periodical indexes, statistical, biographical, and review materials. It provided abstracts for each title, library location information (including address, telephone number, hours, collection description, floor plans, and campus map) and accessed LCS and eighteen networked CD-ROMs.

Custom programming on The Gateway simplified difficult search languages. All electronic resources were given a common front end. Users were not only led to the relevant resources, but found they could connect and search LCS and other databases from Wilson, UMI, and SilverPlatter, with the same interface. No longer did users need to remember tls/ for an LCS title search or t = for a database title search. Instead, they merely clicked an on-screen box marked "Title Search," typed the title, and pressed the Return key (Figure 2). In June, 1990, after extensive testing with users, consultants, and Libraries' personnel, The Gateway was made available to OSU Libraries' users. By 1991 it was the interface for the University Libraries, available on over fifty public computers.

UVC classes began to use The Gateway for their assignments. Reference questions from UVC students about LCS dropped by over 50 percent during Fall 1991. LCS brochure production dropped from 10,000 to about 6,000 per quarter. Over 10,000 evaluations from users over the next four years showed 80

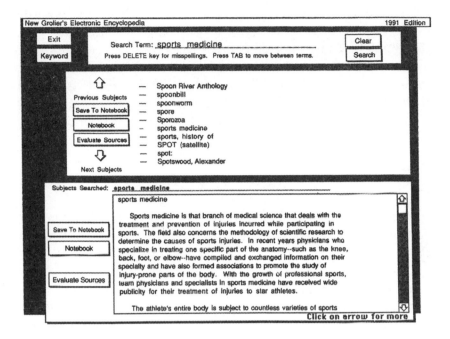

Figure 2. Mac Gateway Database Search Screen

percent of all users were completely or mostly satisfied with their searches, and 85 percent said they would like to use it again for research. The Gateway also was used in the Young Scholars Program to help 2,400 Ohio minority junior and senior high school students organize a research project and access resources. The program director for the Young Scholars became a staunch advocate for The Gateway and library user education. No workshops were required for understanding The Gateway. No instructional brochures or staff were needed by users to successfully find resources. Novice researchers were on their way to becoming independent information users.

LESSONS LEARNED FROM THE GATEWAY

The Gateway proved the Office of User Education could take advantage of technology to deliver time-of-need instruction to a large audience. It demonstrated that users could successfully and independently identify, locate, and evaluate resources, regardless of format, without brochures, workshops, or staff intervention. But The Gateway itself needed to expand. Users could not access The Gateway from dorms, computer labs, offices, or homes due to the hardware and software limitations, as well as the licensing restrictions of the electronic databases. Again, there were no Libraries' personnel or funds available to support this development.

REACH EVERYONE

In 1994 a Gateway Task Force was created to re-examine The Gateway's design, content, and limitations. Its goals were to update and simplify the current HyperCard screens and work towards an eventual move to a format available to remote users. When Mosaic and HTML (HyperText Markup Language) programming came to the attention of the User Education Office, these tools seemed the ideal solution to The Gateway's expansion. Mosaic was free software, stable, and fast. Programming with HTML tags was simple enough to not require a high-level programmer. Best of all, an HTML version of The Gateway would be available to remote users.

Unfortunately, in early 1994 few people in the Libraries knew about HTML programming. Those few who did had no time to convert the HyperCard stacks of the Macintosh Gateway into an HTML version. Therefore, the User Education/Gateway librarian became a self-taught HTML programmer, tagging and then converting revised HyperCard screens designed by The Gateway Task Force for access on the Web. Within a matter of weeks from its completion and testing, the HTML version of The Gateway to Information was made available to OSU users, particularly UVC students for their library assignments.

While it met the goals to provide speed, stability, and remote access, the first HTML version of The Gateway was merely a HyperCard design readable by a web browser. Its card-like screens and simple pathways did not take advantage of all the exciting capabilities of HTML. Almost immediately after installation on the server, the User Education Office decided to

The Gateway to
Information

Instructions:

To identify specific types
of information, click on
the boxes in the graphic.

For the most thorough
research, click on all boxes
from top to bottom.

For location, call number,
date, and other information,
click on any title.

Navigation Note:

To return to this screen
from any Online or WWW
resource, click on the
BACK button above.

Search Tips

Main Menu

OSU Libraries
Information

Comments

Advertising

Useful Sources for Information in a Search Strategy Format

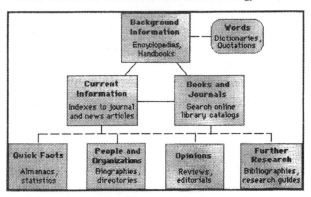

Background Information | Words
Current Information | Books and Journal Titles
Quick Facts | People and Organizations | Opinions | Further Research

Background Information

(General and Subject Encyclopedias, WWW Subject Guides)

Encyclopaedia Britannica *[WWW - OSU users only]*
Concise as well as scholarly articles on a wide range of subjects.

International Encyclopedia of Communication
Provides information on all aspects of communication, including
speech, language, mass media, communication theory and technology
as well as biographical information and references.

[Top of Page]

Words

(Dictionaries, Thesauri, Quotations)

Key Concepts in Communication
Provides extended definitions for communication's major forms,
uses, contents, and research approaches, with extensive historical
detail, and cross references to related terms.

Figure 3. WWW Gateway Subject Screen

completely re-design the HTML version to implement a new
look and functionality.

This new version is subject-based. Users access relevant
resources by subject (e.g., "Advertising") then select a resources
type (e.g., by encyclopedias, periodical indexes, statistical

resources). Known titles will be accessed through an alphabetical lists of all resources available via The Gateway.

A graphical representation of the search strategy provides an index for each page of subject resources. This graphic divides the relevant subject into "Background Information," "Words," "Current Information," "Quick Facts," "People," "Opinions," and "Topical Research," the same divisions taught by the Office of Library User Education for years to help users organize their research. A new content area, "Further Research," has been added to include this new technology, linking users to Web-based sites. Users are able to view titles and descriptions for individual areas or page through the entire list of subject resources (Figure 3). The new Gateway to Information on the Web (http://www.lib.ohio-state.edu/gateway/) provides instructional information at the point of need, whether in the Libraries, dorm, computer lab, offices or home. It is fast, stable, and easily updated to provide the most relevant research assistance to a wide audience.

LESSONS LEARNED FROM THE GATEWAY ON THE WEB

User demands for instruction about the technology drove the project forward; the technology of HTML programming helped create the answer for all users. Again, no workshops, brochures, or staff intervention are required for even novice researchers to use The Gateway successfully. Being on the Internet projected The Gateway beyond a narrow perception of "useful only to undergraduates," and made it advantageous for subject-specialist librarians to adapt a section for their advanced users' needs. For example, the business librarian has helped to build The Gateway's business page into a list of resources useful to his novice users, with a link to his own bibliography of more advanced materials for his sophisticated users. The expansion on the WWW has broadened The Gateway's reach and its support base as subject specialists rely on it to provide links to core resources.

Unfortunately, The Gateway no longer provides a front-end to databases. Custom programming on the old HyperCard Gateway required an advanced programmer and was difficult to maintain.

Users of the current version of The Gateway can find instructions both electronically through the Libraries' Web page or in print by public computers. But because the catalogs for OSCAR and OhioLINK, as well as sixty OhioLINK databases are from the same vendor, users are able to search quite a few core resources with a common interface. The CIC (Big 10) catalogs are available with a Z39.50 interface, so they may be searched using the same screen layout and commands as OSCAR. Also, users today tend to be more experienced with technology than in the past, and find searching easier with the OhioLINK interfaces, or can locate and use print and electronic instructional guides for more complex resources. While the lack of front ends is not the ideal situation, The Gateway will still focus on its original goals: to guide users to the best resources for their needs regardless of format.

MORE ADAPTATIONS

Now the Libraries have a Web page, Web-based catalogs (OhioLINK and OSCAR), and department library home pages. The technology is again expanding. Providing resources on the Web is important, but users still face the same problems of identifying, selecting, and evaluating relevant materials. Adding access to Web sites increases the importance of evaluating and selecting quality information resources. The Gateway will add a section on evaluating materials, but further expansion of user assistance is necessary.

To address these issues of access and critical evaluation, the OSU Libraries sought and received a university grant to fund a full-time user education faculty position in the Libraries to develop, test, and implement an Internet tutorial. This new, interactive tutorial, net.TUTOR (http://gateway.lib.ohio-state.edu/tutor/), helps users find and evaluate resources on the Internet.

In addition, user educational instructional brochures are migrating to the Libraries' Web pages (http://www.lib.ohio-state.edu/guides/). The User Education Office is re-tagging existing brochures using HTML programming to provide specific, in-depth help on the Libraries' Web pages. A user who has difficulty searching OSCAR for journal titles can soon follow a link to the OSCAR/OhioLINK User's Guide online brochure, link to the relevant instructional section, and then continue with the OSCAR search. Additional links to citing print and electronic resources and searching electronic databases will also be available.

The Library User Education Office is expanding in other directions, as well. In order to understand where to allocate funds and create programs, the office set out to learn about current perceptions of the Libraries from users. In March, 1996 OSU teaching faculty were surveyed on their perceptions of the Libraries' services and technology. This data will help determine how the Libraries set priorities for the coming years.

As long as technology continues to dictate access to information, the Office of Library User Education will continue to develop new solutions and adapt services to maintain its usefulness to the OSU Libraries and its users.

COLLABORATIVE LEADERSHIP FOR LEARNING

Sharon Mader

ABSTRACT

Through a series of individual and group activities, this active learning workshop highlights librarian and faculty expectations of each other's roles, explores the factors contributing to successful library/faculty collaborations, and examines the nature of leadership, which builds on many of these same factors. The qualities of leadership identified are those which instruction librarians generally exhibit to be successful at their jobs, and so instruction librarians are likely candidates for leadership roles. The nature of leadership is changing, as the traditional hierarchical leadership structure is being replaced by a new team-based model which merges collaboration and leadership. Instruction librarians must meet the challenge of assuming a leadership role in transforming their organizations for new collaborative and virtual realities.

LIBRARIAN'S EXPECTATIONS OF FACULTY

Let's start out with what we know very well. What do you think librarians expect of faculty?

Individual Activity

- Write down three adjectives to describe what you think librarians expect of faculty.
- Examples will be solicited and shared with the group.

At the 1982 annual meeting of the American Council on Education, William Moffett, an outstanding library leader who died at too early an age last year, participated in a panel discussion on what librarians expect of teaching faculty and administrators and vice versa. In preparation, he had solicited input from a wide range of academic librarians across the country. He found a clear consensus about what kind of support his colleagues felt was needed most. In spite of the double-edged sword of inflation and budget cuts, the primary need expressed was not financial. His survey group agreed that "above all, librarians require the kind of collegial trust and understanding upon which ultimately the quality of their own service to the institution depends."[1] Further, he elaborated on what librarians expect (but do not always find) of their teaching and administrative colleagues:

- a genuine understanding of the library's mission in higher education
- a clearer recognition of the professional librarian's craft and an acceptance of the librarian as a peer in the educational enterprise, and
- a reliable flow of communication and consultation.

FACULTY ATTITUDES TOWARDS LIBRARIANS

Individual Activity

- Write down three adjectives describing faculty attitudes toward librarians and the library's role.
- Examples will then be shared with the whole group.

Let's compare our ideas about faculty attitudes with those reported by Moffett in his survey of colleagues. These included:

- apathy
- benign neglect
- librarians as "technicians and bureaucrats" who have little grasp of what the "real faculty" do, rather than being viewed as teachers or researchers
- reluctance to accept librarians as peers, regardless of whatever official status they may be accorded by the institution, and
- difference in attitude between faculty who make active scholarly use of the library and those who don't.

Another perspective is presented in a study conducted at California State University, Long Beach, of faculty attitudes concerning library instruction.[2] This 1990 survey replicated an earlier one from 1982, with modifications to reflect the effects of library automation. There was no significant change in the response from 1982 to 1990 concerning the view of faculty that they were generally not responsible for assuring that their students develop library skills, whether traditional or electronic. What reasons were identified by faculty respondents to this survey for not making library instruction available to students? Fifty percent of the respondents said the curriculum was too full (as compared to 16% in 1982). The second most prevalent reason was that library research was inappropriate to the class (20% of responses, down from 25% in 1982). The third most frequent reason was the familiar "students should learn on their own" (10%, as opposed to 15% in 1982).

COLLABORATIVE RELATIONSHIPS

From our own experience and what is reported in the literature, we have the uncomfortable sense of dissonance between the expectations of librarians and faculty concerning each other's roles. Since it is essential that we work together, it will be helpful to explore collaborations we have had with teaching faculty in the past and to understand how different variables might have affected our relationships. Let's elaborate on how we collaborate, using the Think-Pair-Share process: first, think and reflect on your own, then exchange with a partner, and finally, share with the group.

Think-Pair-Share Activity

- You will have two minutes on your own to reflect and write down ideas about the following topic, "Describe your most successful collaboration with a faculty member or unit outside the library."
- Then you will pair off with the person next to you; each of you will have two minutes to describe your experience to the other person.
- Now it's time to come back together in small groups. Choose a recorder at your table and brainstorm on what factors made the collaborations successful. The recorder will make a list, using the pink sheet in your folder labeled "Elaborate on How We Collaborate." You now have two minutes to brainstorm and develop your lists.
- Now pass your list to a partner table next to yours. The recorder will read the list, and you should identify any new items created by the other group. Star these items. You now have two minutes to review the list from the other table.
- Ideas were solicited from several tables to share with the whole group. Factors identified included the following: learning from each other in a non-threatening exchange, sharing expectations, the sense of discovery, and a willingness to maintain a commitment.

DEFINITIONS OF COLLABORATION

Before we explore further some of the factors affecting collaboration, let's get a working definition. Michael Schrage, in his book *Shared Minds,* says that collaboration is "an act of shared creation and/or shared discovery."[3] He also emphasizes that collaboration results in the creation of value.

Another definition is that strategic collaborations are "durable commitments created for mutual gain."[4] The key adjectives here are strategic, durable, and mutual. In order to maximize benefits and minimize risks, there are several essential elements in establishing a successful collaborative relationship. These elements have already been mentioned in a number of the sessions at this conference: set goals, build consensus, build trust, communicate, define leadership roles, and commit adequate resources. We can test the collaborative waters by asking a series of questions:

- What are my goals or interests?
- How do these fit with the goals of the other party? With the goals of the library or the institution?
- What resources and expertise are currently in place to accomplish the goal?
- What resources and expertise are needed?
- What level of commitment in terms of time, energy, and other resources can I offer?
- What is the library's commitment?
- How willing am I to work with others to shape, develop, and implement the idea?
- Can I incorporate the viewpoints of others, see new perspectives, and let go of some of my own notions and be flexible?

In your groups, you have identified elements which made your own collaborations successful. Let's examine further some factors that may affect collaboration.

FACTORS AFFECTING COLLABORATION

Factors affecting the success of collaboration include gender, faculty rank, subject discipline, learning style, and research-based versus practice-based perspectives. There has been a dramatic increase in the number of female faculty members, and they bring a new perspective. More than male counterparts, they use collaborative teaching methods and a learning environment that values questions, and they tend to be involved in more interdisciplinary research. In Thomas's study of California State faculty,[5] female faculty were more likely to ask librarians for help in providing class instruction, especially about computer searching.

Female faculty also reported a slightly higher tendency to use the library regularly.

Rank can be another influencing factor. A new finding in Thomas's 1990 study (as compared to the 1982 survey) was the relationship between faculty rank and attitude toward library instruction. A higher proportion of tenured faculty believed that students learned library skills on their own. Lower ranking faculty were also less likely to feel the curriculum was too full to offer library instruction.

Subject discipline (as well as willingness to engage in interdisciplinary dialogue) should also be considered. Thomas's survey showed some variations in responses attributed to discipline, which is not surprising, since information structure and use varies by discipline. In addition, the literature on collaborative learning indicates that one of the initial obstacles is that current educational practices are competitive and tend to foster individualism. Academic institutions themselves are not structured to foster collaboration. Tenure and promotion processes, for example, do not often favor faculty who venture into interdisciplinary endeavors. However, research in many fields is increasingly interdisciplinary and the curriculum also spans these boundaries. Thus faculty in all areas are now seeking (or being forced) to develop interdisciplinary relationships and in essence learn a new language.

When we reflect on what we perceive as our own problems in developing relationships with faculty (which, of course, are interdisciplinary), we should realize that these collaborations present problems for all faculty, and that, indeed, we may be better positioned to deal with them. Librarians, because they tend to be generalists and because they serve and interact with many, if not all, areas of the curriculum, have more experience with an interdisciplinary perspective. They can also serve as a link to bring faculty members from different disciplines together. So, we all need to reach outside of our own boundaries. It can be very exciting and rewarding, but it will take time and nurturing.

Learning style is a factor to consider, because it definitely affects personal interactions. We are all familiar with studies of students' learning styles and academic performance. Your

Myers-Briggs personality type or whether you are field-dependent or field-independent will affect your role as a team member.

Trying to bring together different disciplines can also be complicated by the differences between research-based and practice-based perspectives and experiences. In effective collaborative teams, experts from different disciplines are linked in such a way that they build on each other's strengths, backgrounds, and experiences, and together develop an integrative approach.

We can look to other fields for examples of successful team building. Literature in the health care field, for example, describes numerous examples of the development of teams of researchers and practitioners for projects and problem-solving. This can be compared to teaching faculty and librarians working together. So even with the best intentions, we know that collaboration works better with some faculty and some disciplines than with others.

How can we be more successful? Perhaps it would help if we examined more closely faculty culture, since we may not be speaking the same language or seeking the same goals. In a recently published study, Larry Hardesty illustrates how some strongly held values of faculty culture—which may be at odds with our own values—inhibit our instruction efforts.[6] In recognition of the contribution of this study to the literature of the field, Hardesty received the ACRL Instruction Section's Publication Award for 1996.

Hardesty points out that faculty culture in the United States places an emphasis on research and de-emphasizes teaching, in that there is little professional preparation or discussion with colleagues. Teaching is viewed as an art, not a science. Faculty culture is content-driven and discipline-based, while librarians might be viewed as process- or skills-based and not grounded in a subject discipline. Faculty have been valued for what they know rather than what they can help other people learn; they feel as if they are under constant time pressures; they have strongly-held values of autonomy, independence, and the sanctity of the classroom; they may value the library, but not necessarily the librarians, who they do not see as sharing fully in the faculty culture; and faculty are well-known for resisting change.

In spite of this mismatch of cultures, Hardesty's advice to us is to keep at it—persist in our efforts to involve faculty, since that is essential to achieving our goals. But we should be armed with knowledge of faculty culture and "stop talking just to ourselves," as William Moffett advised.[7] Hardesty encourages us with a finding from one of the studies on faculty attitudes (Oberg, Albion College) that the greater the faculty contact with librarians, the more likely teaching faculty are to accept them as academic equals.[8]

Another way of understanding the relationship between faculty and librarians is to look at the characteristics of professionalism and collegiality. Jean Major, in a 1993 study of librarians' acceptance as colleagues by teaching faculty, distinguishes between professionalism and collegiality. Professionalism is often viewed as the framework for librarians and is characterized by the requirements of formal training and specified credentials, the existence of a code of ethics, autonomy in performing work, and the delivery of expert services for a client. In comparison, collegiality "defines relationships and interactions among members of an academic community." Collegial relationships are defined by "mutual respect for expertise in research and teaching, shared values, and a decision-making style based on participation and consensus," regardless of field or discipline.[9]

Major cites the results of four previous surveys in which faculty regarded librarians as professionals but not as academic or faculty equals. Her paper describes an exploratory study of eighteen experienced librarians who are viewed as colleagues by faculty. The librarians surveyed did not see their professionalism as part of their quest for acceptance as faculty colleagues. Rather, they spoke of the "mutual respect of collegiality, rather than the respect a client has for a professional."[10] We can see that both professionalism and collegial relations form the foundation for collaboration with teaching faculty.

What contributes significantly to acceptance as an academic colleague? Here are the most important factors, as identified by respondents in this study:

- Performing the liaison role of a librarian, that is, making contacts and developing relationships with faculty through

activities such as collection development, periodicals evaluation, instruction, service desks
- Shared values of teaching and learning
- Common interests in research and scholarship
- Integration into campus governance activities and exploitation of these opportunities
- Supportive library administration, who serve as effective models and mentors for learning to be faculty members
- Self-confidence as a librarian—*this was the most important factor*.

Librarians who participate as peers, on an equal basis, have a much greater chance of developing successful collegial relationships with faculty. We can see that both professionalism and collegiality form the foundation for collaboration with teaching faculty.

While librarians have often been successful in developing collaborative relationships with individual faculty, they may not always move to the next stage of team building at the organizational level. As we face increasing pressures and complexities in our organizations, it will be essential that we develop the skills necessary to take a leadership role in institutional transformation. What, then, are the qualities of leadership?

LEADERSHIP

Small Group Round Robin Activity

- Pass the green sheet headed "Leadership is..." around the table; everyone writes down one item or phrase to complete the sentence, then reads the contribution aloud and passes the sheet to the next person.
- After one round has been completed, pass the sheet around again and everyone stars their favorite item.
- After everyone has voted, the last person reads out the item with the most votes.
- Favorite definitions are solicited from several tables and shared with the entire group.

Let's hear how some experts have described leaders and leadership. Peter Drucker, in his new collection of essays, *The Leader of the Future*, emphasizes that "leadership can and must be learned..."[11] Peter Senge tells us that "leadership is about learning how to shape the future."[12] The Center for Creative Leadership believes that "the task of a creative leader is to envision and bring about changes which have beneficial long-term consequences not only for his or her part of the organization but for the organization as a whole and the total society of which that organization is a part."[13] There are definite distinctions between managers and leaders:

Manager	*Leader*
• administers	• innovates
• how & why	• what & when
• bottom line	• horizon
• status quo	• change
• does things right	• does the right thing

Thus we see that managers are efficient, while leaders are effective. Managers meet current commitments through the traditional functions of planning, budgeting, organizing, staffing, controlling, and problem-solving. Leaders meet future commitments by establishing a vision, setting directions toward the vision, and aligning followers who will work toward the vision. They can really be seen as opposites: management controls change and leadership creates change. While managers generally outnumber leaders at most organizations, developing a new crop of leaders will be essential if we are to move to the organization of the future.

Individual Activity

- List two managers and two leaders you know.
- Then think about the leaders: How have they inspired and motivated you to do your best? Write down some adjectives that apply.
- Input is solicited from the whole group by the seminar leader.

LIBRARY LEADERS

Brooke Sheldon, in a very interesting book entitled *Leaders in Libraries*, interviewed sixty library leaders to identify the key qualities they had in common.[14] Using a study of corporate leaders by Bennis and Nanus as her model, she hypothesized that the differences between the corporate and library leaders' basic qualities would be insignificant. Indeed, this proved to be true. There were four "kernels of truth," or strategies for taking charge, that emerged in both studies.

- Vision: Achieving results by securing commitment
- Communication: Using it as a tool to achieve organizational goals; inspiring others to align themselves with your goals
- Trust: Gaining trust through consistency; empowering others
- Self-confidence: Building strengths and compensating for weaknesses; taking action

She also found a new focus on creativity, innovation, and risk-taking and emphasized that mentors, networking, and role models are crucial for leadership development.

Now here is where I think instruction librarians have a natural advantage. The qualities we have been talking about are those which instruction librarians generally exhibit or develop in order to be successful at their jobs-vision, creativity, communication, self-confidence. Instruction librarians by their training, attributes, and role are prime candidates to become leaders, both within the library and the university. Indeed many already have become leaders, but we will need many more. And, as others have already said at this conference, we will have to move outside the library and assume a very active role in the university. Cerise Oberman, whose wise voice has been guiding instruction librarians over the years, gives us this vision: "Bibliographic instruction is the lens through which every function in the library needs to look through."[15]

ASSESSING LEADERSHIP QUALITIES

It is fairly easy and relatively painless to discuss the qualities of leaders and recognize leadership when we see it, but it is much more difficult to realize what we know through action. So how does this happen? We have to make a conscious effort, and we have to begin with ourselves and then help each other. Let's take a few minutes to assess our own strengths and weaknesses and see where we need to grow.

Individual Activity

- Take the blue sheet labeled "Leadership Assessment Inventory" from your folder. This is taken from Bennis and Goldsmith's *Learning to Lead* handbook.[16]
- For each item, circle the number on the scale that best represents where you fit on the continuum between leader and manager. For example, if you seek situations that are stable more than situations that involve change, circle 1 or 2 for the first item, depending on how often you seek these situations. If you fall between the two situations, circle 3. If, however, you are more drawn to change, circle 4 or 5.
- Think about how you usually function and try to be honest with yourself, since only you will see the results.

When everyone has finished:

- Mark the items for which you scored 3 or below. These are the areas where you are behaving more like a manager than a leader. These will help to direct your personal leadership agenda for change that you can begin to develop at the bottom of the inventory.
- Review these target areas again and choose two of them that are most important to you. Note the behaviors you want to change and then identify the barriers that are blocking you.
- Now list supports that can help you develop your leadership potential.

Small Group Activity

- Consider each table as a team. What can you do to help each other develop leadership skills?
- Examples are solicited from several tables to share with the whole group.
- Take your agenda back with you and use it as a tool. It should change as you grow and develop!

Developing as a leader is no longer a choice, but a necessity. As Carla Stoffle reminds us in her "Choosing Our Futures" article, "all library personnel need to receive leadership decision-making, conflict resolution, and budget and project management training because all will be required to assume leadership roles at some point or other."[17]

COLLABORATIVE LEADERSHIP FOR NEW ORGANIZATIONS

So, if everyone is a leader, who are the followers? In the new organization, the hierarchical leadership structure will no longer be functional. Until recently, leadership theory and practice focused on the individual as leader. Now, we are moving to team-centered leadership, where leadership is a shared process that is better able to deal with complexity and change. Team-centered leadership is collective and interactive, providing the opportunity to act with others to accomplish things that couldn't be done alone. Team-centered leadership demands shared responsibility for thinking as well as for doing.

So we are really talking about all of us working together in an environment of collaborative leadership. What will our organization look like? Let's explore for a moment the nature of the virtual organization. In the library literature, "virtual library" is often used synonymously with "electronic library" or "digital library." A virtual library is a concept rather than a place with remote users enjoying electronic access to a vast range of information resources—universal access to knowledge anytime, anywhere. A virtual organization, as used in the business and social sciences literature, has a broader meaning.

The virtual organization is a new organizational model that uses information technology to share skills, costs, and access across partnerships of real organizations. Here are the main characteristics as identified in a *Business Week* cover story on the virtual corporation:[18]

- Opportunism: Partners band together to deal with a specific opportunity and can then disband when the need is gone—"Opportunity-pulled and opportunity-driven."
- Excellence: Each partner brings its core competencies— what it does best—so the partnership can be compared to an all-star team, something that one organization could not do by itself.
- Technology: Information networks provide the link-ups for collaborations that would not otherwise be possible.
- No borders: The traditional boundaries of the organization are being redefined. More cooperation among organizations or units blurs their boundaries.
- Trust: These relationships make the organizations much more reliant on each other, since success depends on their joint effort.

A simple example of the partnering aspect of a virtual corporation, as described in the *Business Week* article, is when Apple Computer lacked the capacity to produce its entire line of Power-Book notebooks and turned to Sony to manufacture the least expensive version for the first year. Another example is a management consulting firm that consists of four partners. When working for a client, they assemble a "just-in-time" team of appropriate talent to address the problem. Once the job is completed, the team disbands.

In reflecting on this new trend in business circles, it struck me that libraries, being the cooperative entities that they are, have actually led business in creating virtual organizations. Then, in reading an article on the topic in the *Harvard Business Review*, I came across this quote: "Libraries, whose lifeblood is information, were always likely to be among the first to confront the challenge and opportunity of virtuality."[19] Libraries have practiced resource sharing and consortial agreements for years as a means of expanding their own collections and providing for customer needs. Librarians have certainly been in the forefront in using technology to digitize materials and to network information resources to eliminate barriers of place. Instruction librarians, in particular, have gone beyond boundaries to create partnerships within the university to improve instruction. A prime example, which has been discussed in sessions at this conference, is the convergence of libraries and computer centers.

Much of this approach is not new to us, while this cooperative mode requires a major shift for the competitive corporate mind set. It was interesting to read in the *Harvard Business Review* article noted above, about the new corporate leader who is moving "from the sage on the stage to the guide on the side." Where have we heard that before? But while we can feel encouraged that we can put principles of cooperative learning to work in making organizational changes, and that we can continue to use technology to link users and information, we should realize that we have been using the pieces without really taking the big leap of turning our organizations upside-down.

I return again to Carla Stoffle's provocative and exciting article in *College & Research Libraries* on "Choosing Our Futures." She is exactly right that the time is upon us to radically change our organizations to meet new realities. Right now, I would like each group to work on a challenge issued in that article: "If we were creating an academic library today, knowing what we know now, how would we organize ourselves and our work to ensure that the library is actively contributing to the achievement of institutional goals?"[20]

Small Group Activity

In your groups, you will create a capsule description of the organizational structure and functioning of this transformed library you have created. Here are some of the questions you should address:

- What is the mission of your library? Who are the staff? Who leads? Who are your partners?

- What traditional or current services will you eliminate or cut back in order to offer new services and resources for a collaborative and virtual environment?
- What will be one of the biggest barriers to making this transformational change?

WRAP-UP: SHARPENING THE SAW

Now that we are nearing the end of this conference and are filled to the brim with ideas and inspiration and questions, we can practice Stephen Covey's seventh habit: Sharpening the Saw.[21] We learn, commit, do, and then follow the cycle again in an upward spiral.

Individual Activity

- As your final activity this morning, everyone can make a commitment to action after the conference. Take out the white sheet at the back of your folder (Appendix I). This will be a contract with yourself. Read and complete the two statements.
- Then put the sheet in the envelope, self-address it, and leave it on the table. It will be mailed to you at the end of the summer.

Remember that neither change nor collaboration are easy or quick, but we must assume a leadership role so we can shape the future. Good luck to us all!

Note: Appendix II provides the slides used during the workshop. The blank ones were used to record group responses.

APPENDIX I

 Commitment to Action

The purpose of this commitment is to help you transfer to your work setting what you have thought about and discussed this morning. Respond to the statements below and place this sheet in the envelope provided (which you will self-address). It will be mailed to you at the end of the summer.

1. Here is one behavior I will work on changing in the next two months to improve my personal leadership skills:

2. When I return to my library, one specific action I will undertake to advance collaborative leadership within the college or university will be:

Signed _____ Date _____

APPENDIX II

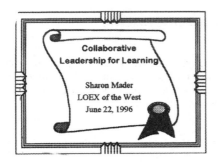

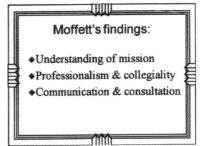

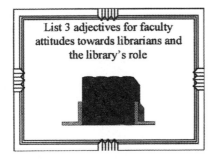

Elaborate on how we collaborate:

◆Think

◆Pair

◆Share

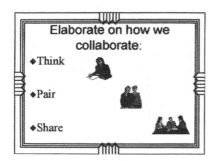

Describe your most successful collaboration with a faculty member or unit outside the library...

What made the collaboration successful?

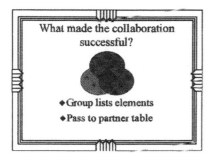

◆Group lists elements
◆Pass to partner table

Likely Partners: Factors Affecting Collaboration

◆Gender
◆Rank
◆Discipline
◆Learning style
◆Research vs. practice

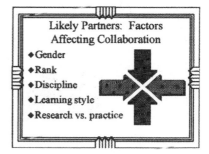

Collaboration

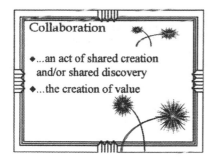

◆...an act of shared creation and/or shared discovery
◆...the creation of value

Strategic collaborations are durable commitments created for mutual gain.

Maximize benefits &
minimize risks:
- Set goals
- Build consensus
- Build trust
- Communicate
- Define leadership roles
- Commit adequate resources

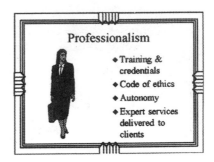

Professionalism
- Training & credentials
- Code of ethics
- Autonomy
- Expert services delivered to clients

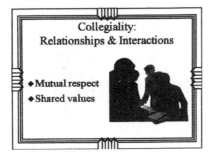

Collegiality:
Relationships & Interactions
- Mutual respect
- Shared values

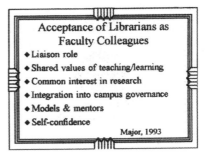

Acceptance of Librarians as
Faculty Colleagues
- Liaison role
- Shared values of teaching/learning
- Common interest in research
- Integration into campus governance
- Models & mentors
- Self-confidence

Major, 1993

MANAGERS & LEADERS
- administers
- how & why
- bottom line
- status quo
- does things right

- innovates
- what & when
- horizon
- change
- does the right thing

List two managers and two
leaders you know:

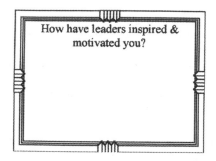

How have leaders inspired & motivated you?

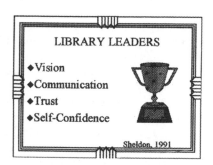

LIBRARY LEADERS

◆ Vision
◆ Communication
◆ Trust
◆ Self-Confidence

Sheldon, 1991

Bibliographic Instruction...

"the lens through which every function in the library needs to look through."

Cerise Oberman

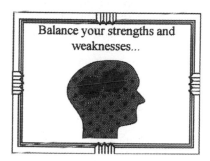

Balance your strengths and weaknesses...

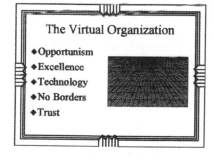

The Virtual Organization

◆ Opportunism
◆ Excellence
◆ Technology
◆ No Borders
◆ Trust

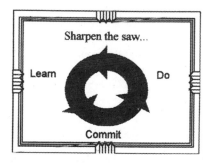

Sharpen the saw...

Learn   Do

Commit

NOTES AND REFERENCES

1. William A. Moffett, "What the Academic Librarian Wants from Administrators and Faculty," *New Directions for Higher Education* 10, no. 3 (1982), p. 14.

2. Joy Thomas, "Faculty Attitudes and Habits Concerning Library Instruction: How Much Has Changed Since 1982?" *Research Strategies* 12, no. 4 (1994), pp. 209-223.

3. Michael Schrage, *Shared Minds: The New Technologies of Collaboration* (New York: Random House, 1990), p. 6.

4. Joanne Scheff and Philip Kotler, "How the Arts Can Prosper Through Strategic Collaborations," *Harvard Business Review* 74, no. 1 (1996), p. 53.

5. Thomas, "Faculty Attitudes," pp. 212, 220.

6. Larry Hardesty, "Faculty Culture and Bibliographic Instruction: An Exploratory Analysis," *Library Trends* 44, no. 2 (1995), pp. 339-367.

7. William A. Moffett, "Guest Editorial: Talking to Ourselves," *College & Research Libraries* 50, no. 6 (1989), p. 610.

8. Hardesty, "Faculty Culture," p. 360.

9. Jean A. Major, "Mature Librarians and the University Faculty: Factors Contributing to Librarians' Acceptance as Colleagues," *College & Research Libraries* 54, no. 6 (1993), p. 464.

10. Ibid., p. 468.

11. Francis Hesselbein, Marshall Goldsmith, and Richard Becker, *The Leader of the Future: New Visions, Strategies, and Practices for the Next Era* (San Francisco: Jossey-Bass, 1996), p. 14.

12. Peter Senge, "Introduction," in *Synchronicity: The Inner Path of Leadership*, ed. Joseph Jaworski and Betty S. Flowers (San Francisco: Berrett-Koehler, 1996), p. 3.

13. Jay Alden Conger, *Learning to Lead: The Art of Transforming Managers Into Leaders* (San Francisco: Jossey-Bass, 1992), p. 115.

14. Brooke E. Sheldon, *Leaders in Libraries: Styles and Strategies for Success* (Chicago: ALA, 1991).

15. Cerise Oberman, "Avoiding the Cereal Syndrome: or, Critical Thinking in the Electronic Environment," *Library Trends* 39, no. 3 (1991), p. 201.

16. Warren G. Bennis and Joan Goldsmith, *Learning to Lead: A Workbook on Becoming a Leader* (Reading, MA: Addison-Wesley, 1994).

17. Carla Stoffle, Robert Renaud, and Jerilyn R. Veldof, "Choosing Our Futures," *College & Research Libraries* 57, no. 3 (1996), pp. 223-224.

18. John A. Byrne, "The Virtual Corporation: The Company of the Future Will Be the Ultimate in Adaptability," *Business Week*, no. 3304 (1993), p. 99. See also Steven L. Goldman, Roger N. Nagel, and Kenneth Preiss, *Agile Competitors and Virtual Organizations: Strategies for Enriching the Customer* (New York: Van Nostrand Reinhold, 1995) for a clear description of virtual organizations.

19. Charles Handy, "Trust and the Virtual Organization," *Harvard Business Review* 73, no. 3 (1995), p. 41.

20. Stoffle, "Choosing Our Futures," p. 219.

21. Stephen R. Covey, *The Seven Habits of Highly Effective People: Restoring the Character Ethic* (New York: Simon & Schuster, 1989).

ABOUT THE AUTHORS

Kari Anderson is Reference Coordinator and selector for general science and history of science materials at the University of Washington's Natural Sciences Library. She regularly conducts library instruction for undergraduate classes in psychology, biology, and the history of science. Kari served as conference co-chair with Theresa Mudrock.

Elizabeth Babbitt was Reference/Assistant User Education Librarian at the Odegaard Undergraduate Library at University of Washington until 1996 and also worked for the King County Library System in Washington. She is currently working in a school library in Bozeman, Montana.

Andrea Bartelstein is UWired Librarian at the University of Washington. She teaches classes on using and evaluating information resources and technology and consults with faculty on the integration of information literacy skills into the curriculum. Prior to her involvement with UWired, Andrea was Reference/User Education Librarian at the Odegaard Undergraduate Library, University of Washington.

Laura Bender is a librarian on the Science-Engineering and Undergraduate Services Teams at the University of Arizona Library. Before joining the University of Arizona Library in 1994, she served as Business Reference Librarian at the University of Hawaii at Manoa, and as a corporate librarian in Tempe, Arizona. She received her M.L.S. and M.A. from the University of Arizona, and her B.A. from the University of California, Santa Barbara.

Larry Berk, Head Librarian at Ulster Community College, New York, has experience in small and large community colleges, schools, and universities. He received his M.S.L.S. from the University of Kentucky and has taught writing and literature as well as library courses. He was a recipient of the SUNY Chancellor's Award for Excellence in Professional Service, 1984-1985. He currently serves as President of the Board of Trustees, Southeastern NY Library Resources Council.

Michael Bertsch is an instructor of composition at Butte and Shasta Community Colleges in Northern California. He regularly teaches writing in networked classrooms and has his students use technology in many forms. He also serves as the director of academic affairs at Athena University, a virtual online university. His most recent activities include writing about online education and training teachers to use MOO platforms for education.

Patricia Carroll-Mathes, Associate Librarian, Coordinator of Information Literacy, Ulster Community College, New York, has twenty-five years of experience at UCCC, after earlier experience as a school librarian. She received her M.L.S. from SUNY Albany. She served a ten-year term on the Board of Trustees, Southeastern NY Library Resources Council, including Treasurer and Vice President. She received the Innovation in Instruction Award from the Instruction Section, ACRL, in 1996.

Jan Deardorff has been a teacher in Corvallis, Oregon since 1976. Currently, she is the Library/Media Coordinator, working with all the school libraries, curriculum divisions, technology and media services in the district. Jan has a B.A. in Sociology from the University of Puget Sound and an M.S. in Education, Standard Teaching certificate, and Standard Educational Media endorsement from Portland State University. Before entering education, she was an inner-city social worker, psychometrist for Stanford Research Institute, and a private preschool teacher.

Karen Diller, Assistant Campus Librarian at Washington State University Vancouver, has been a reference and instruction librarian at both large and small institutions. Currently she is designing a Web-based course on researching in the electronic age.

Kyzyl Fenno-Smith is Instruction Librarian at Pierce College in Tacoma, Washington; she is a member of state and national organizations including ALA, ACRL, and CLAMS (College Librarians and Media Specialists, a Washington state organization of community college librarians). She is active in outcomes assessment at Pierce College and statewide.

Louis B. Fox is the Associate Vice Provost of Undergraduate Education at the University of Washington and has recently been appointed the Associate Vice Provost for Interinstitutional Initiatives. In his new role, he is working to create new educational opportunities with four-year public and private universities, community and technical colleges, and K-12 school districts around the state. His other primary areas of responsibility include curriculum, outreach, facilities, and technology. He has been a co-administrator of UWired since its inception.

Debra Gilchrist is Director of Library/Media Services at Pierce College in Tacoma, Washington. Previously, she was instruction librarian at Pacific Lutheran University. Her research interests include outcomes assessment, effective teaching, and administering a teaching library.

Keith Gresham is Central Reference Librarian and Undergraduate Collections Bibliographer at the University of Colorado at Boulder where, among other duties, he serves as coordinator of library instruction for the social sciences and humanities and teaches an undergraduate credit course on research methods in the electronic environment. He is currently serving a two-year appointment as the ACRL Instruction Section Newsletter Editor.

Diane Gruber is currently an instructor in the Department of Communication Studies at Arizona State University West in Phoenix, Arizona, where she teaches courses in professional writing, persuasion, and gender. Previous to this appointment, she worked as the Assistant to the Director for the Center for Writing Across the Curriculum also at ASU West.

Chuck Harrsch is the Systems Coordinator for Washington State University Vancouver. In addition to his extensive computer experience, he has taught several workshops and classes on computer software, hardware, and the various aspects of computing.

Randy Burke Hensley manages central reference services of Hamilton Library at the University of Hawaii at Manoa. He was formerly the assistant head of the Undergraduate Library at the University of Washington where he taught the user education theory and practice course for the Graduate School of Library and Information Science. He has made numerous presentations nationally on effective presentation skills and learning styles.

Emily Hull is Networked Information Librarian for the Health Sciences Libraries at the University of Washington. Before taking this position, she was Electronic Resources Coordinator and Reference Librarian at the UW Tacoma Campus Library.

Carolyn Johnson is the Business Librarian at the Arizona State University West Library. She previously held a position as an Instruction Librarian at ASU Main, and has worked for many years in other academic and public libraries. Her areas of expertise in library instruction include the application of cooperative learning and critical thinking in course-integrated instruction.

Lisa Kammerlocher is the Social and Behavioral Sciences Librarian and the Coordinator of Course-Integrated Instruction at the Arizona State University West Library. During the implementation of the Gateway course, she served as the Interim Business Librarian. Her areas of expertise in library instruction include the application of cooperative learning and critical thinking in course integrated instruction.

Nancy Lombardo is a Client Services/Systems Librarian at the Spencer S. Eccles Health Sciences Library at the University of Utah in Salt Lake City. She was the principal investigator and coordinator of the Internet Navigator project and has been an Internet trainer for the past five years.

Sharon Mader is Library Director at Christian Brothers University in Memphis, Tennessee. Her invited presentations include active learning workshops at the 1992 ACRL National Conference, the 1993 LOEX Conference, and several state and local conferences. Her professional activities include serving as Chair of the ACRL Instruction Section and as a member of the editorial board of *Research Strategies*.

Buhle Mbambo is Assistant Librarian at the University of Botswana, and is Coordinator of the Social Sciences Unit. She was part of the team which developed the Information Literacy Skills Program at the University of Botswana.

Theresa Mudrock is History Librarian at the University of Washington Libraries. She was previously User Education Librarian for Reference and Research Services, Suzzallo Library, and was involved with the UWired program during its first year. She provided the initial inspiration for the second "LOEX" of the West after attending the first conference in Salem, Oregon in 1994, and served as conference co-chair with Kari Anderson.

Emily Okada served as the Undergraduate Library Services' Librarian for Reference Services at Indiana University Bloomington from 1985 until August 1995. At that time she and her colleague and co-presenter Mary Strow switched responsibilities and she took over as Librarian for Instructional Services. Emily has been active in bibliographic instruction during her entire career at Indiana University. On a state level, she is the co-founder of the Indiana Library Federation's Bibliographic Instruction/User Education group and currently serves on the Steering Committee. On a national level, she has been an active member of the ALA Library Instruction Round Table.

Loretta Rielly is Sponsor of the Instruction and Training Team and the Reference and Research Consulting Team at Oregon State University where she has worked since 1990. Before becoming a librarian, she taught writing at Northern Illinois University and University of Wisconsin-Platteville.

Fred Roecker is the Acting Director for the Office of Library User Education at The Ohio State University. Currently, he oversees the design and distribution of all instructional brochures for the University Libraries. In addition, he coordinates the development and testing of The WWW Gateway to Information.

Ann Roselle served as Assistant Librarian in the Education Unit at the University of Botswana Library, where she coordinated the initial stages of the Information Literacy Skills Program. She presently is working in Cheney, Washington, as Reference/Government Documents Librarian at Eastern Washington University.

Ann Scholz-Crane has been the User Instruction Librarian at Purdue University since 1995. At Purdue, she provides support for the Libraries' active instruction program. Prior to that she served as the User Instruction Coordinator at the University of Wisconsin-Parkside Library/Learning Center.

Karen Smith is currently Director of the Faculty Center for Teaching and Learning at the University of Central Florida. In the past she held various positions at the University of Arizona, including Coordinator of the College of Humanities' Instructional Innovation Projects, Faculty Associate to the Provost for Faculty Development, and Acting Head of the Department of Spanish and Portuguese.

Pamela Stewart is Director of Planning and Facilities Infrastructure in the office of Computing & Communications at the University of Washington. Her responsibilities include planning for the incorporation of voice, data, and video technologies into campus renovation and construction projects. She has been a co-administrator of the UWired program since its inception.

Carla Stoffle is Dean of Libraries at the University of Arizona; previously she held positions at the University of Michigan and the University of Wisconsin-Parkside. She has written three books and numerous articles in the area of academic librarianship, including library management, user education, public services, and budgeting. She is also a past president of the Association for College and Research Libraries, and was the recipient of the ACRL Academic Librarian of the Year Award in 1992. In 1991, she was the ACRL Bibliographic Instruction Librarian of the Year.

Mary Strow began her duties as Librarian for Instructional Services in the Indiana University Undergraduate Library in 1989, and has enjoyed switching jobs with co-presenter Emily Okada. As Librarian for Reference Services, Mary supervises Reference Assistants, oversees desk operations, and continues to participate in library instruction. She is also a fund manager for Theatre and Drama in the IU Libraries, and is active in the ACRL Arts Section.

Jennalyn Tellman is a librarian on the Fine Arts/Humanities and the Bibliographic Access Teams of the University of Arizona Library. Before joining the University of Arizona Library in 1990, she had extensive experience in special libraries. She has a M.S.L.S. from Simmons College, and a B.A. from Wellesley College.

Kim Thompson has been the School-Library Liaison for the Corvallis-Benton County Public Library in Corvallis, Oregon since August 1994. She facilitates collaborative efforts between the public library and the school district. She has a B.S. in Child Development and Family Life from Oregon State University. In her role as a parent and local activist she has served her community through volunteer recruitment and training, fund-raising efforts, and leadership positions. Prior to working at the library, she was head teacher in a day care center, a dental assistant, a retail clerk and a Realtor.

John Tombarge was Business Librarian at Virginia Tech from 1991 until 1996, and is currently a Reference Librarian at Washington and Lee University. He taught courses in online searching and electronic communications for both the University of North Carolina at Greensboro and Virginia Tech.

Susan Waterman MacLean is a member of the Reference Services Division at the University of Guelph, Ontario, and is Social Sciences reference coordinator. Previously, she was Library Education Coordinator. Prior to her University of Guelph appointment, Susan worked in both public and special libraries. Currently, she is completing a collaborative filmography of Canadian film.

Margit Misangyi Watts is the director of three programs for freshman at the University of Hawaii. For the past five years she has been researching in the field of innovative educational philosophy, and her recent publications, presentations, and consultations have been within the realm of restructuring undergraduate education. She is the founder of the Walden Pond virtual community.

Deleyne Wentz is a Reference Librarian at Merrill Library at Utah State University in Logan, Utah. She has been teaming with Computer Services personnel to teach the Internet for four years.

Calvin Williams is Head of Technical Services at Ohio's Bowling Green State University Libraries and Learning Resources. He has worked in several library settings, including special, public, and academic.

Helene Williams is English Studies Librarian at the University of Washington Libraries. She has been involved with UWired since 1996, working specifically with the upper-division course pilot program and the interdisciplinary writing links to UWired. Helene came to the UW after serving as bibliographic instruction coordinator at Northeastern University (Boston) and also at

Michigan State University. She would like to note that she does more instruction than ever, now that she is not a program coordinator.

Karen Williams is the Social Sciences Team Leader at the University of Arizona Library. She has team taught Internet and Web authoring sessions with partners from the Center for Computing and Information Technology for several years.

Lizabeth Wilson is the Associate Director of Libraries for Public Services at the University of Washington. She is responsible for the overall administration of the Libraries' user services and public units with primary focus on information literacy, digital library services, and user assessment. She has been a co-administrator of the UWired since its inception. Prior to her position at the UW, she was Assistant Director of Libraries for Undergraduate and Instructional Services at the University of Illinois at Urbana-Champaign.

Anne Zald is Geography/UWired Librarian at the University of Washington Libraries. Currently, she is working on the curriculum development efforts for the UWired program and leads the Core Curriculum Team in planning for the Libraries' user education programs for computer-based resources. Prior to her involvement with UWired, Anne was Government Documents Reference Librarian at the University of Washington, Oberlin College and Wayne State University.

Margaret Zarnosky received her M.L.S. from the University of California, Los Angeles, and has worked at Virginia Tech since 1993. She served as Library Instruction Coordinator and Librarian for the College of Human Resources; she is currently the Librarian for the Northern Virginia Graduate Center, in Falls Church, Virginia.

INDEX